POWER SW   **DATE DUE**

ENERGY RE   GULATORY GOVERNANCE

IN THE TWENTY-FIRST CENTURY

In the energy sector of Canadian economic and political life, power has a double meaning. It is quintessentially about the generation of power and physical energy. However, it is also about political power, the energy of the economy, and thus the overall governance of Canada. *Power Switch* offers a critical examination of the changing nature of energy regulatory governance, with a particular focus on Canada in the larger contexts of the George W. Bush administration's aggressive energy policies and North American energy markets.

Focusing on the key institutions and complex regimes of regulation, Bruce Doern and Monica Gattinger look at specific regulatory bodies such as the National Energy Board, the Alberta Energy and Utilities Board, and the Ontario Energy Board. They also examine the complex systems of rule making that develop as traditional energy regulation interacts and often collides with environmental and climate change regulation, such as the Kyoto Protocol on reducing greenhouse gas emissions. *Power Switch* is one of the first accounts in many years of Canada's overall energy regulatory system.

G. BRUCE DOERN is a professor in the School of Public Policy and Administration at Carleton University, and the Politics Department at the University of Exeter.

MONICA GATTINGER is an assistant professor in the Public Administration Program at the University of Ottawa.

POWER SWITCH

Energy Regulatory Governance in the Twenty-First Century

G. Bruce Doern
Monica Gattinger

UNIVERSITY OF TORONTO PRESS
Toronto Buffalo London

© University of Toronto Press Incorporated 2003
Toronto Buffalo London
Printed in Canada

ISBN 0-8020-3753-4 (cloth)
ISBN 0-8020-8536-9 (paper)

Printed on acid-free paper

National Library of Canada Cataloguing in Publication

Doern, G. Bruce, 1942–
    Power switch : energy regulatory governance in the twenty-first
century / G. Bruce Doern, Monica Gattinger.

    Includes bibliographical references and index.
    ISBN 0-8020-3753-4 (bound)   ISBN 0-8020-8536-9 (pbk.)

    1. Energy policy – Canada.   2. Energy policy – United States.
I. Gattinger, Monica   II. Title.

    HD9685.A2D63 2003   333.79′0971   C2003-902504-7

University of Toronto Press acknowledges the financial assistance to its
publishing program of the Canada Council for the Arts and the Ontario
Arts Council.

University of Toronto Press acknowledges the financial support for its
publishing activities of the Government of Canada through the Book
Publishing Industry Development Program (BPIDP).

For Joan, Shannon, Chris, Kristin, Rob, and Jake,
and
For Cameron

Contents

Preface

In addition to the literature and sources cited, this book is based on over seventy interviews with current and former staff and with other persons in government, business, and academe who are knowledgeable about the various energy and environmental regulatory bodies it describes. These interviews were conducted during the period from 1999 to 2002 and dealt with – as does the book – major energy events and developments up to November 2002. They were granted upon an undertaking from the authors that no person so interviewed would be quoted or directly attributed. The interviews thus complement other sources but were conducted to enhance the authors' understanding of the subtleties and dynamics of institutional and regime change in energy regulatory governance.

Many thanks are due to all these individuals who gave unstintingly of their time, particularly those who further commented on draft chapters and sections. Two anonymous referees also provided very constructive comments. These individuals helped to make the book a better product but bear no responsibility for any remaining errors or omissions, which are our responsibility alone.

Special thanks are also due for the research funding for this book, which has come from a variety of sources, including the Social Sciences and Humanities Research Council of Canada, the Carleton Research Unit on Innovation, Science and Environment (CRUISE) at the School of Public Policy and Administration, the Politics Department, University of Exeter, Natural Resources Canada, Environment Canada, Industry Canada, the Department of Indian Affairs and Northern Development, the Canadian Electricity Association, and the Canadian Association of Petroleum Producers.

G. Bruce Doern and Monica Gattinger
February 2003

Abbreviations

ADR	appropriate dispute resolution
AE	Alberta Environment
AECL	Atomic Energy of Canada Ltd
AEP	Alberta Environmental Protection
AEUB	Alberta Energy and Utilities Board
AGS	Alberta Geological Survey
AIT	Agreement on Internal Trade
ANWR	Arctic National Wildlife Refuge (Alaska)
APPs	affiliated power producers
CANDU	Canada deuterium uranium (reactor)
CAPP	Canadian Association of Petroleum Producers
CASA	Clean Air Strategic Alliance
CCAP	Climate Change Action Fund
CEA	Canadian Electricity Association
CEAA	Canadian Environmental Assessment Agency
CEPA	Canadian Environmental Protection Act
CFCs	chlorfluoro carbons
CNSC	Canadian Nuclear Safety Commission
DFAIT	Department of Foreign Affairs and International Trade
DFO	Department of Fisheries and Oceans
DIAND	Department of Indian Affairs and Northern Development
DIR	Director of Investigation and Research
EC	Environment Canada
EMR	Energy, Mines and Resources
ENGOs	environmental non-governmental organizations
EPAct	Energy Policy Act (U.S., 1992)
ERCB	Energy Resources Conservation Board (Alberta)

EU	European Union
EWGs	exempt wholesale generators
FERC	Federal Energy Regulatory Commission (U.S.)
FTA	Free Trade Agreement (Canada-U.S.)
GHG	greenhouse gas
IAEA	International Atomic Energy Agency
IEA	International Energy Agency
IMO	Independent Market Operator
IOU	investor-owned utility
IPCC	Intergovernmental Panel on Climate Change
IPPs	independent power producers
ISO	Independent System Operator (U.S.)
LDCs	local distribution companies
MMT	methycyclopentadienyl manganese tricarbonyl (gasoline additive)
MOUs	memoranda of understanding
MPMA	Market Power Mitigation Agreement
NAERC	North American Electricity Reliability Council
NAERO	North American Electricity Reliability Organization
NAFTA	North American Free Trade Agreement
NEB	National Energy Board
NEP	National Energy Program (of 1980)
NGAct	National Gas Act (U.S., 1938)
NGOs	non-governmental organizations
NGPAct	National Gas Policy Act (U.S., 1978)
NOP	National Oil Policy (of 1960)
NOX-VOCS	nitrogen oxides and volatile organic compounds
NPM	New Public Management
NRCan	Natural Resources Canada
NSPI	Nova Scotia Power Inc.
NUGs	non-utility generators
OEB	Ontario Energy Board
OECD	Organization for Economic Cooperation and Development
OPEC	Organization of Petroleum Exporting Countries
OPG	Ontario Power Generation Inc.
PCO	Privy Council Office
PUB	Public Utilities Board (Alberta)
PUCs	public utility commissions (U.S.)
PURPA	Public Utilities Regulatory Policies Act (U.S.)

PX	Power Exchange
QFs	qualifying facilities
RTGs	regional transmission grids
RTOs	regional transmission organizations
SDTF	Sustainable Development Technology Fund
TCPL	TransCanada Pipelines Ltd
UARB	Utilities and Review Board (Nova Scotia)
UNFCCC	United Nations Framework Convention on Climate Change
US NEP	U.S. National Energy Policy (of 2001)
WTO	World Trade Organization

POWER SWITCH:
ENERGY REGULATORY GOVERNANCE
IN THE TWENTY-FIRST CENTURY

Introduction

In the energy sector of Canadian economic and political life, power always has a double meaning. It is quintessentially about the generation of power and physical energy. It is also about political power, and hence about the relative ascendancy and decline of institutions and interests, and about what ideas and values are central in the overall governance of energy in Canada, as well as, of course, continentally and globally. The 'power switch' that has occurred in the last two decades needs a careful examination, one that enhances understanding of the new regulatory governance of energy and explains how it came about.

Canadians take their abundant energy resources for granted and usually think little about how they are delivered and regulated and what ideas and values underlie these processes. Energy issues seem to rise to high levels of political consciousness only when oil and gas prices increase at abnormal rates, as they did in 2000–1, or when electricity prices soar and supply shortages occur, as they did in 2002 under Ontario's transition to competitive electricity supply. However, occasionally energy issues have polarized national politics, as in the great pipeline debate of 1956–7, which helped defeat the St Laurent Liberal government, the 1973 energy crisis, and the 1979–80 energy crisis, which ushered in the era of the 1980–4 Liberal National Energy Program (Doern and Toner 1985; Lucas 1977; McDougall 1982). In the early twenty-first century, the policy and regulatory actions needed to reduce Canada's emission of greenhouse gases in the name of climate change policy are again polarizing national politics. Issues of national and continental energy security are also never far from the political surface and emerge in times of crisis, for example, following the terrorist attacks of 11 September 2001 in the United States.

The election in 2000 of the Bush administration in the United States has elevated Canadian, continental, and global energy issues into a potent political-economic cocktail. The Bush National Energy Policy is an aggressive continental energy policy. Indeed, one of the first things the Chrétien Liberal government had to do, following its own 2000 election victory and that of Bush, was to create a reference Cabinet committee on energy. In essence, the Chrétien Cabinet had to re-educate itself about energy policy because, for most of the previous fifteen years, such policy seemed to tick along in a familiar way, sheltered by the pro-market consensus and low, stable oil and gas prices.

The purpose of this book is to examine how and explain why the regulatory governance of energy in Canada has changed in the last two decades, and to explore the critical challenges facing energy regulatory governance in the first decade of the twenty-first century. There has been no book on overall Canadian energy regulation for many years, and certainly none that looks at developments from a comprehensive regulatory institutional and governance perspective as this book does. To this end, it draws on, and contributes to, two broad strands of academic and policy literature and research: energy policy and regulation; and regulatory governance and institutions, more generally. Energy regulatory governance, in Canada in the early twenty-first century is a changed system of governance, the central features of which are the following: complex distributed systems of decision-making with multiple centres of power; an emphasis on flexible, incentive-based regulation and less adjudicated forms of rule-making; and a preference for market over state mechanisms, but with a growing case being made for increased intervention and rule-making for environmental policy reasons and to ensure sustainable development. The acid test of the latter is undoubtedly the debate about, and regulatory and policy responses to, global warming and the Kyoto Protocol on reducing greenhouse gas emissions. Crucially, we also probe some of the central ideas underpinning the new energy regulatory governance system.

Key Themes

Four key themes and arguments are developed throughout the analysis. The first is that energy regulation has changed markedly in the last two decades, and in a way which we characterize as 'less regulation but more rules.' This has been caused by a number of factors, but at its core it is the result of the contradictory pressures of sectoral deregulation, on the one hand, and, on the other, expanded rule-making on the horizontal regulatory front, an area encompassing health, safety, and the environment, as well as competition (and related trade regulation). We argue that the regulatory governance of energy in Canada has been transformed from a relatively uncomplicated and clear system of sectoral energy regulators overseeing the activities of a small number of large homogeneous industrial players, to a far more complex, dense, and opaque system of multiple sectoral and horizontal regulators regulating the activities of a large number of diverse energy companies. In this sense, contemporary energy regulatory governance constitutes a power switch from a relatively centralized and jurisdictionally insulated governance arrangement to a far more decentralized governance structure, in which power, in the form of information, financial, and other resources, and statutory jurisdiction are distributed among multiple public, private, and civic players. Canada's institutions for energy regulation have changed because they now consist, to an ever greater extent than in the past, of a very complex and dense interplay between two *regimes* of energy regulation, one sectoral and the other horizontal. These regimes are composed of sets of regulators interacting with each other both cooperatively and conflictually.

The second analytical theme is that while energy regulatory governance has been moving in a pro-competition direction, with the implication that energy can be treated as just another set of products and services, we believe that the system still needs to be seen as one encompassing managed competition rather than as competition per se. We argue that Canadians, as well as sectoral and horizontal regulators, are much wiser to think of energy as an essential service industry rather than as just a set of discrete products. Historically, the energy industry has been considered both politically and economically as an industry with natural monopoly features and therefore one in which society would be better served by substituting government regulation for market forces. Thereby, consumers were to be protected from abuse of monopoly power, but also, importantly, their right as *citizens* to access an essential service industry was protected. In the contemporary energy regulatory environment, lessened public intervention in the sector is premised on an understanding that certain elements of the energy industry are no longer natural monopolies.

While citizens are of course consumers desiring reasonably priced and delivered energy products and services, they are still, importantly, citizens of diverse socio-economic circumstances. These citizen-consumers may be poor, vulnerable, or sick, and therefore political and social considerations such as equity, access, and need continue to be crucial components of government, intervention in the energy industry. Contemporary energy regulatory governance involves a power switch from the citizen, government, and energy industry to the consumer, in the form of more choice for consumers through competition and therefore a certain power to consumers through their energy-spending decisions. Some of this is desirable but there are limits to the notion that energy is like any other market product, especially in the electricity sector, but in other ways as well.

Thus, even if the *direction* of regulatory governance is towards more competition, this does not mean that more competition per se is the net resultant *destination*. The destination, in fact, is a world of workable competition. This is so not only because monopoly aspects remain, but also because existing political institutions and political-regulatory authorities seek accommodations with each other and ultimately must manage both a networked industry or grid and an interacting world of imperfect markets and imperfect governments, neither of which has been designed by some single all-knowing all-purposeful actor. It may be tempting to regard everything as moving towards a more perfectly competitive world, but we argue that this is an illusion. Governments and particular regulatory bodies also compete for regulatory space, and hence for the chunk of territory they need to manage markets. The workable electricity competition experiments and/or debates in Alberta, Ontario, and Nova Scotia, with the California crisis as a cautionary backdrop, are an important change in energy regulation and governance, but one whose outcomes are not wholly predictable or desirable. Again, this is because inter-regime accountability and coordination are more complex and opaque than in earlier eras.

Our third key theme is centred on the concept of regulatory 'stacking' as a major feature of energy-environmental regulation. Our argument here is that the overall pattern of change in the last decade is not that of the replacement of command and control regulation with incentive-based regulation. Rather, the institutional pattern is one of regulatory *stacking* in which regulatory systems are layered on top of each other, but often not in an orderly fashion. Partly, this is because of the pressure and demands of business and non-governmental organizations (NGOs) operating through complex sets of environment and energy regulators within Canada (as well as throughout North America, and globally). But it is also because of the central reality that effective incentive-based environmental regulation demands, and crucially depends on, some form of 'command' in the setting of reduced pollution levels or levels of sustainability. We show the continuing importance of traditional environmental regulation or so-called end-of-pipe regulation or emission and pollution control, but also the regulatory institutional change which has accompanied the adoption of the paradigm of sustainable development. Though the latter's intergenerational time frame tends to imply that regulation becomes more incentive-based and flexible rather than founded on 'command and control' approaches, we argue that 'command and control' remains crucial. Our examination is centred on the regulatory and institutional implications of climate change policy and of Canada's commitments under the Kyoto Protocol to reduce greenhouse gases, but also touches other examples. Not only does it take into account the obvious global regulatory dimensions, but it also discloses an energy and environment regulatory challenge that engages both the 'clean-up' and hence 'command' aspects with the 'preventative' and incentive aspects of environmental regulation. The analysis also shows the massive cooperation, and ultimately learning, that must take place between the two core federal departments involved, Natural Resources Canada and Environment Canada, as well as the serious tensions and conflict between them.

The fourth theme centres on the nature of political accountability in the new energy regulatory governance system, in which energy is regulated not just by particular regulators but by complex regimes of regulation. The recent changes in Canada's energy regulatory governance system render basic political accountability much more difficult in a number of ways. Rules are a more complex melange of statutes, normal regulations (i.e., delegated legislation), guidelines, codes, and memoranda of understanding (MOUs). The system consists to a greater extent than even a decade ago of regimes of regulators watching over each other, with Canadian citizens left relying on dense opaque institutions and with sets of regulators essentially saying 'trust us' to watch each other. We examine this regulatory network grid by exploring the necessarily related questions of accountability by whom, to whom, for what, and over what time frame.

While these four themes are central to the book, it must be stressed from the outset that Canada's main energy regulators, such as the National Energy Board and its provincial counterparts, often scarcely register as institutions in the day-to-day consciousness of Canadians.

This is hardly surprising given there are now over sixty departments, agencies, and boards that regulate energy in some way. Nonetheless, key changes have occurred in the way in which Canada's energy regulators function. These changes have been spurred on by the introduction of new technologies of energy supply and demand; ideological shifts in views advocated by industrial interests, non-governmental organizations, and governments about the nature of state intervention; federal-provincial and inter-regional politics; globalization and trade liberalization; and the emergence of the sustainable development paradigm, climate change, and competition policies.

We also stress from the outset that, despite its breadth, this is not a book about energy *policy* as a whole or about all areas of energy regulation. A more complete examination of Canadian energy policy and regulation in the early twenty-first century would have to take into account numerous separate and detailed aspects of oil, gas, electricity, nuclear power, coal, wind power, and newly emerging sources of alternative energy such as fuel cells, a range that is impossible to cover in any single book. It would also have to examine the federal, provincial, and territorial levels of government, and the energy policy delivered through policy instruments other than regulation, which include taxation and expenditure or incentive programs such as those for new energy technologies and supplies. This book clearly cannot deal with all of these dimensions or with all of energy policy, but it must still have a reasonably broad scope in order to do justice to the changes under way in energy regulatory governance in Canada and elsewhere.

As such, the book examines the nature of, and the major factors driving, some of the key changes in contemporary energy regulation, and identifies a number of crucial challenges facing energy regulators and Canadians as a whole. Our focus, as discussed below, is on a handful of key institutions involved in energy regulation in Canada, and we pursue the four themes above throughout the analysis.

The Energy Policy and Political Context: The U.S. Bush Energy Plan and Federal Liberal Energy Policy

The Bush administration's National Energy Policy, ironically another 'NEP,' has changed the political economy of energy policy and regulation in several respects (Government of United States 2001). The Bush NEP report is titled 'Reliable, Affordable, and Environmentally Sound: Energy for America's Future,' and the first three goals in the title are in order of priority. Bush's Republican administration is concerned about reducing U.S. dependence on oil from the Middle East. It also faces high electricity prices, shortfalls, and power outages in California that have been caused by a less than ideal adoption of electricity deregulation combined with failures, partly because of environmentalist pressure, to build new power plants as well as serious failures to regulate at the national level (Duane 2002; Jaccard 2002; Sioshansi 2001). It favours a supply-side solution centred on its own untapped Alaska reserves located in pristine and ecologically crucial wildlife lands. But it also seeks secure long-term access to Mexican and Canadian energy, including Alberta's natural gas and its vast oil sands supply. There are environmental and conservation components of the Bush NEP, but they are clearly not central to it. The Bush administration deeply opposes the Kyoto Protocol and hence direct regulatory measures to reduce carbon emissions. It refuses to commit to the Kyoto reductions and instead has announced its own very modest and slow reductions centred on voluntary action and incentives for new technologies (Bush 2002). A further but crucial aspect of early Bush era energy policy was added when the giant energy company Enron collapsed and raised a host of direct and indirect regulatory inter-regime issues, ranging from financial regulation, accounting ethics and practices, to the political funding of parties and elections. These developments and problems go beyond energy policy per se, but they are germane to our focus on the larger issue of regulatory governance through complex regimes of regulation.

On the Canadian side of the political-economic and energy-environment equations sits a Chrétien Liberal government, returned to power in 2000 for a third majority mandate but with serious political fences to mend in Western Canada, where it won only a handful of seats. Mindful of not wanting to repeat the sins of the 1980 National Energy Program (a policy very much despised in Alberta), the federal Liberals this time were initially determined to make gains in Alberta by supporting Western Canadian energy producer ambitions rather than restraining them (Tupper 2002). But after Prime Minister Chrétien announced in August 2002 that he would be leaving office as a result of the leadership challenge of his finance minister, Paul Martin, the core politics changed. Chrétien then announced in Johannesburg in September 2002 that his government would ask Parliament to pass a resolution ratifying the Kyoto Protocol. This decision, before federal-provincial consultations had seriously begun, triggered open antagonism with the Alberta Conservative government of Premier Ralph Klein. The Canadian record on Kyoto had from the outset been little better than that of the United States, but it is clear there are difficult issues with respect to Alberta-federal relations in Canada's own effort to implement any plan for major reductions in greenhouse gas emission. Hence the macro political-economic stage is set for a considerable re-politicization of energy policy and politics in Canada.

It is crucial in this context to see how, in the early 2000s, the Chrétien Liberal government defines first its energy policy and then the regulation of energy within that larger energy policy context. The Liberals argue that since 1993 energy policy has been 'guided by the principles of sustainable development' and consists of three main objectives:

- to develop a competitive and innovative energy sector – by implementing a framework that promotes the long term development of Canadian energy resources, encourages wise use of energy resources and maximizes economic opportunity in the energy sector for Canadians (which reflects the government's goal of promoting jobs and growth).
- to encourage environmental stewardship – by addressing the environmental impacts of energy development, transportation and use and by integrating environmental objectives into all policies and programs.
- to establish secure access – by ensuring that current and future generations of Canadians have enough competitively priced energy and by taking measures that make efficient use of existing resources and provide reliable energy services to Canadians. (Natural Resources Canada 2000: 9)

As we will argue, the Liberal claim that its energy policy is 'guided by the principles of sustainable development' is a questionable one, or, at the least, these principles are applied in a highly selective way. However, within this very broad and complex notion of energy policy, the Chrétien Liberals do see energy regulation, like all regulation, as having evolved considerably over the last twenty years, 'driven by the same global trends – globalization, deregulation, increased environmental awareness, and the overall theme of reliance on markets' (Natural Resources Canada 2000: 137). Federal energy policy sees energy regulation as being quintessentially federal and provincial in nature, and increasingly continental and global as well, and assumes that managing energy markets means 'more markets – less government.' But having established this market-reliance principle, the same statement goes on to say in the very next breath that 'environmental concerns are growing' and that 'contrary to the trend towards trusting markets and competition, environmental concerns, particularly those related to energy, often call for more regulation' (Natural Resources Canada 2000: 138). The federal view also stresses that energy commodities are 'no longer considered "unique" or "special"' and that contemporary energy regulation must be contrasted with that of the 1970s and early 1980s, when it was driven by several different precepts:

- A perception of scarcity – The world's energy resources were finite, while demand for energy would inevitably rise. The demand for energy needed to be regulated.
- An emphasis on security – Western countries were susceptible to disruptions in their supply.
- An emphasis on self-sufficiency – Canada sought to reduce its vulnerability by protecting and increasing its domestic supply of energy.
- An expectation of rising prices – With scarcity came the belief that prices for energy would rise.
- A perception of market inadequacy – Oil markets, in particular, were distorted and concentrated which led to oligopoly control. (Natural Resources Canada 2000: 137)

At the beginning of the twenty-first century, the federal government sees the core of federal energy regulation as consisting of several key regulatory elements and treaties (Natural Resources Canada 2000: 139 and Appendix I):

- The National Energy Board and the *National Energy Board Act*
- *Canadian Environmental Assessment Act*
- The North American Free Trade Agreement (NAFTA) – Energy Chapter
- Agreement on Internal Trade – Energy Chapter
- *Energy Supplies Emergency Act*
- Energy Efficiency Regulations and the *Energy Efficiency Act*
- Canadian Nuclear Safety Commission
- The 1997 Kyoto Protocol (and the related National Implementation Strategy)

Clearly, federal energy policy is complex and needs to be a key part of the regulatory-institutional story. But even the above federal list of regulatory elements, complex as it is, does not do justice to the nature of contemporary energy regulation for the country as a whole.

Energy Regulatory Governance: The Nature of Energy Regulation, Regulatory Regimes, and Regulatory Institutions

Any book on regulation has some definitional realms to set out and, where feasible, clarify. In this book these definitional and analytical realms centre on the following: the definition of regulation itself; the concept of energy regulatory governance and regulatory regimes as employed in this book; and regulatory institutions.

Regulations in a fundamental sense are 'rules of behaviour backed-up by the sanctions of the state'(Doern, Hill, Prince, and Schultz 1999: 2). Alas, regulations can come in the form of rules expressed:

- as constitutional or quasi-constitutional rules (e.g., the Charter of Rights and Freedoms, and the 1994 Internal Trade Agreement);
- in statutes and laws (e.g., Canadian Environmental Protection Act);
- in delegated legislation or 'the regs' (e.g., rules regarding the safety of nuclear reactors);
- as guidelines (e.g., the merger guidelines under the Competition Act);
- as standards and codes (e.g., for the selling practices of door-to-door gas or electricity marketing companies).

As one moves across these modes and levels of regulatory expression, the extent and nature of the sanctions by the state (from strong to virtually non-existent) is wide, and, of course, the range is itself fought over by key interests. For some interests, the solution to a problem is that there should be a new statute or a regulation passed, but for other interests, a flexible guideline will do or no rules at all would be even better. Or even more broadly in the governance spectrum, some would prefer incentives or tax breaks.

In this book, we have erred on the side of breadth in defining regulation. This is because, in part, the argument of 'less regulation but more rules' implies that more than one type of rule-making is occurring. Thus, for example, there could be a lessening of regulation defined as delegated legislation, but a great expansion of rule-making through guidelines or codes. Though we err on the side of breadth in the above list, it is important to realize that a logical conundrum eventually arises. The wider regulation is defined to be, the more it becomes equated with government as a whole. But, at some point, governing is not just about regulation, and the state is more than just a regulatory state. Governance also involves taxation, spending, persuasion, and other means of trying to ensure that diverse energy (and other) policy goals and values are implemented in democratic life.

Moving to the second concept, *regulatory governance*, what we mean by this is that it involves not just regulations themselves, but the processes and structures through which regulations are developed and implemented, and the ideas and ideals underpinning decision-making. In essence, one is adding to the instrument of regulation the larger nexus of organizations and processes in which it occurs.

Regulatory regimes are the third definitional starting point. We view regulatory regimes as being nested within the larger concept of energy regulatory governance. They are an interacting set of organizations, statutes, ideas, interests, and processes engaged in rule-making and implementation. In other words, the first test of there being a regime is that there is some inner core of such features and characteristics that warrant such a designation for analytical purposes. Building on earlier work on regulatory regimes (Doern and Wilks 1998; Doern, Hill, Prince, and Schultz 1999), we examine Canada's energy regulatory governance as an interplay among two regimes, a *sectoral* energy regime and a *horizontal* energy regime. The concept of regimes is a prism through which some aspects of change in Canada's energy regulatory governance over the past two decades can be better mapped and understood.

These regimes are set out in more detail in chapter 2. But in essence, the *sectoral energy regulatory regime* refers to a set of regulatory laws, agencies, interests, values, and processes which govern energy as a vertical industrial sector. At the core of this system of rules are the various energy boards, federal, provincial, and territorial. In this book, we are focusing on three such boards (the National Energy Board, the Ontario Energy Board, and the Alberta Energy and Utilities Board), but the sectoral energy regime in fact is a larger set of players across all the provinces and territories. The *horizontal energy regulatory regime* refers to a set of regulatory laws, agencies, interests, values, and processes which govern energy from a horizontal perspective in which energy is simply one among many industrial sectors governed by general rules regarding health, safety, environment, fairness, and the quality of products and services, including the nature and quality of competition. This is also a vast and complex terrain which this book will explore only through two aspects: horizontal *competition* regulation and rule-making, and *environmental* regulation. A proper institutional mapping of this regime would necessarily include not only particular regulatory bodies (such as the Competition Bureau, and environmental regulatory bodies and departments, both federal and provincial) but also ministries of environment and industry, which possess some share of rule-making powers and coverage. Our regulatory focus here is largely on the interactions of two key federal departments, Natural Resources Canada and Environment Canada. But we also refer in an illustrative way to provincial energy-environment regulatory interactions and conflicts.

The fourth and final definitional realm is that of *regulatory institutions*. By regulatory institutions, we refer to particular individual departments, boards, and agencies which carry out significant regulatory tasks but which may also, now or historically, have performed or perform other energy policy tasks as well. In terms of the total gamut of energy regulatory institutions in Canada, we explore in closer detail only a handful, although they are certainly key agencies. As already mentioned, the sectoral regulatory institutions we focus on are the National Energy Board (NEB) and two provincial energy boards, the Ontario Energy Board (OEB) and the Alberta Energy and Utilities Board (AEUB), but with analysis extending also to the U.S. Federal Energy Regulatory Commission (FERC), whose influence in liberalizing markets and in deregulation has been important for Canada in the last decade. The horizontal regulatory institutions we examine are environmental regulators and competition regulators, with the focus on Environment Canada, Natural Resources Canada, and the federal Competition Bureau. Both of these horizontal realms have new and expanding links with, and incursions into, energy regulatory governance. The book thus seeks to provide an enhanced understanding of energy regulatory governance, through examining the links energy regulatory institutions have with each other in networked systems of regulators. Accommodations and conflict must be negotiated and managed between sets of sectoral utility regulators (such as the three boards) and sets of horizontal regulators such as those for the environment and for competition.

These are by no means the only analytical realms to be encountered. Energy regulatory systems have always been technical in nature, and the core energy boards such as the NEB, OEB, and AEUB are rightfully seen as technical and expert, with their primary emphasis on engineering and related economic competence. But horizontal energy regulation brings with it a far greater range of science-based regulation, in which scientific advice, including that of a diversely interdisciplinary environmental science, is brought to bear. Natural Resources Canada and Environment Canada are both science-based regulators and policy-makers in this sense, and indeed up to 70 per cent of the staff of these departments are persons with scientific backgrounds (Doern and Reed 2000). Thus an analysis of these departments as science-based regulatory institutions is also a feature of Chapter 8.

As political scientists, our basic approach to analysis as a whole is an institutional one. Institutional approaches or neo-institutionalism (Peters 1999; Reich 2000; Lowdnes 1996) have a variety of features, but broadly they refer to exploring governing bodies or the organizations of the state more generally, in terms of how they have been influenced by policy norms and values and their own distinctive culture as expressed in routines, inertia, and traditions. To these core approaches, we add inter-regime regulatory analysis, which refers broadly, as introduced above, to the need to factor into the analysis the ever more complex interplay among the sets of sectoral regulators (such as the energy boards) and the sets of horizontal regulators (such as environmental and competition regulators).

Inevitably, in a topic as broad as energy regulation, the approach and framework adopted lead to certain areas of emphasis with other factors being given much less attention. In the book as a whole, we accord significant attention to the role of institutions and their core ideas and mandates. There is undoubtedly less concerted analysis in the book on the precise nature of interest groups and policy communities and how these have changed. But we do examine in an illustrative way how some aspects of the pressure exerted by energy business interest groups and NGOs are also key factors of change and regulatory resistance. Indeed, institutional analysis usually requires such inquiry, in part because the agencies and regulators have been shaped by such forces, but also because such interests are, in some sense, represented inside these structures, or have become a part of the changed regulatory regime because they are seeking self-regulatory roles in which they themselves have governance responsibilities. Thus, interest group change is commented upon at different points in the book, but this commentary tends to arise only in an illustrative way to help us say more about the key regulatory bodies or about the two interacting regimes.

Structure and Organization

The analysis proceeds in two parts. Part 1 of the book provides the macro political-economic history of energy, the book's basic dual regime framework, and U.S. energy regulatory influences. Part 2 of the book then zeroes in more closely on the nature of energy regulatory regimes and inter-regime institutional change.

More particularly, chapter 1 sets out the macro history of energy policy and regulation in Canada through a basic look at five key imperatives of energy policy and regulation seen during three broad periods of national political and policy change (1947 to 1973, 1974 to 1984, and 1985 to the present). Chapter 2 takes a closer look at several key factors which have driven regulatory change more recently, including more on the Bush administration's NEP and alternatives to the Kyoto Protocol, and then provides the central framework for the book, showing why it is important to see the changing interaction between the sectoral energy regulatory regime and the horizontal energy regulatory regime as an integral feature of contemporary energy regulatory governance. Chapter 3 explores U.S. influences, over the last decade in particular, on energy regulation, particularly the direct impact of the Federal Energy Regulatory Commission (FERC) policies on Canadian regulatory thinking and practice. These ideas and practices have had implications in such areas as natural gas regulation and the electricity sector.

Part 2 of the book contains five chapters on the two regimes and their interactions. Chapters 4, 5, and 6 look, in turn, at the NEB, the OEB, and the AEUB. While some common questions are raised about each board and its institutional journey across the last decade or so, it is also necessary to tell each board's institutional story in a different way. This is because each board displays a different pattern of change and continuity. The NEB experienced a more stretched out and even pattern of change across the last decade, while the OEB experienced a veritable burst of change from 1998 on, when electricity restructuring sharply changed the rules and the players in Ontario's energy industry. The AEUB is somewhere in the middle in the temporal concentration of change, but it had to deal with significant change resulting not only from pro-market pressures (in an already pro-market province) but also from the merging of two main regulators into one single institution in the mid-1990s.

A natural question arises regarding why these three boards were chosen as exemplars of larger energy regulatory governance changes. The NEB was a fairly obvious choice because it is the main federal energy regulator. To complement the federal level, it was appropriate to choose Alberta's AEUB to capture energy regulation in Canada's largest energy producer province, while the OEB was chosen because Ontario is a large industrial province and the largest energy consumer province. Both the latter boards were also engaged in electricity restructuring, albeit at different stages of development.

In chapters 7 and 8, we deal with key features of the horizontal energy regulatory regime. Chapter 7 is centred on a discussion of the nature of competition and of competition regulation, but in the context of the issues of a networked essential service industry versus claims that energy is becoming just another product or service. It examines the federal Competition Bureau's evolving approach to sharing regulation with industry sectoral regulators, such as the energy regulators, and also explores developments in the transition to competitive electricity regulation in Alberta, Ontario, and Nova Scotia. This chapter also explores the California electricity crisis and its implications for Canada, as well as the issues of accountability in complex networked inter-regime regulation. The focus of chapter 8 is on energy and environmental regulation, and it further explores the theme of regulatory 'stacking.' Centred on a closer look at both Natural Resources Canada and Environment Canada as interacting regulatory institutions, it examines three kinds of evolving change as revealed by so-called traditional 'end of pipe' regulation, regulation functioning under the paradigm of sustainable development, and the regulation of greenhouse gas emissions under the climate change and Kyoto Protocol process. Chapter 8 also comments illustratively on some provincial developments of an inter-regime kind.

A concluding chapter follows. These final observations deal not only with the four main themes previewed above, but also with a discussion of some of the unresolved regulatory policy and institutional issues that Canada's energy regulators face in the twenty-first century, including the overall federal Liberal response to the aggressive U.S. energy agenda under the Bush administration.

PART 1

HISTORY, FRAMEWORK, AND GLOBAL CONTEXT

1 Canadian Energy Policy and Regulation in Historical Context

Energy policy and regulatory development in Canada has historically been a function of five political-economic imperatives: a rich and diverse energy endowment of oil and gas, hydroelectric power, coal, and nuclear fuels; a Canadian dependence on U.S. continental markets to make feasible most energy developments; divided political jurisdiction over energy policy between the federal and provincial governments, but with resource ownership powers residing mainly in the hands of the latter; the pan-Canadian spatial reality of energy resources located in regions distant from consumer population centres, thus triggering significant transportation problems but also entrenched political-economic divisions among Canada's regions, especially between the producer regions of Western Canada and the heavily populated consumer regions of Ontario and Quebec; and the growing desire for a better marriage between energy and the environment through the achievement of sustainable development, a part of which implies the reduction of carbon emissions and the management of climate change.

Each of these macro-historical imperatives is discussed briefly and then related to three broad periods of energy policy and regulatory development since the Second World War: 1945 to 1973, 1973 to 1984, and 1984 to the present. These periods, in turn, must be linked to the broader political context in each period. As previously indicated, the remainder of the book then focuses on the more immediate and middle-level policy, regulatory, and institutional changes over the last decade extending into the early twenty-first century. The three periods sketched in this chapter correspond roughly to different levels of reliance on markets versus government intervention to influence the pace and nature of development. The first and last periods have been very market-oriented, while the middle period, influenced greatly by the two world oil crises of 1973 and 1979–80, witnessed a surge of government intervention. Each period can also be seen as embracing the emergence of a new 'ascending' or dominant fuel. But cumulatively a situation has evolved in which, in the early twenty-first century, there are more and more economic opportunities for inter-fuel substitution and competition in industrial production and consumer use and a much greater presence of a global and North American energy market.

The Five Imperatives

The Rich Fuel Endowment: The Problem of Too Many Choices

Canada's huge land mass is a resource haven. Its abundant supplies of fuels – oil and gas, coal, and uranium for nuclear power – as well as of hydroelectricity give it energy assets that are the envy of most countries (McDougall 1982; Canada 1988; Economic Council of Canada 1985). At the same time, the immense continental expanse and cold northern climate make it one of the world's most prodigious per capita energy users and wasters. Canada's use of its energy base as an explicit development strategy has led many to conclude that successive efforts to 'live off' its resources have resulted in a lack of national attention to the manufacturing components of its economy. Even as recently as 1981, the federal government defined its 'industrial' policy as the management of spin-offs from resource mega-projects (Doern 1982). According to this policy, several planned giant energy projects would be the engine of a national strategy. Past energy developments, in concert with other resource development in the grain and mineral sectors, have also led to 'boom and bust' cycles of economic activity in response to price changes and world sales (Pratt and Richards 1980).

Countries with lesser energy endowments have no option but to choose the obvious. Canada's multiple endowments have often led to the problem of too many choices, or at least a tendency to think the country's endowments permitted the luxury of shielding itself from energy realities. In both the 1973 and 1979–80 energy crises, it was argued by many that Canada tried to shield itself unrealistically from the effects of rising world prices by establishing a two-price policy for exports versus domestic users of oil and gas (Watkins 1991).

Dependence on U.S. Continental Markets

The unalterable fact that the United States has ten times the population of Canada, combined with the equally unalterable fact that Canada's resources are usually located in its more sparsely populated regions, has meant that Canadian energy decisions are almost always simultaneously American decisions (Canada 1988). The fact that the Canadian oil and gas industry has been extensively American-owned only adds to this energy market dependence. Foreign ownership has been as high as 70 per cent; it was reduced in the 1970s and 1980s to about 40 per cent, but had edged upwards in the last decade.

Scarcely any major energy development beyond the exploration stage – in short, any decisions regarding the financing and building of production facilities – involves not only American influence but decisions by American authorities and regulators. Over 40 per cent of oil and gas transported from one part of Canada to another traverses the United States. While hydroelectric development was for a long period somewhat isolated from these continental realities, it too has increasingly been tied to the desire of provincial governments, which own hydroelectric resources, to export ever growing amounts of electrical power to the United States. The huge James Bay projects in Quebec typify this trend.

Canadian energy development has also been adversely affected by U.S. energy protectionism. This has come in the form of import taxes and fees, regulatory rules, and outright prohibitions (Doern and Toner 1985). To a significant extent, when U.S. energy policy changes, Canadian energy policy changes too, albeit not always in lockstep. For example, the partial deregulation of natural gas in the United States in the late 1970s and early 1980s certainly helped precipitate the Canadian effort to deregulate in 1985 and 1986. The same can also be said with respect to electricity competition in the 1990s (see chapter 3).

Divided Political Jurisdiction

Compared with other Western federal countries, Canada probably has the most divided and decentralized jurisdictional arrangement for making energy policy. This arises primarily because of the great extent of direct provincial ownership of lands containing energy resources and because of strong provincial managerial powers over resource extraction (Pratt and Richards 1980). The federal government also has substantial powers that can directly and indirectly influence energy development.

More specifically, provincial powers are derived from section 109 of the Canadian constitution, which confers all lands, mines, minerals, and royalties to the provinces. Provincial ownership is reinforced by the property and civil rights clause (92-13), the power to levy direct taxes (92-2), and the authority over management and sale of public lands (92-50). Federal power resides in the trade and commerce clause (91-2), which confers powers over interprovincial trade, and clause (91-3), which gives the federal government the power to tax by any mode or means, as well as emergency and declaratory powers and treaty powers. The federal government also has direct ownership of the vast Canada Lands (the North and offshore), in which it has all the powers that a province has, as well as powers of owner. Some of these latter powers have been involved in two types of dispute: in some cases, offshore areas, such as those off Newfoundland, raise provincial-like disputes; and in some cases, Native people's land claims are in dispute.

Divided jurisdiction means that energy policy-making is always a process of federal-provincial bargaining, which has been most intense over oil and gas issues. In the realm of hydroelectric power, which is also a classic area of monopoly economic activity, provincial ownership has been the norm. Moreover, with only limited interprovincial trade in electricity, it has generally escaped significant federal-provincial dispute. With regard to uranium and other aspects of nuclear power development, the federal government has the upper hand mainly because of powers granted to it at the beginning of the nuclear age during the Second World War. Even here, however, there are important elements of shared power. For example, Ontario is by far the largest producer and user of nuclear power, and Saskatchewan has huge uranium reserves (Doern and Morrison 1980; Doern, Dorman, and Morrison 2001).

Regional/Spatial Realities and Producer-Consumer Tensions

Within Canada, the major population concentrations are in Ontario and Quebec, and most of these are located in the Montreal to Windsor corridor hugging the American border. Energy sources, by contrast, tend to be in the less populated West (especially oil, gas, and coal), in remote hinterland regions within each province (hydroelectric projects), or in the vast northern and offshore territories known as the Canada Lands.

One consequence of this, in concert with divided jurisdiction, is that Canada has replicated within its borders some of the basic producer-consumer conflicts seen on the world stage between the Western OECD consumer countries and OPEC oil-producing countries. Canada's western producer provinces and its eastern consumer provinces frequently have fundamentally different interests. These different material interests emerged most starkly when world oil prices shot up in 1973 and then again during 1979–80. Western producer interests believed they should have been entitled to receive the world price, but they were denied it by national (in their view 'eastern') policy (McDougall 1982; Pratt and Richards 1980). These resentments are not just a product of energy issues. They reflect a larger historical view, especially in Western Canada, that national economic policy as a whole has favoured Eastern Canada, especially Ontario and Quebec. Thus battles over energy become extremely emotional and symbolic in inter-regional terms.

The second result of these spatial imperatives is that most energy developments involve extensive transportation links to bring the energy fuel to market. Individual projects, usually mega-projects, therefore become highly visible because of their cost and risk. Both political and business careers are 'on the line' in the full glare of national and regional media coverage. Governments at the federal and provincial levels have both risen to and fallen from power on the basis of the promises, successes, and failures of such projects.

Energy, Environment, and Sustainable Development

There is a strong sense, with Canadians clustered near the American border, that the North and its energy and other resources are Canada's 'environment.' With the political emergence of an environmental movement in the late 1960s, the sense of linkage between energy and environment has intensified and become both more complex and more specific. The increased political visibility of the moral case advanced by Native peoples for their land claims in energy-rich areas has also enhanced the links.

Environmental-energy issues first peaked on the national political-economic agenda in the mid-1970s when a major commission of inquiry, the Berger Commission, examined the desirability of building the proposed Mackenzie Valley gas pipeline. Because of the Berger hearings and the sensitivities they raised, the project was put on hold (Bregha 1980).

In the 1980s, there was a gradual increase in regulatory requirements at both the federal and provincial levels to protect environmental values. In the late 1980s, the federal government formally committed itself, along with other G-7 countries, to adopting the 'sustainable development' concept advocated by the prestigious Brundtland World Commission on the Environment (Toner 2000). As will be evident throughout this book, policies on climate change became increasingly contentious and were responsible in part not only for resurrecting new forms of East-West suspicion in Canada but also for creating more complex relationships between traditional energy sectors and sectors such as forestry (Natural Resources Canada 2000).

Key Historical Periods

In addition to the five historical imperatives highlighted above, energy policy and regulation needs to be seen in the context of three key periods of historical development in energy policy: from the end of the Second World War to 1973; 1973 to 1984; and 1985 to 2000. Each period is profiled below and located within its larger political context.

Second World War to 1973: Regulatory Nation- and Province-Building

As the post–Second World War period began, the dominant fuel was coal, with significant use of electrical power within each province (McDougall 1982). All this changed with the discovery in 1947 of major oil and gas reserves in Alberta. Almost immediately, these discoveries resulted in a battle for jurisdiction. Alberta strengthened its powers with legislation to ensure that Albertans had primary access to their own resource. It also established the Alberta Gas Trunk Line as a single-system gas gatherer within the province. The federal government also passed laws to battress its role in interprovincial and international energy trade.

Federal policy differentiated clearly between oil and gas, especially as related to the early approval of the first pipelines. The main concern with oil was to move it and sell it efficiently so as to earn the highest rate of return. Thus the early pipelines were linked to U.S. markets. For natural gas, however, federal policy was different. Natural gas would not move across the border until the government was convinced that there was no economic use, present or future, for that gas within Canada.

The first post-war decade ended with a major national political battle over the construction of the trans-Canada pipeline, in which the federal St Laurent government had to compromise somewhat on its initial promises. This, plus the perceived arrogance of the sponsoring minister, the legendary C.D. Howe, in pushing the necessary legislation through Parliament, eventually led to the defeat of the entrenched Liberal government, which had been in power for over twenty years. Though the Liberals had continued some of the wartime nation-building spirit in such projects as the construction of St Lawrence Seaway, they had increasingly practised a centralized managerial approach that included massive encouragement of foreign ownership, including of the new oil and gas industry.

With the election of the Conservative Diefenbaker government in 1957, political priorities shifted towards those advocated by a government whose leader had a Saskatchewan and Western Canadian base. The 1956 pipeline debate had not only helped defeat the St Laurent Liberals, but it had also led directly to a royal commission. The tabling of the report of the Royal Commission on Energy ushered in a period of relative energy policy and political serenity.

The focus of policy from 1960 until 1973, during a period of both Conservative rule and then Liberal rule under Prime Ministers Lester Pearson and Pierre Trudeau, was almost exclusively on the expansion and development of the oil industry (Doern and Toner 1985). Within the decade, oil became the dominant fuel, supplanting coal. The centrepiece of this development was the Diefenbaker government's 1960 National Oil Policy (NOP). The NOP ensured that consumers east of the Ottawa Valley would be served by cheaper Venezuelan imports (as the U.S. major oil companies were urging), while consumers to the west were supplied by Alberta oil. Alberta oil was more expensive, and hence Ontario consumers would pay a premium price for national development purposes. All the main industrial, national, and regional players were accommodated by this policy. In 1959 the National Energy Board (NEB) was also established to preside over this basically dynamic developmental phase of nation-building, much as an earlier era had seen the building of the national pan-Canadian railways (Lucas 1977, 1978).

The other major development of this period, though largely outside national political attention, was the consolidation and expansion of provincial hydroelectrical utilities and their increasing use as tools of provincial economic development. While the timing varied among the provinces, most of the hydros had been brought under provincial ownership by the 1960s. Alberta was a significant exception to this trend.

Electricity, unlike oil and gas, is a natural monopoly and is characterized by significant economies of scale, prompting pressures for public ownership. This pressure came mainly from the business community, which feared monopoly exploitation. This was certainly the impetus in Ontario, where ownership by the province dates back to 1904 (Armstrong and Nelles 1986). Later takeovers by other provinces also arose out of fears over foreign or non-provincial ownership as well as out of positive desires to use the hydros as tools of development. The nationalization of hydroelectric utilities in Quebec in the 1960s, and the later development of the huge James Bay projects, were a central feature of Quebec nationalist sentiment.

The main development tool with respect to the hydros was pricing policy. Promotional rate structures were introduced in which major customers were charged lower rates for each succeeding block of power purchased (Canada 1988). These policies lured major customers, such as forestry and mineral companies. Pricing policy was also intended to keep electrical prices for general consumers as low and as uniform as possible across the province in question. By the early 1970s, the hydros were among the largest of Canada's corporations; virtually all were state-owned, and they were key players in the political economy of each province. For the most part, however, they were energy traders within their own provinces, rather than interprovincially or internationally.

1974 to 1984: The Energy Crises and Government Intervention

The benchmark events for Canadian energy development during this period were the two energy crises. But these events also occurred with – and were linked to – periods of overall economic stagnation, with double-digit inflation and unemployment, and eventually a full-scale recession in the early 1980s and an increase in the federal fiscal deficit from about $10 billion in 1979 to over $30 billion in 1982. Thus energy policy was crafted within a much larger and very intense debate about the state of the economy and about the degree to which extensive government intervention was the cause of, or the cure for, economic malaise. The period as a whole was dominated by Liberal federal rule under the Trudeau government, interrupted only by the short-lived

Clark Conservative government in 1979. But crucially, when the Trudeau Liberals won power again in 1980, they had almost no MPs from Western Canada.

The first energy crisis occurred in 1973 when the OPEC oil embargo helped precipitate a sudden fourfold increase in the world price of oil. The second occurred during 1979–80 when, in the wake of the revolution in Iran, the world price for oil doubled. Both of these price shocks led to bursts of policy intervention and international and federal-provincial political conflict (Pratt and Richards 1980; Doern and Toner 1985).

Criticized for its lack of preparedness, the federal Trudeau Liberal government responded in 1973 by announcing in quick succession a series of initiatives, including oil export controls, a freeze on domestic oil prices, an oil import compensation program to protect consumers who were dependent on imported oil, and the establishment of a new state-owned oil company, Petro-Canada. Many of these initiatives where the result of the federal government's frustration over its own lack of good information about Canada's reserves, and over its dependence on a largely foreign-owned industry for strategic energy policy and regulatory information.

The federal policy initiatives were viewed by the main producing provinces as a major invasion of their areas of jurisdiction. The old NOP consensus of the 1960s was decimated. The provinces strengthened their own legislation and added their own provincially owned energy companies to fend off Ottawa. In subsequent negotiations over prices, later in the 1970s, Ottawa pulled back from its two-price position and gradually let oil prices approach quite closely to the then prevailing world level. Then suddenly came the second oil crisis, when, following the Iranian revolution of 1979, world prices shot up again.

It was indicative of the intensity of this next inter-regional conflict within Canada that not even newly elected Prime Minister Joe Clark, himself an Albertan, could solve the growing dispute with fellow Conservative and Albertan, Premier Peter Lougheed. The Clark government, after barely nine months in office, was defeated in the House of Commons, in part over its budget proposals for new energy taxes. The core political issue, as in 1973, was that Alberta believed it was entitled to ask the world price for its depleting resource, while the federal government pressed again for lower prices to assist Central Canadian consumers and industries. Ontario Conservative governments also basically backed the federal approach. As well, there was intense dispute over how the new windfall resource revenues should be managed to promote economic development.

Each of the political protagonists had its own new institutional symbol that served to gall the other. In the latter part of the 1970s, the Liberal government of Pierre Trudeau had facilitated the expansion of Petro-Canada through takeovers of private oil companies. This angered the oil patch as well as free enterprise Albertans, and the Clark government promised to privatize Petro-Canada. For its part, Alberta had established the Heritage Trust Fund, into which it deposited a portion of its burgeoning oil and gas revenues. The exponential growth of this fund meant that any Alberta claims to be an aggrieved and economically vulnerable region fell upon deaf ears in Eastern Canada (Pratt and Richards 1980).

The sudden defeat of the Clark government in 1980 brought with it the equally sudden return to power of a refurbished Trudeau Liberal government, with its previously mentioned dearth of representation from Western Canada. In their first budget in the fall of 1980, the Liberals announced the National Energy Program (NEP). The NEP was a massive act of federal intervention premised on the Liberals' campaign promises of fair 'made in Canada' prices, 50 per cent Canadian ownership of the oil and gas industry, and the promotion of energy security, with self-sufficiency in oil by 1990. The NEP was premised on absolutely bullish expectations about rising future energy prices, which failed to materialize (Doern and Toner 1985; Desveaux 1995).

With the NEP, the federal Liberals had thrown down the gauntlet, precipitating angry negotiations and acts of political brinkmanship that seriously threatened national unity. Nonetheless, a pricing agreement was eventually reached in September 1981, in part because both the federal government and Alberta believed their own forecasts of ever-increasing prices and hence thought they were sharing a very large revenue pie. The NEP also angered the newly elected free enterprise–oriented Reagan administration in the United States, as well as major parts of the energy industry and Canadian business community as a whole. It was, however, initially a popular policy in Ontario and Quebec.

The NEP had barely commenced, however, when many of its underpinnings fell away. High interest rates and the 1982 worldwide recession dealt an initial blow. Oil prices were softened by reduced demand brought on by the recession itself, by political splits in OPEC, and by the cumulative effects of past conservation programs and the discovery of new world supplies. When these factors were combined with the new energy taxes and the uncertainties of the new NEP regime, the energy industry in Canada nosedived. By mid-1982 the Liberal government was already offering to change its policy.

The NEP did increase Canadian ownership as well as produce a level of exploration in the frontier areas that increased knowledge of the reserves in those regions. The gas industry infrastructure was expanded further into Quebec, and Petro-Canada became a formidable and symbolic presence in the consciousness of Canadians. But the opinion of the great majority of energy policy professionals was that the NEP was a mistaken and seriously flawed policy. The view increasingly became that energy issues were too volatile economically for any policy to anticipate or encompass all the changes taking place. Massive intervention only made things worse. The stage was being set politically and economically for the return of pro-market energy policy under the Mulroney Conservative government elected in 1984.

Politically, however, the NEP left a bitter taste, particularly regarding relations between Central and Western Canada. It became the quintessential example, especially in Western Canada, of how not to make policy. It was seen as a combative unilateral act by an unsympathetic Eastern-dominated government. This lesson was a major contributing factor in later discussions during 1987–8 when energy free trade was secured through the Canada-U.S. Free Trade Agreement. From the Western Canadian perspective, energy free trade ensured that there could never again be 'another NEP.' Debates over the Kyoto treaty on climate change have also resonated with the view that Kyoto would be 'another NEP,' that is, another unilaterally imposed policy by Eastern governments over Western oil and gas. We return to this argument, and the extent to which it is valid, in later chapters.

Operating far in the background, but nonetheless still important to Canadian energy development in the 1970s and early 1980s, was Canada's nuclear industry (Morrison 1998). Following its earlier research and development phase under federal auspices at Atomic Energy of Canada Ltd (AECL), the industry moved into its commercial stage. The Canadian-designed CANDU reactor became the basis for Ontario Hydro's extensive movement into nuclear power. Ontario became Canada's main nuclear province. The federal government also tried to persuade and induce other provinces to adopt the CANDU, but only New Brunswick and Hydro-Québec did, and the latter to only a very limited extent.

Ottawa's ambitions for developing foreign markets for CANDU reactors did not enjoy much success. In part this was because of the novelty of the design of the CANDU system compared to other reactor systems, but also because of the contraction of the world reactor market in the wake of the shutdown of the Three Mile Island plant in the United States. But to an even greater extent, the lack of foreign market development for CANDU reactors was also caused by the ambivalence of Canada's views about nuclear reactor sales and nuclear proliferation. This came to a head in the mid-1970s when India, using nuclear materials from a Canadian-sponsored research reactor, exploded its first nuclear weapon. The issue of nuclear safeguards escalated even further into policy consciousness and divided the federal Cabinet over just how hard to push sales, especially to countries with dubious records on non-proliferation issues (Doern and Morrison 1980).

Compounding these dilemmas were some serious financial and accountability problems at AECL. Questionable sales practices and costly oversupply problems concerning heavy water brought AECL into political disrepute. By the mid-1980s the CANDU program and AECL were facing at best a steady-state situation and at worst a seriously deteriorating one.

The Mid-1980s to the Early 2000s: Energy Deregulation, Free Trade, and Sustainable Development

Each era of Canadian energy policy reacts to the previous period while at the same time seeking to deal with what the future might bring. It is also propelled by realities that may bear only limited resemblance to the rhetoric used to describe that them. The election of the Mulroney Conservative government with a massive majority in 1984 certainly brought a new energy agenda and a pro-market approach to national policy in general. Ideologically, the Mulroney Conservatives favoured a return to strong pro-market policies on energy and the economy (Toner 1986; Watkins 1991; Canada 1988), while politically, especially regarding Western Canada, the new government sought national reconciliation and an end to the energy wars. Internationally, it sought closer relations with the United States, eventually through the Canada-U.S. Free Trade Agreement.

In their last days of opposition and during the transition period to power, the Mulroney government probably spent more concerted time on developing their energy policy than on any other policy field. A task force had worked for over a year in close cooperation with the oil and gas industry. Accordingly, once in power, they moved swiftly and sure-handedly on the energy front, with the prime task being the dismantling of the NEP. The decisive pro-market conciliatory slant of federal policy was reflected in four initiatives, the net effects of which have been to create a free market in energy trade that exceeds even the pre-1973 era, when the National Oil Policy (NOP) was in operation.

The first initiative was the signing of the Western Accord between Ottawa and the western producer provinces. This accord deregulated oil and restored continental oil markets. The Atlantic Accord was an agreement primarily with Newfoundland which settled the long-festering and divisive issue of jurisdictional control and management of offshore resources. The Atlantic Accord was not itself particularly pro-market in its content but certainly exhibited commitment to national reconciliation. The Western Accord was followed by an agreement to phase in the deregulation of gas. This would allow more direct buy-sell relationships between gas producers and gas users with a consequent weakening of some of the previous monopoly powers of pipelines and distribution companies. Because of long-term contracts, this new gas policy was difficult to implement, but it was nonetheless a significant change. The extent of gas deregulation eventually included an end to the postwar policy which had required surplus reserve tests for exports of gas. These had required a 25-to-30-year domestic supply cushion before exports were allowed.

The final arrow in the Mulroney energy policy quiver came in some key provisions of the Canada-U.S. Free Trade Agreement (FTA), which came into effect on 1 January 1989 (Hart 1994; Doern and Tomlin 1991). The FTA further opened the continental boundaries, mainly by preventing the future use of two-price systems and by restraining the Americans from using many restrictive measures that they had resorted to in the postwar era with respect to Canadian oil and gas (and uranium) exports. The quid pro quo for this more secure access to the massive American market, which had been long saught after, was the so-called proportionality clause. It provided that Canada could not arbitrarily cut off contracted American buyers of Canadian oil and gas. If declared shortages occurred, Canada could only reduce supply proportionately over an agreed three-year base period. The FTA did protect Canada's existing foreign ownership laws regarding energy investments, but for the most part the FTA provided the capstone to the Mulroney government's pro-market energy policies, in effect quasi- 'constitutionalizing' them.

The degree to which this was achieved in the FTA is in part the result of the anger left over from the political legacy of the NEP. The federal government may have given up more of its energy powers in the FTA negotiations than it would have needed to, had the Liberals practised a more conciliatory approach in 1980. In any event, there is little doubt that as the 1990s began, the pro-market approach was clearly in the ascendancy.

One of the policy events that further reflected the intellectual underpinnings for the pro-market focus was the Energy Options report published in 1988 by the minister of energy's Energy Options Advisory Committee (Canada 1988). After an elaborate public consultation exercise, it concluded that energy policy participants had rejected the 'hoarding' approach, for a 'development' approach. By a development approach, it meant an approach that relies on free markets, and by a hoarding approach, policies that slow the rate of development below what is economically viable under prevailing conditions to ensure that future generations are left with an adequate supply. The Energy Options committee concluded that the latter policies were fundamentally flawed for four reasons. First, they presumed that policy-makers had the wisdom to forecast the future. Second, they frustrated the very mechanism, namely market pricing, most likely to bring on the growth of needed oil and gas reserves. Third, they divided the nation by frustrating the needs and aspirations of the producing regions. And finally, they assigned to governments the responsibility for prescribing choices as opposed to allowing Canadian producers and consumers to generate the needed solutions through their diverse market interactions (Canada 1988).

While the implicit and explicit claims for the development model are somewhat overstated in the above critique, they nonetheless capture the real changes in energy markets and in views about how past policy had worked or failed to work. For example, unknown to the general public, profound changes had occurred in energy markets in the 1980s. Several layers beneath the policy rhetoric, both interventionist and pro-market, a situation had emerged in Canada in which massive new opportunities now existed for inter-fuel substitution. Policy no longer just fostered or followed the rise of a newly dominant fuel – first coal, then oil, then gas. There was a new maturity to markets in which one could now more readily say that inter-fuel 'energy' markets truly existed. Industrial production could increasingly switch to different fuels depending on price and other factors. Conservation and softer energy alternatives were beginning to have an effect on the range of energy choices available.

As already mentioned, electricity production and distribution had remained the last bastion of state monopoly activity, but in the 1990s this changed with the advent of competitive or quasi-competitive markets, first in Alberta and then in nuclear Ontario. The U.S. pressures that partially precipitated both of these changes in electricity policy are examined in chapter 3, but the essence of the Canadian changes, especially the crucial ones in Ontario, can be sketched in a preliminary way here.

Nuclear energy is at the centre of the Ontario changes, but so are political and technological advances (Freeman 1995; Vollans 1995). Ontario's electricity was largely generated by nuclear-powered CANDU reactors, which had been developed in relatively close partnership between AECL and Ontario Hydro. But by the mid-1980s, and certainly into the 1990s, this Ontario-federal relationship had grown strained (Doern, Dorman, and Morrison 2001). Ontario Hydro's focus had clearly been on the investments of tens of billions of dollars it was making in a thirty-year construction program of twenty nuclear power plants. Through decades of steady growth in electricity demand, averaging close to 7 per cent per year, Ontario Hydro had invested in expanded generation capacity, using dams, coal-fired generation, and, in the 1960s and 1970s, nuclear power, on assumptions that rested seemingly on the continuation of this ever-expanding demand. However, the rate of demand growth in electricity consumption fell, initially in the 1970s and then extensively in the 1980s and 1990s, as a result of the combined effects of economic recession and effective energy conservation measures. The fact that Ontario was gradually becoming more of a service economy than a manufacturing economy also affected electricity demand, since the service sector uses less electricity. The size of Ontario Hydro's debt was exceeded only by the growing concerns about a public enterprise which no political authority seemed able to control and whose accountability was oblique at best (Ontario 1996).

In the 1990s the intensity of these political-economic pressures increased. Their political salience was propelled in particular by a 30 per cent increase in power rates for consumers in the early 1990s, at a time of recession when many ordinary Ontario citizens were again facing economic hardships. Ontario's electricity demand remained below its 1989 value for the better part of a decade. Anticipated load growth of 3 per cent per year, or more than 30 per cent for the decade, failed to materialize. When the Darlington nuclear station, with four large CANDU units, came on line in the early 1990s, its capacity was surplus to Ontario's needs. The rate increases were a direct result of the inflated debt taken on by Ontario Hydro to pay for the nuclear plants and for other mechanisms to reconcile supply and demand. Other factors were also coalescing to produce change in the 1990s. These were expressed in various ways by the Macdonald Committee (Ontario 1996) and other advisory bodies, and eventually by the Harris Conservative government's own 1997 White Paper (Ontario Ministry of Energy, Science and Technology 1997), which heralded Ontario's decision to break up Ontario Hydro (see chapter 5) and which announced that competition in electricity supply would be introduced.

The White Paper identified four main factors driving change:

1. *Deregulation in the United States*: Federal regulators in the United States had recently mandated competition among wholesale electricity customers (municipal and rural distribution utilities) and many states were passing legislation creating choice for retail electricity customers.
2. *Economic Competitiveness*: The globalization of Ontario's economy meant greater competitive pressures for industry. Industries were looking to cut costs, including that of electricity, and were looking to the success of deregulation elsewhere (the natural gas sector) in driving prices down.
3. *Technology*: New generation technologies could provide financially and environmentally attractive alternatives to large-scale, capital-intensive electricity generation.
4. *Financial Soundness*: Concern about public sector debt.

Other assessments of the causes of change focused on nuclear power per se. Some authors explicitly linked Ontario Hydro's problems regarding the over-estimation of future demand to the 'over-expansion and related borrowings with respect to its nuclear facilities in the 1970s and 1980s' and to the 'substantial cost over-runs and disappointing operating performance of a number of these facilities, in part itself a function of a federal-provincial industrial strategy designed to promote the atomic energy sector in Ontario through the Atomic Energy of Canada Ltd.' (Trebilcock and Daniels 1995: 6). This assessment also drew attention, in the economic sphere, to 'an anachronistic regulatory structure characterized by dispersed and fragmented authority that has at times subverted public transparency and fostered government micro-management.'

Ontario Hydro's management of its nuclear operations was severely criticized in August 1997 by a special team of U.S. nuclear experts who had been called in by Ontario Hydro's president. The president subsequently resigned, and the U.S. experts were put in charge of the nuclear operations. They decided to shut down seven reactors in order to focus the company's efforts on getting the other twelve operating reactors back up to top performance.

The key feature of the competitive Ontario electricity market is that CANDU reactors will have to compete with newer, mainly gas-fired sources of electricity generation, which will now be able to enter the Ontario electricity market under private ownership (McNeil 1999). AECL is affected negatively by these choices with respect to domestic CANDU reactor sales (which seem highly unlikely in this decade), but also positively, because new opportunities for commercial service and refurbishment work will emerge as Ontario tries to get its nuclear plants into competitive shape with a view to penetrating the neighbouring U.S. market.

While the overall direction of energy development became market oriented in this period, there is one contrary trend that implies a potentially greater, rather than reduced, governmental role in Canadian energy development. This potential arose out of the adoption by federal and provincial governments, in principle, of the concept of 'sustainable' development in their environmental policies (Toner 2000). As defined by the Brundtland World Commission, sustainable development is development which ensures that the utilization of resources and the environment today does not damage prospects for their use by future generations. In theory, this is a radical concept, but its meaning in practice depends upon a host of decisions and bargains by public and private decision-makers. In 1993 the new statute for Canada's reorganized 'energy' department, Natural Resources Canada (NRCan), gave it a legal mandate to foster sustainable development (Doern and Gattinger 2001).

The other new element to enter this complex realm is the Kyoto Protocol, the international agreement which Canada signed and whose purpose is to fight global warming by reducing carbon emissions on a global basis. Canada had made commitments to reduce by 2012 its greenhouse gas emissions by 6 per cent below the 1990 levels. But such was the policy failure with respect to this commitment that by 2001 it would have to amount to a 26 per cent reduction below the increased levels of 2001. The failure to meet commitments is partly the result of a new confrontation between the federal Chrétien Liberal government and the oil-and-gas-producer provinces, led by a popular and also thrice-elected Klein Conservative government in Alberta. A more detailed examination of the complex Kyoto debate is given in chapter 8.

A further environmental policy change during this final historical period was the general movement of federal environmental assessment policy from being a policy based on federal guidelines to one based on statute law. In 1995 the Canadian Environmental Assessment Act (CEAA) took effect. The environmental assessment process of the federal government as a whole had been transformed largely by court rulings initiated by environmental activists. These court decisions had determined that the federal 'guidelines' previously in existence were in fact law-like in their nature (Doern and Conway 1994). As a result of the CEAA, energy regulators such as the NEB (as a 'responsible authority' under the CEAA) have to work closely with Environment Canada's Canadian Environmental Assessment Agency to ensure that their assessments are efficient, avoid duplication, and are environmentally effective (Sato 1997).

The concept of sustainable development, the pressures of the Kyoto Protocol and the climate change debate, and the overall strengthening of environmental assessment are by no means the only environmental elements to enter into energy policy. But they are a crucial part of any minimum list such as that presented in this initial account of energy policy imperatives. Later chapters return to the crucial nature of the sustainable development debate and the degree to which such a paradigm has been institutionalized in federal (and provincial) energy regulation.

Conclusions

To provide a broader historical context for the book as a whole, this chapter has traced the five key historical imperatives of Canadian energy policy and overall regulatory development. Energy riches have been central to this story, as have energy nation-building and nation-dividing, always couched in the practical need to deal with, and respond to, the American energy and political giant to the south of the Canadian border. Divided political jurisdiction is a given, as is the need to cooperate in some fashion, however begrudgingly, to bridge the interests of producers and consumers in a geographically vast country. And unfolding through the last two decades of this history has been an ever more complex and insistent global and national agenda on the environment and on sustainable development. So also has a fuel-by-fuel story that has increasingly melded, both through new technology and through some policy successes, into a world in which inter-fuel substitution and competition is a reality. But energy policy is still partly a sectoral world as well, comprising oil and gas, electricity, nuclear energy, and new alternative energy technologies.

The broad picture over the three energy policy periods covered has been one of changing degrees of market primacy versus state intervention. This is also a crucial backdrop for the analysis to follow and must be located within the larger patterns of political change, including partisan politics and the overall state of the economy in each period. Sandwiched between two periods of relative pro-market policies was one decade of significantly increased state intervention. But there is a crucial residue from all three periods, deriving not only from the actual effects of each period's policies, but from the myths they have created and their effects on the political memory of politicians and voters alike.

While we have gone into some areas of detail, this chapter has necessarily presented a macro view of the key periods of change. This initial picture now needs to be complemented in the next chapter by a closer, more middle-level view that focuses on particular aspects of institutional change and change in the energy regulatory regime over the last decade.

2 Analysing the Power Switch: Factors and Framework

This chapter provides a basis for analysing the power switch in energy regulatory governance through a closer look at the key factors driving recent change and through a framework of contemporary energy regulation cast as a system of interacting energy regulatory regimes, one largely sectoral and the other horizontal. The resulting interplay of institutions (and related interests) thus shows energy regulation as involving the governance of a complex networked essential service industry. But crucially, energy regulatory governance also consists of networked cooperating and competing regulators with partially contending views of what essential service means. Though the energy regulatory system has been heading in a pro-competitive direction, it is still not a regulatory realm that can easily be encompassed by conventional notions of full competition. Rather, it is more accurately seen as a system of ordered or managed competition. Nor does the system evoke a clear separation between the role of the state and the role of markets or of conventional notions of selling products and services. But in what sense is the industry a complex networked essential service industry? This question is explored in this chapter because it is also central to the question of networked and interacting regulatory regimes and the mechanisms of accountability within and between these regimes.

Key Factors for Change: A Closer Look

The account in chapter 1 of Canada's energy policy and regulatory history presented the broad sweep of change in the post–Second World War period as a whole, casting it widely as periods of pro-market, then state intervention, and then pro-market policies. However, an examination of energy regulatory governance in the present period of Canada's energy policy evolution needs to zero in first on a sharper account of the more specific factors driving change in the early years of the twenty-first century. These factors are the following: the Bush administration's U.S. National Energy Plan (NEP), announced in May 2001; the emergence of ideologically driven concepts of incentive-based regulation; the role of economic ideas which, when combined with technical change, reduce the monopoly rationale for regulation; the institutionalization of the sustainable development paradigm and the related Kyoto commitments to reduce greenhouse gas emissions, particularly in the context of the role of Natural Resources Canada (NRCan), the lead federal energy department; the role of free trade commitments (including internal trade) and their links to continental energy markets and a far more integrated Canada-U.S. economy and business climate; and the reconfiguration of energy interests and interest groups.

The Bush Administration's NEP and Alternative to Kyoto

In many respects, until the Bush NEP was announced on 17 May 2001, Canadian energy policy as such might well have stayed on the back-burner of federal priorities. Nothing is more ironical than an American 'NEP' bringing energy policy back with a vengeance not seen since the rise and demise of Canada's NEP twenty years earlier. The trauma of the terrorist attacks of 11 September 2001 on the United States added a further security dimension to U.S. policy in general, including energy security (security of supply) and the physical security of energy pipelines and nuclear power plants. This was followed in February 2002 with the Bush administration's announcement of its own unilateral alternative to Kyoto, centred on voluntary approaches for U.S. energy producers and incentives for new developments in alternative energy technologies.

But the Bush NEP undoubtedly has the broadest implications for pan-Canadian energy policy. Drafted by Vice President Dick Cheney in a Bush administration whose Cabinet contains several ex–energy industry executives, the Bush NEP is unabashedly a supply-driven and -dominated policy (Government of the United States 2001). The policy was forged in the midst of rapidly rising gas prices, both at the pump and for home heating, and in the midst of the electricity crisis in California (see chapters 3 and 7), where soaring electricity prices and frequent blackouts were disrupting a booming Internet-driven knowledge economy (Jaccard 2002).

The central features of the Bush NEP are as follows:

- Ease restrictions on oil and gas development on public lands.
- Open part of the Arctic National Wildlife Refuge (ANWR) in Alaska for drilling.
- Reconsider requirements for 'boutique' gasoline blends that contribute to supply shortages.
- Streamline the approval process for siting power plants.
- Government authority for takeover of private property for power lines.
- Provide tax breaks for developing clean coal technologies.
- Ease regulatory barriers, including clean-air rules, to speed up expansion of existing plants or building of new plants.
- Speed nuclear safety reviews in the relicensing of reactors and the licensing of new plants.
- Limit industry liability from a nuclear accident.

The Bush NEP also includes some tax breaks for renewable energy and conservation, but these are decidedly secondary in the plan as a whole.

These plans affect Canada simply because they affect the full North American energy industry. But the Bush plan also speaks of energy security for the United States in terms of North American energy supply, and thus Canada's oil and gas reserves, along with those of Mexico, are a key part of the continental plan. During 2001 and 2002, with a U.S. Senate controlled by the Democratic party and a House of Representatives controlled by the president's Republican party, there was no guarantee that the U.S. NEP would be approved in its entirety. This still remains true even though the Republicans regained a narrow majority control of both Houses in the November 2002 mid-term elections. Regardless, the Bush NEP is clearly the agenda to which everyone is now reacting (see more below).

The Bush NEP received a relatively smooth ride in the Republican-controlled House of Representatives. The House bill, passed in August 2001, closely reflects the president's goal of increasing domestic energy production, including the Bush NEP's continued emphasis on fossil fuels. The bill permits oil and gas exploration in Alaska's Arctic National Wildlife Refuge (ANWR) and creates tax incentives, concentrated largely on fossil fuels, for the production of new forms of energy. The

NEP did not receive such a warm reception in the Democrat-controlled Senate, however, whose energy bill was debated for close to two months, though finally approved in late April 2002 with a wide margin (88 to 11). The Senate bill places somewhat more emphasis on conservation and renewable resources than its House counterpart, with some modest measures for conservation and renewable resources.

The two versions of the legislation differ markedly in some areas, most notably with respect to ANWR, a core item in President Bush's domestic agenda. Whereas the House bill permits ANWR exploration (provided development is limited to a surface area of 2,000 acres), the Senate bill contains no provisions on ANWR, following the senators' rejection of ANWR exploration by a vote of 54 to 46 in March 2002. And while both bills contain tax incentives, over the next decade for energy production, the Senate bill's incentives, though less sizeable ($14 billion versus the House's $33 billion), encourage conservation and renewable energy sources, whereas the House tax breaks emphasize fossil fuels. There is an additional difference between the two bills in the area of renewable energy sources. While the House bill contains no provisions on renewables, the Senate bill requires energy utility companies to increase the proportion of electricity they derive from renewable sources to 10 per cent by the year 2019.

At the time of writing, the bills had yet to go before a House-Senate conference committee, which will try to draft compromise energy legislation. Given the Senate's rejection of ANWR exploration, it is unlikely that the resulting legislation will permit oil and gas development in ANWR. Of consequence for Canada, the House and the Senate seem to concur on the route for a northern gas pipeline and its construction; both bills encourage pipeline construction from the northern slope of Alaska, but specify a route through Alaska rather than mostly through Canada.

At the same time as these two bills were being debated in committee and passed on the House and Senate floors, both the House and the Senate were working on new legislative measures in the wake of the collapse of the giant energy company Enron. On the same day as the Senate passed its energy bill, the Senate Judiciary Committee approved a bill that would establish a new felony in federal securities fraud for any scheme to defraud shareholders in publicly traded companies, would provide prosecutors with additional means of prosecuting white collar crime, and would strengthen protection for whistle-blowers. A similar measure was passed by the House of Representatives. The day before the Senate passed its energy bill, the House approved an accounting reform bill that would create a new audit oversight board under the auspices of the Securities and Exchange Commission and would bar accounting firms from providing certain consulting services to firms they audit. Two weeks prior, the House approved a pension reform bill seeking to protect workers from substantial retirement-plan losses like those experienced by Enron employees.

The interplay of issues arising from the Bush NEP, the U.S. alternative to Kyoto (discussed more fully in chapter 8), the Enron collapse, the California electricity crisis, and September 11th terrorism brought energy issues into the North American media and public eye during 2001–2 in a way that had not been seen for two decades. The new energy policy context would undoubtedly affect Canada, but exactly how, both in general and in regulatory terms, remains to be seen.

Meanwhile, underlying these developments was the need to keep in mind the basic patterns and growth of energy trade in a NAFTA market context. In recent years, North American energy commodities trade has been rising. As shown in Table 1, the value of bilateral trade in energy products between all of the parties to NAFTA has grown quite rapidly over the past decade. Energy trade between Canada and the United States almost tripled between 1990 and 2001, rising from U.S. $13.1 billion to U.S. $37.3 billion. Canada-Mexico trade multiplied many times over during this same period, from U.S. $53 million in 1990 to U.S. $295 million in 2001. U.S.-Mexico energy trade also increased markedly over the past ten years, from U.S. $6.1 billion in 1990 to U.S. $13.5 billion in 2001.

As these figures reveal, the largest bilateral energy trading relationship in North America is the Canada-U.S. relationship. The value of bilateral Canada-U.S. trade is roughly triple that of U.S.-Mexico trade, at U.S. $37.3 billion in 2001, compared with U.S. $13.5 billion worth of U.S.-Mexico energy trade in this same year. These two bilateral trade relationships dwarf by many orders of magnitude the value of energy commodity trade between Canada and Mexico.

Over the past decade, the United States was a net energy importer in its trading relationships with both Canada and Mexico, in some years importing close to twelve times more energy from Canada than it exported, and importing anywhere from three to six times more energy from Mexico than it exported. In the relatively small energy trading relationships between Canada and Mexico, Canada is a net importer of energy.

Table 1
Value of North American energy commodities trade

Year	Canada–United States		Canada–Mexico		Unites States–Mexico	
	Imports	Exports	Imports	Exports	Imports	Exports
1990	2,104*	10,990	49	4	5,288	827
1991	1,261	11,710	85	16	4,672	868
1992	1,293	12,529	156	32	4,737	1,239
1993	1,162	13,536	173	16	4,875	1,038
1994	1,212	13,955	111	19	5,112	1,013
1995	1,348	15,097	81	38	6,251	1,277
1996	1,766	18,791	142	16	8,114	1,506
1997	2,220	19,585	193	19	8,443	1,992
1998	2,546	15,929	139	10	5,290	1,772
1999	2,151	18,873	180	12	7,284	2,258
2000	2,657	35,457	267	11	12,779	4,279
2001	3,512	35,810	278	17	10,213	3,255

Sources: Statistics Canada and the U.S. Census Bureau (data compiled on strategis.gc.ca).
Note: Value of trade in Harmonized System (HS) Code 27 – mineral fuels, mineral oils, bituminous substances, and mineral waxes (includes petroleum and petroleum products, natural gas, coal, and electricity). Imports are total imports, and exports are domestic exports.
*Millions of current U.S. dollars.

Petroleum dominates energy commodities trade in North America, followed distantly by natural gas. Over 90 per cent of Canada's exports to the United States consists of petroleum and natural gas, with petroleum exports accounting for the lion's share of this amount, at roughly twice the level of natural gas exports.[1] U.S.-Mexico energy trade follows a similar pattern, with petroleum making up over 95 per cent of energy commodities trade between these two countries in recent years (natural gas accounted for roughly 4 per cent of energy traded).[2] In addition to petroleum and natural gas, Canada, the United States, and Mexico also trade coal, electricity,[3] and uranium.

---

1 Natural Resources Canada, *Energy in Canada 2000*, Statistical Series 12.03a, Canadian Energy Trade with the U.S. – Value of Exports.
2 U.S. Census Bureau, Foreign Trade Division, Data Dissemination Branch.
3 While there is some evidence that energy market continentalization has enabled Canada to sell electricity into Mexico (Dukert 2000), this is not as yet reflected in Canadian trade statistics.

Ideology and Incentive-Based Regulation

A second key factor driving change has been the role of pro-market ideologies and the general advocacy of incentive-based regulation. We have already seen this in chapter 1 in a broad overall way, but the exact nature of this catalyst for change needs to be appreciated further. Indeed, paradoxically, the Bush NEP seems to contain provisions that, while pro-market, are decidedly not incentive-based. Some very heavy-handed command-and-control-style rules are a part of the U.S. NEP arsenal. Nonetheless, in the larger scheme of things, the shift towards incentive-based regulation has been unmistakable in recent years in the United States and Canada.

Incentive-based regulation refers to efforts to craft rule-making in energy and other policy realms in more flexible ways (Grabosky 1995; Doern, Hill, Prince, and Schultz 1999). Typically contrasted with rigid, detailed 'command and control' regulation, incentive-based regulation takes far greater cognizance of the different commercial situations faced by the diverse firms being regulated, and seeks to use a broader tool-kit of rule-making and behaviour-inducing approaches. These include such approaches as price-capping rather than detailed rate of return regulation the use of guidelines and voluntary codes, and, even more broadly, the use of tax incentives and tradeable permits.

The three energy boards explored in Part 2 of this book, but also the environmental and competition regulators whose work intersects with them, have all been influenced by this general global ideological shift to incentive-based regulation (Braithwaite and Drahos 2000). But these shifts are also aligned broadly with the general reforms in so-called *reinvented government*, including reforms in service delivery and compliance. Changes in public administration and the management of government are of key importance in understanding the three boards and the two networked energy regulatory regimes. At one level, these changes have been characterized in terms of the rise of the New Public Management (NPM) and or 'reinvented' government, and the decline of traditional hierarchical and bureaucratic government (Aucoin 1997). They are also entwined with the implications of governing through and with the new information technologies (Bellamy and Taylor 1998). The NPM and reinvention ethos essentially argued that public service bureaucracies need to focus much more on service to customers and on the quality of service, and to downplay their focus on top-level policy development roles. Rigid accountability concepts also had to be changed

(Aucoin 1997; Ford and Zussman 1997; Ferlie et al. 1997). Reforms have led to new ways of funding regulators and programs through user fees, and also to new ways of negotiated regulation-making and rule-making. They have also led to the previously mentioned increase in use of guidelines and voluntary codes (Ayres and Braithwaite 1992; Grabosky 1995; Sparrow 1994; Webb 2002).

These changes in public administration are well under way and are part of the energy regulatory story, but they also raise questions about the extent to which energy users are customers as opposed to being citizens, and, if they are customers, about what kinds of customers they are. These questions are also tied to the issue of how much of the energy industry is a series of products like any other as opposed to an essential industry or service as a whole (see further discussion below).

Economic Ideas, Technical Change, and the Reduced Monopoly Rationale

A further variant of the shift to incentive-based regulation, but one deserving separate mention in an energy context, is the emergence of economic ideas that, when linked to technological change, upset or overturn some of the classic rationales for regulation based on the existence of natural monopolies. The transformation of electricity regulation has been significantly affected by such combined forces. It is occurring in Canada, but its roots are best seen in earlier U.S. developments and in the U.K.'s electricity markets. We discuss this further in chapter 3 regarding the particular influences of the FERC on gas and electricity, but an initial discussion is needed in the context of the purposes of this chapter.

In the United States (as in Canada), the electricity supply industry has been heavily regulated since the 1920s (Norman 1999). Electricity generation and transmission has been viewed as a natural monopoly and regulated as such: the government grants utilities monopoly control over geographical service territories in exchange for obligations to provide universal and affordable service on a non-discriminatory basis. Sidak and Spulber (1998) summarize the resulting 'regulatory contract': 'in return for assuming an obligation to serve and charging not more than "just and reasonable" prices on a nondiscriminatory basis, the utility is guaranteed a franchise protected by entry regulation and income sufficient to recover and to earn a competitive rate of return on its invested capital' (4). This regulatory framework is in the process of significant change.

Numerous countries throughout the world are rapidly restructuring and partially deregulating their electricity supply industries. A variety of reasons have been cited for these changes in the American context, including the energy crisis of the 1970s (Czamanski 1999), energy security concerns, and changing views about regulation's role in the American economy (Norman 1999). The energy crisis is said to have focused attention on certain aspects of the demand and supply sides of the industry that prompted change. On the demand side, energy shortages drew attention to the over-consumption of electricity, while on the supply side, large, vertically integrated electricity suppliers, particularly publicly owned utilities, were deemed inefficient. The resulting pressures to promote electricity conservation and increase efficiency in electricity production led to restructuring and some related deregulatory initiatives.

Energy security issues also contributed to these changes. Immediately prior to the commencement of electricity industry liberalization, U.S. dependence on imported oil had grown to nearly 50 per cent, prompting action to reduce this dependence. Deregulation has been a partial response to this concern. Finally, beginning in the 1970s, American economists increasingly questioned regulation's effectiveness in supplying lowest cost electricity, arguing that regulators were susceptible to capture, that regulation stifled innovation, and that many of the original economic rationales for regulation had been weakened by technological change.

Historically, the electricity industry was treated as a natural monopoly. There are significant economies of scale in the industry because electricity cannot readily be stored (it is less expensive to invest in redundant capacity than it is to store electric power), demand is highly variable, and capital costs are both substantial and specific. The conventional view held that optimal efficiency in electricity supply could be achieved by capitalizing on these scale economies. This required an integrated network system of electricity generation and transmission, and some mechanism of coordinating investment decisions between the generation and transmission sides of the business. Regulation attempted to strike a balance between the goals of public policy (i.e., reliability of service, security of supply, accessibility/affordability, price stability, etc.) and the requirements of investors for sufficient rates of return.

But the traditional economic view of the electricity industry as a natural monopoly has given way to a 'new concept' of the industry as composed of five distinct functions, only some of which are monopolistic (Hunt and Shuttleworth 1996). These functions are *generation* (the production of electricity), *transmission* (bulk electricity transfers across the country), *system control* (coordinating the transmission of electricity throughout the network), *distribution* (bulk electricity delivery over local networks), and *supply* (wholesale and retail sales). Only transmission, system control, and distribution are viewed as natural monopolies, while it is held that competition can improve allocative efficiency in generation and supply because there do not exist sufficient economies of scale and scope to merit monopoly treatment. The United States is introducing competition into both of these sectors, as have other countries such as the U.K. (Helm and Jenkinson 1998). Deregulation has focused on liberalizing entry restrictions, using competitive bidding for long-term bulk power supplies, and reducing rate of return regulation at the wholesale level (Comnes, Kahn, and Belden 1996).

Not surprisingly, these changes easily emerged in energy debates in Canada in the 1990s, first in Alberta, where electricity utilities were already privately owned, and then in Ontario and other provinces, where the utilities were provincial crown corporations and where restructuring implied not only restructuring markets but also restructuring political assumptions about core institutions such as the hydros, which had been instruments of provincial development (Jaccard 2002).

*NRCan, Sustainable Development, and Kyoto Climate
Change Commitments*

In chapter 1 we briefly mentioned the emergence on the historical energy agenda of the sustainable development paradigm and the Kyoto climate change commitments. Later, in chapter 8, we will look more closely at how these concepts and commitments are a central part of the horizontal regime aspects of energy regulatory governance. Here we highlight the basic ways in which they are influencing the nature of twenty-first-century Canadian energy policy formation and federal energy policy institutions centred in Natural Resources Canada, the lead federal natural resource department. We also refer here to Environment Canada's role but leave our closer look at Environment Canada to the analysis in chapter 8 of the horizontal regime and the Kyoto debate.

The paradigm of sustainable development emerged internationally from the 1987 Brundtland Commission. At its core, the paradigm embraced the notion that the current generation had an obligation to leave the environment and its ecosystems in at least as good a shape for future generations as it had found them. Domestically, within the federal government, sustainable development grew largely out of Environment Canada's advocacy and has gradually been endorsed at a government-wide level as a part of national policy (Toner 2000; Doern and Conway 1994). In many senses, because sustainable development is a paradigm of prevention, it relies on non-regulatory instruments of governance, but only in part. It also involves considerable elements of command and control in setting basic initial standards for reduced environmental pollution or impacts, a theme we pick up later in chapter 8. As a series of preventative actions, it depends upon the ability of a department such as Environment Canada to influence the policies and decisions of fellow departments at much *earlier* stages in the decision process than had previously been the case. This does not mean that sustainable development has been practised as such, but it has been institutionalized to some extent (VanNijnatten and Boardman 2002).

A further element of the institutionalization of sustainable development emerged in the implementation of the Chrétien Liberal's 1993 Red Book commitment to establish an environmental auditor reporting to Parliament. The commissioner of the environment and sustainable development was to work within the Office of the Auditor General of Canada, with the role of scrutinizing and reporting on, on a regular basis, the extent to which all departments were developing and implementing sustainable development strategies (and other environmental measures). Again, this institutional presence does not guarantee changed behaviour, but it does exert pressure, simply because lead energy departments such as NRCan have to continuously report in a more public manner.

As a part of the federal government, NRCan was aware of these key ideas in the Liberal platform, and within its own ranks it had officials who supported them. But, given its core clientele of resource industry sub-sector interests (e.g., oil, gas, mining), it was not at all clear exactly how it could respond to them or embrace them, or how quickly it could move to make them an implemented reality. After all, in the test case of climate change policies and global warming, it is true that during the 1990s, urged on by energy and other business interests, and by Alberta and other key energy provinces, NRCan's core instinct has been to defend the oil and gas industry, and to avoid or slow down precipitous post-Kyoto targets. Nonetheless, in other senses, institutional change is occurring and there is certainly a new institutionalized link between

NRCan and Environment Canada, as well as with business, NGOs, and provincial stakeholders. Chapter 8 examines these institutional changes in the context of the larger environmental aspects of the horizontal energy regulatory regime.

But at another level, NRCan's response has been to try to combat the belief in other parts of the federal government that its industries were to be lumped in with the 'old economy' of Canada's natural resource–dominated past, rather than being considered part of Canada's 'new economy' centred on knowledge and innovation. At the insistence of all of its Chrétien era ministers and key parts of its resource industries, NRCan has sought to reassert that the natural resource industries have always been innovative (and global) and have always been under-pinned by a long-standing and first-class earth sciences capacity. It was quite possible, and valid, for it to argue that the scientific and technical role of its earth sciences branch had always constituted a crucial public good underlying the on-going modernization of Canada's oil, gas, min-ing, and forestry sectors. As a result, NRCan's own presentation of its mandate and mission focuses on sustainable development linked to continuous innovation.

Among NRCan ministers in the Chrétien era, this embrace occurred gradually but unmistakably. In 1993 Anne McLellan was named the Chrétien government's first NRCan minister. An Alberta-based politi-cian, and a lawyer, she was new to elected office and devoid of any previous Cabinet experience when she was given the portfolio. As a new minister, she had limited knowledge of the key NRCan sectors but was personally very interested in the sustainable development aspects which were part of the new NRCan statutory mandate. At the same time, as an Alberta politician, she had to move with great caution on the then looming climate change policy file, which many saw as the ulti-mate litmus test of the sustainable development commitment. Not only was this an intrinsically difficult file, inherently cross-governmental in its complexity, but it was also one with enormous impact on the Alberta and Western Canadian oil and gas industry, whose production of hy-drocarbon emissions was the target of any present and future climate change commitments. Any strong federal intervention in the control and reduction of such emissions through federal tax, environmental policy, or other measures was easily portrayed in Alberta as 'another NEP,' imposed again by an Ontario-dominated federal government. McLellan's tenure saw the initial steps towards the establishment of the Climate Change Secretariat and its joint coordination with Environment Canada. However, for the most part, she did not have the political clout in Cabinet to advance very much of NRCan's agenda, and for much of her tenure, which also coincided with Program Review budget cuts, NRCan seemed to 'hunker down' into a defensive mode of operation.

The second Chrétien era NRCan minister, Ralph Goodale, brought a broader set of experience and skills to the NRCan portfolio. As a Saskatchewan-based MP, he also brought a more diverse set of political contacts with energy and mining interests. He personally, and frequently, reminded his officials that sustainable development is part of the NRCan departmental *legislation*. Unusual for any minister, Goodale also personally wrote the vision statement of NRCan, which emphasizes the importance of sustainable development and innovation:

> As we enter the millennium, Canada must become and remain the world's 'smartest' natural resources steward, developer, user and exporter – the most high tech, the most environmentally friendly, the most socially responsible, the most productive and competitive – leading the world as a living model of sustainable development.

Goodale also had other ministerial responsibilities that appear to have fed into his thinking about NRCan's sustainability and innovation mandates. He is the interlocutor, or lead minister, in dealing with the Métis in federal Aboriginal policy. His role as a Saskatchewan minister, and as minister whose mandate encompasses numerous remote mining and resource communities, led to initiatives from himself and from the Cabinet regarding what innovation and sustainable economic development mean for such communities. And very importantly, he was, until 2002, the Chair of the Cabinet Committee on the Economic Union, which means that he was fully involved in the larger debate about innovation policy, including the ideas and pressures on these fronts emanating from economic departments such as Industry Canada and the Department of Finance.

In these forums, Goodale and senior NRCan officials were also becoming concerned with the degree to which Canada's natural resource sectors were being labelled as 'old economy,' and hence not garnering attention as a still crucial and very innovative part of the Canadian economy. To influence and change this perception, NRCan would have to be more active and aggressive in engaging the rest of the government and being, and being *seen* to be, involved in shaping the new economic agenda. As we have seen, this involved reasserting that innovation has always been part and parcel of the natural resource industries, and that the department's own earth sciences branch played a crucial role in innovative activity in the natural resource sector. The third Chrétien era NRCan minister, Herb Dhaliwal, succeeded Goodale early in 2002 and has continued the emphasis on these twin themes of sustainable development and innovation.

However, as suggested above, it is the Kyoto Protocol of the United Nations Framework Convention on Climate Change (UNFCCC), agreed to in December 1997, which has become the acid test of fostering sustainable development. As previously mentioned, Canada undertook to reduce its greenhouse gas emissions by 6 per cent below their 1990 levels, averaged over the 2008 to 2012 period (Schwanen 2000). But, given a lag in action, that commitment now amounts to a 26 per cent reduction. However, as Schwanen stresses, the problem is how to achieve it:

Unfortunately, the Kyoto targets were set without reference to the cost of meeting them (or of their potential benefits relative to those of following alternative scenarios of emissions reductions and time frames). Considering how far Canada is from reaching its Kyoto target, and how closely the emissions of the principal GHGs (green house gasses) resulting from human activity are linked with the growth and type of economic activity the country has typically enjoyed, a serious attempt at meeting the commitment within a given timetable would likely involve significant changes in the economy and even in Canadian lifestyles. (Schwanen 2000: 1)

In the name of both sustainable development and Kyoto, Canada has taken some initiatives. These have mainly occurred through the various tables functioning under the joint auspices of federal and provincial energy and environment ministers (see chapter 8), but they have focused largely on what might be called 'getting ready to get ready' consultations, and on some useful research on technological options.

The Bush administration's aggressive opposition to the Kyoto Protocol process, and its previously mentioned focus on supply-side energy policy, creates for Canada a curious mixture of both high and low politics. On the one hand, the Chrétien government has played the card of criticizing the Bush policy as the height of international arrogance, and has pronounced that Canada will continue to support its Kyoto commitments. This kind of 'look good, feel good' foreign policy stance is contradicted, however, by the larger reality that Canada's energy policy has scarcely begun to actually comply with its Kyoto commitments, and faces a challenge of an almost identical magnitude to that of the United States. As chapter 8 shows, Canada's consultation paper on climate change alternatives (Canada 2002) reveals to what degree federal policy on Kyoto was on the defensive and in disarray as it sought to square the circle of a climate change policy that was seeking to respond to the Bush energy agenda, keep the peace with Alberta, and respond to a fierce political lobby from some key parts of the Canadian business and energy community (Toulin 2002). Moreover, the economic and political urge is overwhelming to sell more and more Canadian oil and gas to the energy-hungry American economy and to American consumers.

While this section has focused on sustainable development and the Kyoto factors as drivers of change, it is crucial to stress that these are not the only 'environmental' ideas and regulatory concerns that interact with energy policy. Other elements of even longer standing, such as environmental assessment laws and processes, pipeline safety, nuclear reactor safety, and the regulation of long-term nuclear wastes, have yet to be layered into our account of contemporary energy regulatory regimes (VanNijnatten 2002; Doern, Dorman, and Morrison 2001).

Free Trade Commitments and Continental Energy and Industry Markets

Free trade has been a dominant reality since the mid to late 1980s, and energy regulation has been affected by the free trade juggernaut both directly and indirectly, and with respect to both international and internal trade. We draw attention to three aspects of the impact of free trade; the free trade commitments on energy; the greater sensitivity to comparative Canada-U.S. energy costs for Canadian firms, especially in Central Canada; and energy free trade, especially of electricity, within Canada.

With respect to free trade commitments, chapter 1 has already shown that the Canada-U.S. Free Trade Agreement of 1987 greatly liberalized Canada-U.S. trade, and that the energy chapter essentially prevents any actions by the federal government such as those which were at the core of the 1980 Liberal NEP, including two-price systems for oil and gas. It also eliminates any realistic basis for Canada to shut off supply to the United States, should Canadians need more of their own energy in an emergency. Some of the latter provisions for emergency sharing also exist under Canada's larger obligations through the International Energy Agency (IEA), and thus it is not just a free trade agreement provision. In essence, therefore, the Canada-U.S. free trade agreement did entrench oil and gas free trade, in particular. The later 1993 NAFTA deal, which added Mexico to the now continental free trade area, did not significantly alter Canada's energy rules, although Mexico did preserve some powers over its largely state-owned energy industry which Canada had ceded in 1987 (Cameron and Tomlin 2000). The addition of Mexico does mean, however, the competitive presence of Mexican oil and gas supplies in the U.S. market. It also opens up commercial opportunities in Mexico for Canadian energy companies.

The second aspect of the impact of free trade was less the stuff of negotiations and front-page news and much more the result of the growing integration of the Canadian and U.S. economies in the wake of free trade and other globalization pressures. Here attention shifted away from Western oil and gas producers, and their desire to entrench energy free trade, to Ontario-centred mainstream Canadian industry. From the early 1990s extending through to the present, Canadian industries have become more and more sensitive to the cost and competitive situations they face relative to American firms competing with them in U.S. markets, in Canada, and globally. Canadian firms have the advantage of the lower Canadian dollar, but they have been suffering from much lower productivity than their U.S. counterparts, and hence more and more attention has been paid to any area of cost advantage or disadvantage, including energy costs.

The most direct manifestation of this concern has been in electricity costs, and has led, along with concerns about Ontario Hydro's managerial faults and nuclear plant difficulties, to the establishment of the Macdonald Committee in 1996 and then to the eventual restructuring and deregulation of the Ontario electricity industry by the Harris Conservative government. Other threads of this story are picked up in chapter 3 (on U.S. developments and FERC policies) and in chapter 5 (on the Ontario Energy Board).

A third aspect of the free trade influence is found in the efforts to negotiate an internal free trade agreement within Canada. The Agreement on Internal Trade (AIT) was negotiated in 1994 but without an energy chapter. A brief look at these dynamics are instructive to show the underlying politics, especially concerning electricity.

In the oil and gas sectors there was already close to full internal free trade. It was the electricity sector that posed the problems, especially issues regarding the wheeling of electricity between provinces (a controversy between Quebec and Newfoundland was particularly troublesome). Alberta was not prepared to see an energy chapter included in the AIT until all energy sources were included. A draft chapter at the early stages had garnered support for the general proposition that the chapter apply to all energy goods and services. This, however, would be subject to a basic 'notwithstanding clause' which would exempt provincial monopolies. Attention then turned on how to constrain these entities to some extent in a pro-internal free trade direction.

Saskatchewan and Ontario were strong supporters of preserving their monopoly rights for gas and electricity transmission and distribution, as well as provincial rights to regulate these activities. At the other end of the continuum, Newfoundland sought full rights to the wheeling of electricity, including binding dispute settlement provisions. All other provinces, led by Quebec and Ontario, thought in 1993–4 that wheeling and transmission access across provincial boundaries were issues best left for their electrical utilities to negotiate. There was a very real political imperative to this deference as hydro utilities were big players in provincial economies.

The federal government could not play a role in electricity from a position of real strength. It neither owned hydro utilities nor did it have to finance or guarantee their debts. It broadly supported the view that there be open internal trade on all energy products, but it also had to be careful that it did not take sides in the Quebec-Newfoundland dispute over electricity. In the endgame of the 1994 AIT negotiations, the energy chapter was taken off the table by the ministers. Electricity wheeling was undoubtedly the crucial issue, but there were also other underlying concerns that were not, in one sense, about interprovincial trade as such. The concerns in many key provinces were about intra-provincial electricity trade. The hydros were facing many changes that were altering their accustomed and relatively stable lives as regulated public utilities (Vollans 1995). These changes, as we have seen above, included technological changes and co-generation options; relative and inter-fuel costs and pricing choices of a more complex nature; declining economies of scale; and so-called stranded investment assets or over-built capacity.

These changes produced different permutations and combinations of concern in different provinces. For Ontario and Quebec, it was the inherent magnitude of what to do with giant utilities and bureaucracies such as Ontario Hydro and Hydro-Québec. For Saskatchewan, there were concerns that if the province was connected to an interprovincial grid, its internal, relatively high cost, power would or could be supplied by Manitoba or Alberta (both lower cost producers). For Alberta, its bullish position on free trade in electricity was partly premised on its already having an intra-provincial grid that it felt could be the model for Canada. PEI had a vested interest in freer electricity trade because it was dependent on New Brunswick electrical power and believed it could get cheaper power from Quebec.

Newfoundland refused to sign an energy chapter largely because of the wheeling issue. But it was also fiercely critical of its fellow provincial negotiators in that, in Newfoundland's view, they lacked the determination to reach a Canadian decision even though they would likely have to soon reach the same free trade decisions because of U.S. rules. The U.S. pressure to do so (see chapter 3) was largely emerging from rulings by the U.S. Federal Energy Regulatory Commission (FERC). Its rulings regarding regional transmission grids (RTGs), of which Canadian utilities would be a part, would forbid members of the grid from discriminating against one another. In effect, internal free trade for electricity in Canada would become a-made-in-the-U.S.A. policy. In 2000 an energy chapter was ready for agreement because U.S. rules had made wheeling necessary. But the chapter had not yet been signed because of other energy regulation matters, namely the desire of both Newfoundland and Nova Scotia to preserve provisions in their offshore agreements with Ottawa to allow preferences in hiring for local labour.

The Reconfiguration of Core Energy Interests

The final factor to be highlighted is the reconfiguration of core energy interests. We have referred implicitly to many of these interests in the discussion of the preceding five factors, as well as in chapter 1, but we need to appreciate more explicitly some of the patterns of change among energy interests. We seek to describe changes in interest groups, but also in the strategies and lobbying of key firms as individual corporations, of players such as scientists, and of groups such as Aboriginal peoples (who constitute more than just an NGO because they are peoples with constitutional rights and are owners of energy resources). As is the case with each of the other factors in this chapter, we can sketch here only some basic points about the nature of these interests.

A starting point for comparison across time is that although there is still much conflict between energy industries and environmental NGOs as a whole, it is arguably not as great or as intense as in the earlier days of energy regulation, for instance, during the Berger Commission era of the mid-1970s. A key new feature of the role of interests and the pressure they exert is that they are much more complex and and diverse than previously. There are important divisions or sub-elements *within* and also *across* the two overarching interest of categories of 'energy' businesses and 'environmental' NGOs.

In the early 2000s, energy business interests certainly include firms that are polluters and greenhouse gas emitters, but they also include key firms that are known to be environmentally progressive and that see economic opportunity in new green environmental technologies as alternatives to the carbon economy (Macdonald 2002). Thus a global firm such as British Petroleum (BP) changes its logo to mean 'beyond petroleum' and pursues quite different strategies than say Exxon (Rowlands 2000). In Canada, TransAlta has developed strategies for profiting from emission reductions and alternative technologies, and there are many other examples along these lines as well (Toner 2003; Macdonald 2002; Corporate Knights 2002).

A further illustration of the complexity and diversity of contemporary energy interests can be found in energy associations. A key Canadian lobby such as the Canadian Electricity Association used to consist of a handful of big, mainly provincially owned, utilities, but now it also includes dozens of smaller firms that are entering the newly restructured electricity markets. The energy associations have diverse views about the energy-environment trade-offs and linkages, as well as how to profit from them. A core energy lobby such as the Canadian Association of Petroleum Producers (CAPP) has to lobby in ways that recognize its diverse mix of small and large energy players, some of whom see themselves as being in the environmental industries sector.

There are also more numerous and varied organizations on the core environmental NGO side of the interest equation (Parson 2001; VanNijnatten and Boardman 2002). NGOs still seek to mobilize global pressure to ensure that Canada's environmental policy relating to energy and other fields is progressive, but the strategies of groups such as Greenpeace, Energy Probe, Pollution Probe, the Sierra Club, the Pembina Institute, the Canadian Arctic Resources Committee, and the David Suzuki Foundation vary enormously. Environmental advocates also function in and through advisory bodies, such as the National Roundtable on the Environment and the Economy, and in numerous local and provincial-regional settings. Compared to even a decade ago, such interests, while still maintaining overall pressure, are much more literate about, experienced with, and prepared to consider varied ways of dealing with energy-environmental problems (from direct regulation to incentives and tradeable emission systems).

The structure of interests concerning Aboriginal peoples, and other groups such as consumers, has also changed in the energy regulatory context. Aboriginal self-governance in Canada's North has conferred direct powers on Aboriginal peoples, and these have been accompanied by quite a different set of views about energy and resource development than during the Berger era. This time, by and large, Aboriginal peoples tend to favour development, provided there is local control over employment, benefits, and investment (Abele 2002; Poelzer 2002; Doyle-Bedwell and Cohen 2001). But, on other aspects of energy policy, such as climate change, there are major concerns, because Aboriginal peoples in the North are already experiencing adverse climate change effects.

The issue of consumer interests and citizen-consumers is also germane to this brief survey. We deal with consumers in our inter-regime framework in the next section of this chapter, but a key point to note is that there are more arenas for the expression of consumer interests, precisely because markets have gained a greater hold in the energy sphere. Consumer-citizens mount continuous challenges regarding the quality of consumption, that is, not just concerning what products are made but how they are made (Webb 2002; Princen, Maniates, and Comca 2002). Moreover, the growth of business user groups as an organized class of consumers is a significant change in the profile of interest groups and lobbying.

Last but not least – and probably the hardest to pin down – is the role of scientists (inside and outside of government, and internationally). Individual scientist advocates, such as David Suzuki, as well as those who may be members of environmental roundtables and panels, or who have strong university-based reputations, exert considerable influence, certainly in the identification of environmental hazards. Moreover, federal scientists in both NRCan and Environment Canada, and those who belong to global bodies that form around particular environmental agreements, also exert influence (Doern and Reed 2000).

Energy Regulatory Governance in the Twenty-First Century: Interacting Regimes and the Regulation of Energy As an Essential Service Networked Industry

The key factors discussed above range from quite recent policy change (e.g., the Bush NEP) to ideas, interests, technologies, and agreements that span the last fifteen to twenty years. They convey the direction of change, but they do not themselves tell us what the contemporary institutions of Canadian energy regulation are like as a result of them. For this, we need a framework which captures a complex and net-worked set of institutional relations, both cooperative and conflictual in nature. The framework is derived mainly from recent literature on regulation that portrays regulation and rule-making in terms of overarching institutional regimes of regulation within which the role of particular regulatory bodies can be better understood (Doern, Hill, Prince, and Schultz 1999; Doern and Wilks 1998; Vass 1998). We briefly set out this framework with the aid of figure 1. In a very basic sense, figure 1 shows that energy regulatory governance consists of a sectoral or economic regime, represented by the arrows running 'north and south,' and a horizontal regime dealing with social or quality regula-tion, including aspects of distributive equity. The latter elements are represented by the horizontal or 'east-west' arrows in the diagram. Both the vertical and horizontal elements interact with, and cross through, the specific regulatory bodies or institutions, the regulated companies, and consumer-citizens.

Figure 1 therefore provides a framework map of the key elements of Canada's energy regulatory governance, a system containing two inter-acting regimes, the sectoral energy regime and the horizontal energy regime. In this section, we discuss first the sectoral energy regulatory regime. Second, we map the horizontal energy regulatory regime, that for our purposes we will focus on environmental regulation writ large (including sustainable development) and competition regulation (rules regarding anti-competitive behaviour, mergers, and predatory activ-ity). Third, we discuss the two regimes together so as to understand energy regulatory governance. We show how energy regulation is at its core still best understood, politically and economically, as an essential service networked industry governed both by the norms of workable or managed competition, rather than full competition, and by the para-digm of sustainable development. This section of the chapter fleshes out the framework in an initial way in order to discern and classify basic relationships. Later chapters then provide a more detailed look at the core sectoral regulatory bodies (such as the NEB, OEB, and AEUB) and the horizontal framework bodies and processes, such as the Com-petition Bureau, environmental regulators, and ultimately the parent federal ministries, such as Natural Resources Canada and Environment

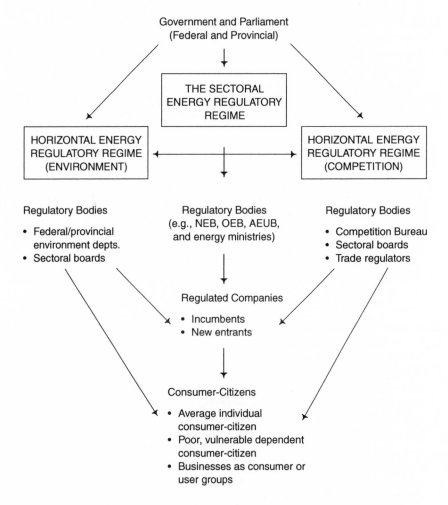

Figure 1: Sectoral and Horizontal Energy Regulatory Regimes in Canada

Canada, which in some fashion must negotiate and mediate disputes which are often disputes *within* the state. In short, they must deal with inter-regime issues which are, variously, confronted, postponed, or finessed in a larger set of national priorities, energy, regulatory, and otherwise.

The Sectoral Energy Regulatory Regime

The sectoral energy regulatory regime refers to a set of regulatory laws, agencies, values, interests, and processes which govern energy as a vertical industrial sector. As figure 1 suggests, at the core of this regime are the various energy boards, federal and provincial. In this book, we are focusing on three such boards, but the sectoral energy regime is in fact a larger set of players across all ten provinces as well as the territorial governments and Aboriginal governance structures in the north. At the federal level, the National Energy Board would be joined by the Canadian Nuclear Safety Commission as well as other federal agencies not shown in figure 1. As figure 1 does show, the sectoral regime necessarily extends to the federal and provincial-territorial parent energy ministries (variously titled), where political control is centred and where ministers typically share some portion of the rule-making power with the regulatory board. At the federal, level these parent ministries extend beyond NRCan to the Department of Indian Affairs and Northern Development (DIAND), which has some key responsibilities in the North.

The other key feature of the sectoral energy regulatory regime is that the core energy boards have historically dealt with an industry which had natural monopoly features, and hence regulation was seen as a substitute for markets to protect consumers but also, quite importantly, *citizens* as consumers of an essential service industry. We have already seen above how some of the monopoly features were beginning to break down, because of new technologies but also because of more market-oriented ways of thinking about how to regulate more flexibly and with efficiency and choice more clearly in mind for at least some consumers (see further discussion in chapter 3).

It is important to see this as a regime because regulatory and political behaviour within the state (federal and provincial) is in effect an interplay among regulatory and ministerial bodies with their own institutional capacities for inertia, change, and experimentation and also with core interest groups and key firms lobbying them and building strategies around their preferred array of regulatory arrangements.

As one mentally and visually goes down through the vertical centre of figure 1, the regime eventually encounters, and is intended to serve, both firms and consumer-citizens. Since private firms are mainly the ultimate deliverers of energy products and services, the regulator not only regulates such firms but has obligations and *commitments* to such firms. In particular, the regulator has to be conscious of these firms' ability to raise capital, which then means also having a capacity to have some reasonable rate of return. As the energy sector becomes more market-oriented but still not a fully competitive market – in effect, a managed market – the structure of firms (and therefore interests) within the purview of sectoral regulatory boards has become much more complex. As recently as fifteen years ago, the typical energy regulator would be dealing with a small set of very large firms. In the early twenty-first century, such regulators must continue to deal with some very large players, but also with numerous new, and typically smaller, incumbent firms or firms seeking entry. As indicated earlier, this is especially the case in restructured electricity markets, but it also is true for oil and gas and alternative energy industrial sub-sectors.

Finally, the south end of figure 1 brings in the consumer-citizen explicitly. When seen as the ultimate beneficiary of regulated energy services and products, it is of course important to cast such recipients as being in some very important sense *consumers* desiring a reasonably priced and efficacious product or service. But these recipients include business users of energy as well as the average individual consumer. When such distinctions are made there is almost immediately a different equation of political and market power, with the power of business users being more concentrated. But the average individual consumer is also just that, an *average*. When *citizen* is hyphenated with *consumer*, one ends up with other crucial categories of consumption and need. Citizen-consumers who are poor, vulnerable, or sick, or who live in remote areas, become a different part of the consumer-citizen realm. Here also emerge different concepts of energy as an *essential* service and socially networked industry.

In this book, we cannot deal with the whole of this sectoral energy regime with all of its regulators, ministries, firms, and citizen-consumer elements. But it is important to see energy regulatory governance at this sectoral regime level. Without such a larger perspective, the behaviour of energy regulatory boards cannot be understood. But even then, our analytical framework is only half constructed.

The Horizontal Energy Regulatory Regime

Figure 1 also shows the horizontal energy regulatory regime. This refers to a set of regulatory laws, agencies, values, and processes which govern energy from a horizontal perspective in which energy is simply one among many industrial sectors governed by rules regarding health, safety, environment, fairness, and the quality of products and services, including the nature and quality of competition. This is also a vast and complex terrain, which this book will explore only through two aspects: horizontal competition regulation and rule-making; and environmental regulation. But one could easily discuss, as we have earlier in this chapter, issues such as framework trade rules (NAFTA and the Agreement on Internal Trade) as a part of this horizontal realm of rules.

This regime is horizontal because it typically contains laws, agencies, values, interests, and processes which apply across the economy and society, in a sense, regardless of sector. And again, figure 1 suggests that a proper institutional mapping of this regime would necessarily include not only particular regulatory bodies (such as the Competition Bureau and environmental regulatory bodies and departments, federal and provincial) but also ministries of industry and environment, with some share of rule-making powers and coverage in these realms.

Whereas the sectoral energy regulatory regime described earlier is a regime in which considerable *deregulation* has been under way, the horizontal regulatory regime has exhibited an *expanded realm of overall rule-making* and pressure for yet more rule-making. Chapters 7 and 8 describe some basic features of these changes in the competition and environmental fields, but the presence of such horizontal aspects of energy regulatory governance also shows up in the chapters on the three energy boards. These chapters show that the boards have themselves taken on some of these tasks, whereas previously they were not a major concern. But horizontal rule-making is also occurring in areas beyond the focus of this book. For example, energy-environment regulation of oil and gas in the North and on Canada's frontiers is now influenced by the Oceans Act, which covers all three of Canada's oceans. Centred in the Department of Fisheries and Oceans (DFO), this legislation extends the authority of DFO but is also supposed to engage other Northern regulators, such as the Department of Indian Affairs and Northern Development (DIAND). The legislation prescribes sustainable development, the precautionary approach, and the eco-system approach, along with the need for integrated management plans. So there is little doubt that the horizontal regime is growing in scope and in the range of concepts that regulators are supposed to bring to bear on energy development.

The horizontal regime can also be seen as simply a system of rules and processes for ensuring the *quality* of energy products and services in an essential service industry or in an industry with essential service elements. We focus on competition and environmental aspects, but, even within these two realms, the issue of quality evokes many variables and values. Competition bodies throughout the world, Canada's included, routinely pronounce that competition is never desirable simply for its own sake, but rather for what it yields with respect to better products and greater choice. They also seek the *fair* functioning of markets – in short, fair competition – so as to prevent predatory behaviour and misleading advertising, and hence are very much concerned about the overall quality of the market place as a functioning institution.

Similarly, environmental quality can refer to any number of risks and third-party effects regarding the energy product or service (e.g., leaded gasoline, new fuel additives); the safety of oil and gas pipelines; environmental assessments of new production plants or coal mines; and sustainable development involving the mandated lowering of the extent of use of hydrocarbon and greenhouse gas emitting fuels.

When one mentally pictures the role of firms and consumers in this 'east-west' axis of figure 1, a different set of dynamics arises. Firms face an array of federal and provincial environmental and quality regulators, and their concerns, some tactical and some principled, are over issues such as multiple requirements for hearings, long or longish time periods to obtain approval for the use of products, and other logistical complexities of dealing with multiple regulatory bodies. The consumer-citizen split becomes even sharper in the environmental realm because, when consuming an essential service product, individual Canadians may think and behave as citizens as much as they do as consumers. In short, they are aware of their own desire to preserve and use energy in an environmentally friendly and sustainable way. They of course do not behave with total consistency on these matters, but there is little doubt that they are interested both in what energy they consume and use, and the quality of that consumption.

In the case of both the vertical and horizontal axes of figure 1, our analytical framework maps an essentially Canadian regulatory realm. But in reality, under increasingly globalized trade and free trade arrangements, as well as global environmental protocols, an international and continental set of actors, processes, and rules also has to be factored in. These include bodies such as the International Energy Agency (IEA), the Organization of Petroleum Exporting Countries (OPEC), the International Atomic Energy Agency (IAEA), and the NAFTA-centred Commission on Environmental Cooperation (CEC), as well as other provisions of NAFTA. Chapter 3 supplies some of this international institutional presence in the case of the FERC and U.S. developments, as do chapters 7 and 8 on global competition and environmental matters.

Interacting Networked Regimes: The Four Key Themes in the Power Switch

The key factors driving change identified earlier in this chapter and the four key overall themes of this book have to be lodged in a framework that can map the existence of two basic regimes of regulation for energy. In the study of energy policy, there has always been some basic understanding of the presence of both vertical sectoral regulation and horizontal regulation of the kinds referred to above. But it is far less clear that the contemporary and evolving interactions between these regimes are well understood. Indeed, this is the first of the four themes developed in this book, that the last two decades have seen a transformation in energy regulation – in a way that we characterize as 'less regulation' and 'more rules' – that is a result primarily of the contradictory pressures of sectoral deregulation, on the one hand, and expanded rule-making in the horizontal regulatory regime, on the other. For example, electricity restructuring was referred to as 'restructuring' because, although it involved some key features of deregulation and market liberalization, it also involved extensive new forms of regulation (see chapters 3, 5 and 7).

The starting point for such understanding, as captured by the framework, is that each regime has had its own partly separate history of evolution and construction at different time periods and with different bursts of development, inertia, and stalemating. What is also clear is that the dual sets of regulators, rules, values, and statutes have not been designed from 'on-high' by some all-seeing, all-knowing political or economic authority. They are not at all the product of the state functioning as some form of rational unitary actor. The systems as a whole and their component pieces and development are the product, 'the resultant,' of myriad political-economic forms of lobbying and institutional adaptation and inertia. Just as plants can grow and die amidst numerous particular micro-climates, so also do energy regulatory entities and regimes emerge from micro-political climates.

This book cannot tell the full story of every aspect of this development, but it is important to begin to understand some of the basic ways in which the two overall regimes are interacting, cooperating, and colliding with each other, within Canada, and of course continentally (or regionally in a Canada-U.S. context for electricity grids) as well as globally. And this relates to our second theme, which is that although energy regulatory governance has been moving in a pro-competitive direction, the overall system must be regarded as a system of managed competition, rather than of competition per se (see chapter 7).

As we have emphasized before, the framework employed and adapted here emerges from a broader comparative and Canadian literature on regulatory institutions and regimes, which we are now seeking to apply to energy regulation. In principle, it could be applied to other realms, such as telecommunications, biotechnology, and financial services, to better understand actual regulatory governance. This literature tends to be anchored in the fields of political science and public administration, but there are interesting complementary ways in which authors from other disciplines have viewed similar concerns.

For example, some economists have focused on the issues of 'deregulation and managed competition in network industries.' Sidak and Spulber address these concerns where there has been a competitive transformation of telecommunication and other 'network industries' (such as energy) in the United States, and where government policymakers are increasingly concerned with the fairness of the resulting deregulatory process and outcomes (Sidak and Spulber 1998). In part, their focus is on how to treat processes of transition to competition, and how to be fair to both incumbent firms and new entrants. Sidak and Spulber urge regulators to resist the temptation to 'manage' competition, but of course this is exactly what real regulators usually have to do. They also refer to 'networked' industries, by which they seem to mean mainly that the industries examined are a set of firms connected and linked to varied market situations, in some of which monopoly situations prevail, while in others, through unbundling, competition can occur and is occurring. But there is not much appreciation in this kind of thinking about *networked regulators* and regulatory regimes, where it is the state writ large which constitutes the bundle of competing and cooperating regulators increasingly engaged in trying to 'manage a network' of regulators and rules.

Business academic John Burton is somewhat more inclined to look at larger sets of institutions. He examines the 'U.K. model' of utility regulation, created virtually from scratch during the last fifteen years, and asks whether it is a system that has produced a 'competitive order' or 'ordered competition.' For Burton, the former means something close to full and real competition, while the latter means managed competition. The U.K. utility model was in fact a model which combined some of what we would label a mixture of the sectoral and horizontal regulatory regimes, especially in the sense that the sectoral regulator (such as the U.K.'s energy regulator) was explicitly given a competition mandate, which was shared with the U.K. central competition regulator (the then Monopoly and Mergers Commission). Burton concludes that in practice what has emerged is a system of *ordered competition*. Burton goes on to argue that a fundamental policy choice emerges as to whether the U.K. system should 'continue as a system or ordered competition as it is now, or whether it should become a regime characterized by open and effective competition (where feasible)' (Burton 1997: 1). But the final caveat, 'where feasible,' is precisely the point, and of course it must be added in theory and practice if one is seeking to be realistic about the competition aspects of horizontal regulation. There is no discussion in the Burton article about the environmental aspects of the 'U.K. model'; nor is their any appreciation that there is, and is bound to be, competition among sectoral and vertical regulators for regulatory space and territory.

Economists Pelzman and Winston have also explored the deregulation of network industries in the United States and essentially ask, 'What's next?' The 'what's next' problem they are most concerned about is the pressure emerging in several utility sectors which they explore to *re-regulate* or *newly regulate* in the face of experience with the imperfections of deregulated markets. As ardent pro-market advocates, the broad remedy suggested by these two authors is to resist the urge and in fact to deregulate even more. This is not dissimilar advice to that inherent in Burton's argument. But again, there is no parallel effort to see why a countervailing or simply emerging set of horizontal regulatory elements might be needed (as seen by some set of political actors).

The framework and the four key themes of the book are also developed to contribute to a further refinement of the literature in political science and public administration. This literature is more inclined by instinct to be leery of institutional forces simply falling into line with market designers and reformers. Key authors here are contributing to a good understanding of how in the real world different countries have shaped deregulatory policies in sectors such as energy and telecommunications (Ernst 1994; Kickert et al. 1997; Levi-Faur 1999, 2001; Muller and Bartle 2000; Prosser 1999: Vass 1998). But none of this literature has made as focused an attempt as we do in this volume to understand complex regimes and changing governance at multiple levels of interaction.

Thus there is a basic need to appreciate at an explicitly institutional level the continued presence of two regulatory regimes cast as sets of laws, regulatory bodies and ministries, interests, and core values. These are also competing in some sense and cooperating in others, and they are themselves networks of interaction and influence. This point bears on our third theme, the concept of regulatory 'stacking' in the realm of energy-environment regulation, whereby command-and-control and incentive-based regulation are layered on top of each other, a feature we examine in chapter 8.

There is also a need, in examining these sectoral and horizontal energy regulatory regimes, to restore to some analytical primacy the core notion of sectors like energy being essential service industries in a modern economy. This raises the question examined by John Ernst concerning 'whose utility' public utility industries serve (Ernst 1994). We examine this theme again in chapters 7 and 8, and pick it up in various chapters in the book in the context of our fourth theme, the nature and challenges of political accountability of contemporary energy regulatory governance.

Conclusions

As a complement to the broader history of energy regulation in chapter 1, this chapter has provided a basis for analysing the power switch under way in the regulatory governance of energy. The key factors driving change during the last fifteen to twenty years have been given a closer look. They are important, separately and in combination, in appreciating both the macro politics of change and pressure, but also the particular ways in which regulation has changed and is likely to change in the energy sector. But these drivers of change, from the Bush agenda to pro-market ideas, and from the reconfiguration of energy interests to trade agreements, the Kyoto Protocol, and technical change in energy production, do not tell in detail how energy regulatory regimes have changed or are structured institutionally as a whole.

The framework provided in the second half of the chapter is presented as a way of mapping and understanding, in a broad overall manner, who now regulates energy in Canada. The existence of sectoral and horizontal energy regulatory regimes is central to this framework and informs the analysis in the chapters which follow. The framework helps understand the nature of interactions between the two regimes insofar as it helps raise questions about both cooperative relations between regimes (and regulatory bodies) and about competition and conflict between them, within the state and outside it. In addition, we have stressed the notion that understandings of networked industries have to be complemented by a better appreciation of networked regulators and regulatory regimes, especially given the reality of energy as an essential service industry.

Our ultimate focus is energy regulatory institutions and regimes in Canada, but the chapter has shown some initial links with global and continental pressures and systems of thinking and regulation. The next chapter adds more comparative background and context for Canada's energy regulatory change, especially since developments in the United States not only provided a laboratory of energy regulatory change, especially in the electricity sector, but also exerted direct pressure and imperatives for change on Canada's energy regulators as continental energy markets became more and more integrated.

3 U.S. Influences: FERC and Alternative Energy Regulatory Models

While this book focuses on Canada's changing energy regulatory institutions, previous chapters have already testified to the overall historical influence of the United States, including the recent initiatives of the Bush administration in 2001 and 2002, on Canadian energy development and regulation. But U.S. influences have also been quite direct and specific during the last decade and in many ways are centred on the role of the Federal Energy Regulatory Commission (FERC) and its adoption of alternative regulatory models. This chapter examines more closely key energy regulatory reforms in the United States and their impact on Canada. The FERC is a federal independent regulatory commission with regulatory authority over a number of integral segments of the oil, natural gas, and electricity industries in the United States. In particular, we examine liberalization of the wholesale electricity and natural gas markets, where the most substantive restructuring and deregulation has occurred.

Following a review of the key developments at the FERC, we then assess the actual and potential impacts of these changes on Canadian energy regulation. The nature and extent of the potential impact is conditioned by a number of factors. These include the relative pace of deregulation in the United States compared to Canada, and the extent to which differences between the Canadian and American regulatory frameworks serve to mobilize constituencies and interests and Canadian institutions, most notably differences in the nature of federalism.

FERC Policy and Regulatory Developments

In the United States, regulatory authority over energy resides at both the federal and state levels. State public utility commissions, PUCs, are primarily focused on intra-state matters, such as energy distribution, retail pricing, and intra-state energy transmission. The federal government, with constitutional authority over interstate commerce and ownership rights over the majority of hydroelectric resources, regulates most wholesale transactions in energy markets, as well as hydroelectric developments. Federal regulatory authority is exercised primarily through the Federal Energy Regulatory Commission, the FERC (first established as the Federal Power Commission by the Federal Water Power Act of 1920).[1] The FERC is an independent regulatory agency and is governed by five presidentially appointed commissioners.

The FERC has four principal areas of regulatory responsibility: interstate sales and transmission of electricity; interstate trade in natural gas; non-federal hydroelectric power-plant construction and operation; and rate regulation of oil pipelines operating in interstate commerce. The FERC has been transforming its regulation of the electricity and natural gas sectors through a series of successive reforms introducing greater and greater elements of competition into wholesale markets. The intended result is non-discriminatory open access transmission and the unbundling of the production and transmission sides of the business at the wholesale level. We look in turn at these regulatory reforms in the electricity sector and then in natural gas.

The Electricity Industry

In the United States, the electricity supply industry has been heavily regulated since the 1920s (Norman 1999). Electricity generation and transmission has been viewed as a natural monopoly and regulated as such: the government grants utilities monopoly control over geographical service territories in exchange for obligations to provide universal and affordable service on a non-discriminatory basis. Sidak and Spulber (1997) summarize the 'regulatory contract': 'in return for assuming an obligation to serve and charging not more than "just and reasonable" prices on a nondiscriminatory basis, the utility is guaranteed a franchise protected by entry regulation and income sufficient to recover and to earn a competitive rate of return on its invested capital' (4).

The Energy Policy Act of 1992 and a number of subsequent FERC policy statements and rule-makings constitute the major regulatory

---

1 Nuclear power is also under federal jurisdiction and is regulated by the Nuclear Regulatory Commission.

and policy changes in electricity regulation over the last decade. These changes followed in the wake of the Public Utilities Regulatory Policies Act (PURPA) of 1978, the enactment of which is generally held to be the watershed of regulatory change in the American electricity industry (Gilbert and Kahn 1996; Kahn 1997). PURPA's primary objective was to promote energy conservation and the use of alternative forms of energy by requiring electric utilities to purchase surplus power from a new class of generators, called qualifying facilities (QFs). PURPA liberalized entry restrictions into the generation market and introduced competition into the wholesale market through qualifying facilities. QFs are small-scale generators using either co-generation or renewable resource technology, and operating at federally prescribed efficiency levels (PURPA prohibited utilities from holding a majority equity interest in QFs). While the FERC initially played a lead role in PURPA by establishing the general framework for QF development, state regulators were delegated the responsibility for PURPA's implementation. States regulate the prices of QF sales and administer the competitive bidding process for bulk power sales in the QF market. The FERC approves wholesale rates for any other kind of private generator.

Although PURPA's principal objective was environmental conservation, it was instrumental in electricity deregulation because it set in motion a dynamic which prompted still further liberalization. 'While the Congress in 1978 may have intended PURPA to encourage energy efficiency and conservation as a primary goal, its historical significance was the introduction of competition in the generating sector of the electric power industry' (Kinnie Smith, Jr 1995: 86). PURPA's purchase requirement led to a substantial increase in the number and variety of wholesale transactions. For example, utilities that had purchased power based on bullish projections began selling the excess at wholesale to other utilities, which led to demands for deregulation of wholesale sales. Some QFs even began seeking access to utilities' transmission lines to wheel power to third parties. Furthermore, numerous independent power producers (IPPs), or non-QF and non-utility generators, entered the wholesale market, requiring clarification of their legal status (prior to PURPA, the investor-owned independent power industry was virtually non-existent). The Energy Policy Act (EPAct) of 1992 was conceived by the American electricity industry (utilities and utility holding companies, with their affiliated IPPs, and independent IPPs) to encourage full competition in generation (Kinnie Smith, Jr 1995).

The Energy Policy Act of 1992 further liberalized the wholesale gen-

eration and supply markets by reducing barriers to entry for independent power producers and expanding the FERC's authority to order
wholesale wheeling. 'The Energy Policy Act of 1992 (EPAct) opened the
door for a competitive multi-state and international independent power
industry and gave the Federal Energy Regulatory Commission (FERC)
power to mandate open access transmission' (Kinnie Smith, Jr 1995:
75–6). The EPAct reduced entry restrictions for IPPs into the wholesale
market by exempting them from the provisions of the Public Utility
Holding Company Act of 1935 (PUHCA). PUHCA required holding
companies acquiring more than 10 per cent of an IPP to get approval
from the Securities and Exchange Commission (SEC). Following SEC
approval, these companies were then subject to SEC regulation for such
activities as mergers and acquisitions, securities issuances, and capital
structure. The EPAct's removal of this entry barrier was also extended
to generators in which a utility had a majority interest (so-called 'affiliated power producers' or APPs). IPPs and APPs now form a new class
of generator, exempt wholesale generators (EWGs), engaged solely in
wholesale transactions (recognition as an EWG also requires FERC
approval). Unlike QFs, EWGs are not prohibited from engaging in
wholesale power marketing. With state authorization, electric utility
companies can liberate specific generation facilities from the yolk of
rate-based regulation by designating them as EWGs. Furthermore, since
EWGs are exempted from PURPA equity restrictions, they can acquire a
majority equity interest in qualifying facilities (which means that a
utility can now own a QF via its ownership of an EWG). The EPAct
permits transactions between electric utilities and their EWGs provided
they obtain approval of their state regulatory authority.

Second, the EPAct enhanced the FERC's capacity to build the wholesale market by ordering wholesale wheeling.[2] Following the EPAct,
electric utilities, federal power administrations, and other wholesale
generators can apply to the FERC to obtain wheeling orders, and the
FERC can order wheeling (provided it does not unduly impair network
reliability, the applicant pays wheeling expenses, and the wheeling
costs include all related expenses). Although wheeling is not a new
phenomenon – it takes place commonly between power pool members – the FERC's authority to mandate wheeling under the EPAct

---

2 Although the FERC previously had the power to order wheeling under the Federal
  Power Act of 1935, it did not tend to exercise this authority because of the act's strict
  rules regarding wheeling orders.

represented a significant change. It permitted a new form of transaction within the electricity industry, whereby non-utility generators could make sales through utilities' transmission networks, bypassing utilities to make wholesale sales to other companies.

In April 1996, the FERC formally laid the foundation for competitive wholesale electricity markets with Order Nos. 888 and 889 (FERC 1999). These rule-makings aimed to level the competitive playing field by preventing vertically integrated utilities from discriminating against non-utility generators seeking access to transmission services. Order No. 888 responded to the FERC's finding that transmission-owning utilities were discriminating against other companies seeking transmission access. Using its new EPAct powers, the FERC issued this rule-making, which mandates public utilities to provide non-discriminatory open access transmission services. Public utilities that own, control, or operate networks used for electricity transmission in interstate commerce were required to file open access non-discriminatory transmission tariffs (the tariffs entered into force in 1997). Furthermore, Order No. 888 required utilities to functionally unbundle the wholesale electricity component of their business from the other components. Under functional unbundling, utilities must determine separate rates for wholesale generation, transmission, and ancillary (i.e., system control) services; they must charge themselves the same fee for wholesale services that they charge third-party users; and they must utilize the same information network that their transmission customers use when purchasing or selling bulk power.[3] Order No. 888 also delineates rules for stranded cost recovery through exit fees or transmission surcharges levied on departing wholesale generation customers. Order No. 889 further contributed to the creation of open access transmission by ordering all public utilities to create, or be a part of, an electronic system to share information about available transmission capacity (the Open Access Same-Time Information System, OASIS). The order laid out standards of conduct to be followed by public utilities engaging in wholesale power marketing, to ensure that employees active in power marketing functions do not obtain preferential access to pertinent trans-

---

3 Functional unbundling is a less intrusive approach than corporate unbundling, which would require firms to sell their transmission facilities or create a separate corporate subsidiary owning the facilities. This being said, prior to deregulation, long-term gas purchase agreements had the effect of vertically integrating the industry (Kinnie Smith, Jr 1995).

mission information in their dealings (e.g., salesmen and purchasers are not permitted to enter the transmission control room).

Common wisdom held that corporate restructuring in the electricity industry would flourish as companies sought to strategically reposition themselves in the new open access environment (Whitfield 1999). In line with this expectation, eight months after issuing Order Nos. 888 and 889, the FERC released a policy statement on mergers (Order No. 592, Electric Merger Policy Statement) to update and clarify Commission procedures, criteria, and policies for public utility mergers. The first aim of the statement was to ensure that mergers would be reviewed according to the FERC's statutory requirement under the Federal Power Act to ensure mergers are 'consistent with the public interest.' Traditionally, the FERC has applied a six factor balancing test in merger assessments. Order No. 592 reduces the number of factors to three: the effect on competition, the effect on rates, and the effect on regulation. In assessing the competition component, the FERC adopts the approach used by antitrust regulators, applying the Merger Guidelines used by the Department of Justice and the Federal Trade Commission. The focus of rate analysis is ratepayer protection. Here, merger applicants are encouraged to negotiate with ratepayers prior to filing with the Commission, with a view to achieving consensus among the parties before the merger. Regulatory considerations relate to the role of state regulators and the Securities and Exchange Commission in pre-merger analysis and post-merger regulation. State regulators can exercise their authority to protect state interests where necessary, and applicants proposing mergers resulting in the creation of public utility holding companies have options regarding the post-merger regulation of affiliate transactions. The FERC's aim with the regulatory criterion is to ensure that newly merged entities do not escape the Commission's jurisdiction by virtue of their new organizational form. The second aim of the policy statement is to increase the certainty and speed of the FERC's handling of merger applications. Order No. 592 outlines procedural innovations to expedite the merger review process.

Neither Order No. 888 nor Order No. 889 required utilities to vertically disintegrate the monopolistic components of their business (i.e., transmission and system control) from the increasingly liberalized generation and supply sides of the firm. The FERC adopted a less intrusive approach to address potential discriminatory behaviour by requiring functional unbundling. It was not until late 1999, with Order No. 2000, that the Commission took a more aggressive stance.

The intervening years between Order Nos. 888 and 889 (April 1996) and Order No. 2000 (late 1999) saw a number of crucial developments in the industry that resulted in new regulatory challenges (FERC 1999). The industrial landscape shifted dramatically, with the entrance of numerous independent and affiliated power marketers and generators (the FERC granted market-based rate authority to more than 800 such entities); the divestiture by many utilities of generating capacity (more than 10 per cent of U.S. generating capacity was sold or was up for sale between 1997 and 1999); and numerous mergers between electric utilities and between electric and natural gas utilities (more than 40 merger applications were filed with the FERC between 1996 and 1999). The growth in wholesale transactions resulting from deregulation began to place increasing strain on transmission networks. In a sense, restructuring and deregulation were becoming a victim of their own success: open access transmission fostered such an increase in the wholesale market that regional transmission networks grew ever more strained. The growth in volume of wholesale electricity transmissions combined with unexpected shifts in the direction and pattern of transmission paths led to concerns over system reliability.

Order No. 2000 responded to the growth and changing nature of wholesale transmission requirements in an open access environment It addressed the FERC's concerns over the industry's ability to operate, maintain, and plan the grid to ensure system reliability, keep pace with new transmission requirements, and eliminate any discriminatory practices. It requires public and non-public utilities that own, operate, or control networks involved in interstate transmission to establish and participate in regional transmission organizations (RTOs). Essentially, Order No. 2000 requires utilities to place their transmission networks under the control of independent, regionally operated transmission grids. The Commission has adopted a voluntary approach to RTO development, laying out the minimum characteristics and functions RTOs must possess, and has left it to utilities to fill in the finer structural details in collaboration with each other. To facilitate RTO formation, the Commission delineated a collaborative process among utilities, state officials, FERC staff, and interest groups.

In summary, PURPA, the EPAct, and the subsequent FERC Orders introduced competition into the wholesale segment of the electricity industry. They reduced barriers to entry into the wholesale generation market, allowing non-utility generators, such as independent power producers and qualifying facilities, to enter the market. Deregulation of the wholesale supply industry, beginning with the FERC's authority to mandate wheeling, and continuing the with the FERC's open access and transmission capacity orders, enabled non-utility generators to increase their wholesale sales volume.

Deregulation has altered the industrial structure of the electricity sector, and it has also massively changed the nature and number of corporate interests, who pressed for further change. As we have discussed, it has transformed a commercial landscape populated by vertically integrated utilities and publicly owned generators and distributors into a landscape which features entities like qualifying facilities, independent power producers, and exempt wholesale generators.

The Natural Gas Industry

The American natural gas industry is much smaller than the electricity supply industry, with an annual turnover of approximately $80 billion versus roughly $250 billion in the electricity industry (International Energy Agency 1998b). In addition to size differences, the industries also differ in their ownership structure. In contrast to the mixture of public and private ownership in the electricity industry, the natural gas industry is almost entirely privately owned. In addition, there is little vertical integration as in the electricity industry: in natural gas, the production, transmission, distribution, and marketing functions of the business are generally under separate ownership. Corporate concentration varies among the different segments of the natural gas business. In comparison to other industries, concentration in natural gas production is relatively low: of the roughly 10,000 producing companies, the 10 largest account for only 37 per cent of domestic natural gas production, and the 20 largest account for only about half (IEA 1998b). In the pipeline sector, concentration is somewhat higher. Roughly 200 pipeline companies are owned by 5 or 6 large firms, and only 25 interstate firms supply the heavily populated eastern third of the United States (IEA 1998b). Natural gas distribution is provided by over 2,000 local distribution companies (LDCs), which vary widely in size from small firms with several thousand customers to companies that distribute gas to over a million end users (IEA 1998b). There are hundreds of gas marketing companies, which range from independent firms to marketing departments or affiliates of pipeline companies, LDCs, or producers. For the most part, marketers are the affiliates of pipeline companies, and they dominate the business of buying natural gas wholesale from producers and selling it to end users (IEA 1998b). The varying degrees of market power between the different industry segments and between different regions of the country have produced two types of market structure in the industry: markets with limited market power, and markets with monopoly or oligopoly structures. The regulation of the different sectors of the natural gas industry tends to differ depending on the degree of existing or potential competition within the sector in question.

The natural gas industry is inherently volatile, owing to seasonal shifts in demand, weather variations around seasonal fluctuations, and uncertainty in the oil market (Lyon 1990). Demand can be twice as high in January as in July, and residential consumption can vary by a factor of seven or more (IEA 1998b). In contrast to the electricity supply industry, where the high costs of electricity storage prohibit the use of inventories to meet demand peaks, natural gas storage is economically feasible and is therefore used extensively to meet fluctuations in demand.

Under the Natural Gas Act (NGAct) of 1938, the FERC regulates pipeline construction and the transportation of natural gas in interstate commerce. Companies engaging in these activities must apply to the Commission for certificates of public convenience and necessity. FERC approval is also required for facility abandonment and rate-setting for facility use and services. Provisions regarding the FERC's regulation of natural gas transportation are also contained in the Natural Gas Policy Act (NGPAct) of 1978, the Outer Continental Shelf Lands Act (OCSLA), and the Energy Policy Act (EPAct) of 1992. In addition, the FERC oversees the construction and operation of facilities and pipelines needed for imports or exports, and regulates certain environmental aspects of pipeline construction. In contrast to the electricity industry, where the FERC has authority over mergers, in the natural gas industry, the FERC has no responsibility for pipeline mergers.

As Lyon (1990) points out, analysis of natural gas industry regulation and market structure must recognize the tension between two regulatory objectives: the goal of economic efficiency, on the one hand, and the equitable distribution of economic surplus, on the other. In the United States, the balance between these objectives has often been struck with greater weight given to distributional considerations. 'Holding down prices to residential customers has been a frequent motivation for legislators and regulators, sometimes prompting them to adopt inefficient practices' (Lyon 1990: 27). Such was the case in the 1960s when the FERC, under the NGAct of 1938 (which controlled virtually every aspect of the industry from well-head to burner-tip), maintained well-head prices at artificially low levels. Price suppression resulted in severe natural gas shortages in the 1970s, as well as the passage by Congress of the NGPAct of 1978 (Reiter and Economides 1998). The NGPAct terminated federal well-head price regulation of 'new' gas as of 1 January 1985, and it represented the first of four milestones in the move to competition in the U.S. gas market (IEA 1998b). The NGPAct commenced the process of well-head price decontrol by legislating rate ceilings for first sales of natural gas at levels higher than those previously permitted by the FERC.

By the mid-1980s, when the next milestone was laid, the structure of the gas industry was beginning to shift radically: partial well-head decontrol catalyzed the growth of new market institutions (e.g., the natural gas spot market); volatility in oil prices exerted competitive pressure on the traditionally rigid contract structure of the industry; and maturation of the interstate pipeline network opened the possibility of competition between pipelines (Lyon 1990). In 1985 the second milestone towards competition was laid with FERC Order No. 436. Order No. 436 began the process of unbundling pipeline companies' merchant and transportation functions by encouraging pipelines to provide open access to their facilities. It sought to increase competition by permitting end users to bypass the merchant function of pipeline companies by purchasing gas directly from producers and shipping it over pipeline facilities. The Order spawned the emergence of an entirely new industry segment, natural gas marketing, a segment which quickly became a dominant business sector, providing marketing and brokerage services to independent producers seeking to make gas sales, and end users looking for less expensive gas (Kinnie Smith, Jr 1995). The Natural Gas Wellhead Decontrol Act (WDAct) of 1989 was the third milestone in natural gas deregulation. By 1993 it removed all remaining well-head price controls, completing the process of well-head price decontrol.

The WDAct was followed in 1993 by FERC Order No. 636, the final milestone in federal deregulation, which mandated pipeline companies to unbundle transportation, storage, back-up, and merchant services. The objective of Order No. 636 (and its progeny, Order Nos. 636-A, 636-B, and 636-C) was to establish open, non-discriminatory access to gas transportation services. 'With its Orders 636, 636-A, and 636-B, FERC completed its rulemaking steps intended to transform the interstate natural gas market into one in which competing gas suppliers sell directly to LDCs and other end users, with equal transportation services available to all shippers' (Farrell and Forshay 1994).[4] The Order permits pipeline companies to engage in merchant functions, but requires them to do so via separate production and marketing affiliates, to which they cannot accord preferential treatment. Furthermore, it brings storage services under the umbrella of transportation, ensuring that pipeline customers have open access to storage facility services. Additional Order No. 636 provisions to increase competition include the establishment of capacity release programs and the creation of electronic bulletin boards showing available capacity. Capacity release programs allow firm transportation customers to sell excess pipeline capacity, thereby creating a secondary market that competes with pipelines' interruptible transportation services. Electronic bulletin boards provide information to market participants on available capacity, including released capacity.

Order No. 636 altered the playing field, as well as the role and risks of all actors, in the natural gas industry. It fundamentally changed the way the gas market operates, prompting widespread market entry of gas marketing companies, expansion in the number, size, and importance of market centres, and rapid growth in spot and futures markets (IEA 1998b). Numerous gas marketing companies have appeared on the gas industry playing field. These firms, largely the affiliates of pipeline companies, dominate the business of buying well-head gas and selling it to LDCs and large end users. Although Order No. 636 enables producers to sell directly to LDCs and large end users, the lion's share of transactions flows through gas marketing firms. Market centres have also expanded in number, size, and importance as a result of Order No. 636. They play a variety of important roles, including assisting shippers to manage their supply, transportation, and storage portfolios, limiting the ability of any one industry player to exercise market power, enhancing the transparency and dissemination of prices, and permitting numerous purchasers and vendors to take or make delivery.

Spot and futures markets for natural gas have also grown rapidly following Order No. 636. Spot markets first emerged in the mid-1980s when producers wanted to sell excess natural gas supplies outside of long-term contracts. Now, active spot markets exist at many hubs and

---

4 This quotation does not refer to Order No. 636-C because the journal article was written prior to the issuance of this Order.

market centres, and futures markets have also developed to hedge against price volatility. Order No. 636 has spawned two markets for trading natural gas: one to transport physical gas from producers to consumers, and the other to provide financial instruments to control for price risk (Reiter and Economides 1998). The existence of spot and futures markets has had an important influence on the natural gas contract market. Contract lengths are shortening, and contract prices are increasingly linked to prices in the spot market. The existence of the spot market has also impacted the role of natural gas storage. Previously, storage served a smoothing function for daily and seasonal demand fluctuations. Now, in addition to system balancing, storage facilitates arbitrage, enabling firms to take advantage of short-term price movements.

The market structure of the natural gas industry is now characterized by four major sectors: production, transmission, distribution, and marketing (Reiter and Economides 1998). Following well-head price decontrol and open access transmission, producers are no longer restricted to gas sales at regulated prices to pipeline companies. They can now sell directly to LDCs and large end users at market-based rates, and have more choice concerning the pipeline companies they deal with. But despite the range of commercial alternatives now available to producers, most producers are rather small firms and lack the economies of scale to profitably undertake the marketing function. As a result, most purchases at the well-head are made by natural gas marketers (IEA 1998b). Before deregulation, pipeline companies had a monopoly on first sales, transportation, and resales of gas. Following open access, pipelines function primarily as transporters of natural gas, but many have created gas marketing affiliates. The distribution sector is composed of LDCs, which handle the largest part of residential and commercial retail sales. The marketing sector of the natural gas business has emerged as an important industry player as a result of deregulation. The sector conducts business along the entire spectrum of the natural gas industry, from producers through to end users. The majority of its business is natural gas trade, and profits are derived from the spread between purchase and selling prices. Restructuring of the natural gas industry has not changed the basic ownership structure of the industry because the production, transportation, and distribution functions of the business have traditionally been under separate ownership (Kinnie Smith, Jr 1995).

Under Order No. 636, the FERC continues to regulate rates for natural gas transportation, unless a pipeline can prove that it lacks market power, in which case it can use market-based rates. Progress towards the use of market-based rates following Order No. 636 has been minimal, however, and the FERC therefore remains an active participant in transportation rate-setting (Chermak 1998). Two factors have been advanced to explain the FERC's continued dominance of transportation pricing. First, relatively high levels of market concentration in the natural gas pipeline sector, particularly in the northeastern United States, mitigate against the use of market-based rates in all regions of the country (IEA 1998b). Second, the FERC itself may be hesitant to depart from cost-of-service regulation because it does not wish to relinquish regulatory control (Bailey 1999).

This being said, on 9 February 2000, the FERC promulgated Order No. 637, which partially decontrols short-term transportation pricing. The Order waives price ceilings for short-term released capacity for a two-year period, enabling captive customers to reduce the cost of holding long-term pipeline capacity. It also provides pipelines with greater flexibility in pricing, by permitting them to file for peak/off-peak and term differentiated rate structures. Peak/off-peak rates are intended to accommodate seasonal variations in demand, while term differentiated rates are meant to enhance pipelines' capacity to manage the risk underlying contracts of varying lengths. Additional provisions contained in Order No. 637 aim to improve the efficiency and competitiveness of the natural gas market by improving reporting requirements to increase price transparency and to more effectively monitor for the abuse of market power; by changing regulations regarding scheduling procedures, capacity segmentation, and pipeline penalties; and by narrowing the right of first refusal of long-term capacity customers. While the regulatory changes contained in Order No. 637 pertain primarily to the regulation of short-term transportation, the Commission recognizes in the Order that the changing nature of the natural gas market challenges its regulatory framework for long-term transportation capacity.

In summary, there were four milestones in natural gas market deregulation: the Natural Gas Policy Act of 1978, which commenced the process of well-head price decontrol; FERC Order No. 436 in 1985, which began to unbundle pipelines' merchant and transportation functions, the Natural Gas Wellhead Decontrol Act of 1989, which completed the process of well-head decontrol; and FERC Order No. 636 in

1993, which mandated unbundling. These milestones have recently been followed by a fifth, FERC Order No. 637 in 2000, which partially decontrols short-term transportation pricing.

This series of regulatory reforms has had a dramatic impact on the structure of the industry, catalyzing the growth of new market institutions like the spot and futures markets, expanding the number, size, and importance of market centres, creating an entirely new industry segment, natural gas marketing, and building a secondary market for natural gas transportation.

Impact on Canada

The actual and potential impact of American reforms on Canadian regulation depends on a number of factors. First is the issue of whether American developments precede or follow Canadian reforms. As chapter 7 shows, electricity market restructuring and deregulation is more advanced in the United States than in Canada. It is therefore more likely to exert greater future pressure on Canadian regulation than reforms in the natural gas industry, which in fact followed similar developments in Canada. In part, this is also because electricity markets and grids are regional in nature rather than fully continental. Second, the extent of the impact is likely to be greater where differences between the Canadian and American regulatory frameworks serve to mobilize constituencies and interests that attempt to influence Canadian regulation. In the context of electricity, exporters are likely to exert pressure on Canadian regulators to adopt similar reforms because of the FERC's reciprocity conditions. These require Canadian electricity exporters to provide open access transmission in order to receive transmission access to the United States. Third, the scope and nature of the impact is conditioned by domestic institutional arrangements. Chief among these is Canada's federal system. Where interprovincial wheeling of electricity is involved, for example, federal-provincial relations and interprovincial relations play a key role in determining the extent of American influence. We discuss these potential impacts on the electricity and natural gas sectors below.

The Electricity Industry

In Canada, a number of factors are driving restructuring in the electricity industry. While domestic consumer demands, international trade agreements, and technological developments in electricity generation are key factors, in the short term, the strongest pressure originates in the increasingly competitive electricity market in the United States. This section focuses on the potential impact on Canada of the regulatory and policy changes at the FERC. Impacts are categorized along three lines: impacts on electricity policy and regulation; impacts on Canada's electricity regulatory regime; and impacts on Canada's trade in electricity. Each of these categories is discussed below.

Faced with the FERC's liberalization of the generation and wholesale wheeling markets, provincial regulators are likely to undertake similar initiatives. Experience to date suggests that regulators are not simply 'following the leader' but, rather, are liberalizing their markets in order to maintain and/or expand Canadian electricity trade with the United States. Indeed, the utilities that are introducing competition into generation and are opening transmission access tend to be those that have direct access to the American market. FERC Order No. 888's open access condition requires 'transmission-owning foreign electric utilities to provide open-access transmission services as a condition to receiving transmission access from transmission-owning public utilities in the United States' (FERC 1996a). British Columbia and Quebec, in an effort to expand their export markets, were the first provinces to introduce transmission rates modelled on the FERC tariff (IEA 1999). But not all provinces have been as quick off the mark. On 2 May 1997 Ontario Hydro requested a stay of the reciprocity provision pending judicial review. The company asserted that its annual $235-million export business would suffer irreparable harm because it could not permit open access transmission without Ontario government approval (which it stated would require significant restructuring of the province's electricity system and the resolution of complex financial issues). In response to this filing, the FERC issued an order clarifying the open access condition and requesting further information from Ontario Hydro (FERC 1997). The Commission stated that the open access condition only applies to sales by Canadian exporters that require delivery to points within the United States (i.e., it does not apply to transactions in which an American company imports electricity for resale) and that pre–Order No. 888 power sales or transmission contracts are exempt from the open access condition.

Through the creation of RTOs, FERC Order No. 2000 addressed the need to maintain grid reliability, keep pace with new transmission requirements, and eliminate discriminatory practices of transmission-owning utilities. Order No. 2000's likely impact on Canada will derive from Canadian transmission-owning utilities' membership in cross-border reliability councils. Utilities in North America have traditionally interconnected their transmission networks to minimize the cost of maintaining spinning reserves, that is, the cost of having reserve generators ready to produce power immediately if an active generator fails. Industry members have voluntarily organized themselves into regional councils that coordinate the generation and transmission of electricity within their jurisdictions with a view to ensuring reliability. Provincial utilities belong to regional councils that cross the Canada–United States border (British Columbia and Alberta are members of the Western Systems Coordinating Council, Alberta and Saskatchewan are part of the Mid-Continent Area Power Pool, and Ontario, Quebec, and the Maritime provinces belong to the Northeast Power Coordinating Council). Together, the regional councils own a non-profit corporation called the North American Electric Reliability Organization, NAERO (formerly the North American Electric Reliability Council, NERC). It will likely be difficult for Canadian transmission owners to remain active participants in regional councils without belonging to a regional transmission organization (RTO). And yet, the FERC requires transmission owners to surrender control of their networks to their RTO. Accordingly, Canadian regulators will be subjected to mounting pressure from the American government and electricity industry to issue regulations along the lines of Order No. 2000.

If Canadian regulation is – either willingly or begrudgingly – 'pulled along' by American deregulation, the key players, key relationships, and balance of power in Canada's electricity regulatory regime may be subject to change. The federal government is likely to become a key player in initiatives that involve uniform national rules, such as wholesale wheeling, because of its constitutional authority to intervene in matters involving interprovincial transactions. However, the federal government currently faces a stumbling block in this regard because the National Energy Board Act only delegates authority to the NEB for the construction of interprovincial transmission lines and electricity exports. Without federal involvement, system-wide solutions to such issues as nation-wide open access transmission may not be possible.

On the one hand, this scepticism may be warranted. The outcome of provincial negotiations leading to the Interprovincial Trade Agreement suggests that interprovincial agreement on open access may be difficult. As we have seen in chapter 2, the provinces were unable to suc-cessfully conclude the energy chapter largely because of disagreements over interprovincial wheeling (Doern and MacDonald 1999). On the other hand, American deregulation may have increased the likelihood of reaching interprovincial agreement by providing a common set of challenges and opportunities to the provinces, as well as a shared sense of urgency. The FERC's open access condition may supply the neces-sary impetus to drive the provinces towards cooperation. As provincial utilities increasingly provide reciprocal access to American firms, the experience they accumulate and the market opportunities they enjoy may increase the attractiveness of interprovincial open access transmis-sion. Moreover, the FERC's open access tariff guidelines may provide a common point of departure for renewed provincial negotiations. How-ever, regardless of the respective roles that the federal government and the provinces will play in electricity deregulation, liberalization may shift the locus of power upwards from the intra-provincial level to the interprovincial, federal-provincial, and federal levels. The key battles, key players, and key challenges are not intra-provincial in nature. In-creasingly, the focus of attention is borders – whether of the provincial or national variety. And the division of powers between federal and provincial regulators plays a key role in determining the pace, extent, and mechanics of deregulation (Hancher 1997).

Canada exports about 10 per cent of its electricity to the United States. If exporters are experiencing significant change and uncertainty as the American wholesale power market moves from agreements with single generators to competitive bidding procedures, and as American utilities move to minimize their risk by using smaller-scale and shorter-term purchases, then Canadian exporters will have to adapt to these market conditions. Canada's electricity exports are also vulnerable via deregulation-induced relative price changes. As Norman (1999) notes, investment and operating incentives in a regulated environment differ from those under competition. In a study of the new incentives facing firms in the American generation sector, Norman contends that the removal of rate of return assurances from regulators could lead to a generation capacity 'bubble' that exerts downward pressure on prices. In the absence of the security of rate of return regulation, firms with existing capacity will be motivated to make investments that maximize the efficiency, utilization rate, and life of their existing plants rather than undertaking new capacity investments. Combined with the addi-tional capacity investments made by new industry entrants, the industry may experience a bubble in capacity that will reduce electricity prices. 'Falling prices will benefit electricity consumers, but they also will put pressure on suppliers of fuels used to generate electricity as well as on firms considering entry into the electricity generation industry' (212). If Norman's prediction is correct, Canadian electricity exports may decline in the face of excess American generation capacity and lower American electricity prices. With fewer Canadian generators dedicated to export production, Canada may also experience excess capacity and a downward trend in electricity prices. But other factors and dynamics are also at play, and we return to some of these in chapter 7, where inter-regime competition aspects of energy regulation are examined, including the demonstration effect of the California crisis on Canada's development of electricity restructuring in Ontario, Alberta, and Nova Scotia.

The Natural Gas Industry

In contrast to the electricity supply industry, where regulatory change in the United States has been cited as the most important factor driving deregulation in Canada, in the natural gas industry, Canada has not been subject to the same degree of bilateral pressure from its southern neighbour. The reason for this stems from the relative pace of the two countries' deregulation. Canada has been a forerunner in natural gas industry deregulation, described as early as 1996 as having 'perhaps the most unfettered natural gas market in the world' (IEA 1996: 61). As indicated briefly in chapter 1, substantial deregulation has taken place at both the federal and provincial levels, including well-head price decontrol, mandatory open access to pipelines, and unbundling of pipeline purchasing, transportation, and sales activities (see further discussion in chapter 4 on the NEB). Well-head gas prices have not been regulated in Canada since 1986, a full seven years prior to complete well-head decontrol in the United States (the Natural Gas Wellhead Decontrol Act of 1989 completed the process of well-head price decontrol in 1993). In Canada, open access to pipelines and unbundling of pipeline merchant and transportation functions also occurred in the mid-1980s, again, prior to the 1993 promulgation of FERC Order No. 636, which introduced mandatory unbundling and established open access in the United States. Even the FERC's most recent initiative to further liberalize the natural gas industry, Order No. 637, only serves to bring American regulation in line with that in Canada, where there were already no restrictions on release and resale of marketers' and LDCs' unneeded pipeline and storage capacity.

Temporal differences notwithstanding, deregulation in the Canadian and American natural gas industries has followed a similar overall path. The initial focus on well-head price decontrol, followed by mandatory unbundling and open access transmission, is evident in both countries (IEA 1998c). But as the leader, rather than the follower, in natural gas market liberalization, Canada does not experience the same sort of pressure from American regulatory change in natural gas as in the electricity market. Instead of being 'pulled along' by change south of the border as may occur in electricity regulation, in natural gas the slower pace of American deregulation means that Canadian regulation is not likely to be impacted by these American developments.

But while American regulatory reform of the natural gas industry may not exert explicit pressure on Canada's natural gas regulation, Canadian regulators may be impacted by the American scene nonetheless. Regulators may find themselves playing a two-level game between domestic and American interests. At the domestic level of the game, domestic private sector interests may press for further liberalization that confers competitive advantage (even if temporary) vis-à-vis American firms. As Lyon (1990) points out, the more integrated the natural gas market, the more impact differences in regulatory structure can have.

The natural gas market between Canada and the United States is highly integrated. Major pipeline links and significant volumes of gas flowing from Canada to the United States mean that the countries' systems can be considered a single market. Given the substantive integration of the two markets, there may be significant advantages for domestic firms located in the country that moves first on new liberalization initiatives. Indeed, prior to FERC Order No. 636, Canadian gas producers enjoyed a competitive advantage over U.S. firms because usage charges were lower in Canada, enabling Canadian firms to ship gas to American markets at a lower marginal cost (IEA 1998c).

At the bi-national level, Canadian regulators may be subject to pressure from their American counterparts, who might prefer a less rapid approach to liberalization. The FERC may be promoting the interests of its own domestic constituency, concerned about being placed at a competitive disadvantage. Or it may wish to allow a longer period for the American natural gas industry to adjust to American regulatory reforms. Alternatively, as has been suggested (Bailey 1999), the FERC may be hesitant to pursue further liberalization because it does not wish to relinquish regulatory control.

There are, of course, other issues in Canada-U.S. natural gas trade arising from the Bush administration's National Energy Policy and from the energy security issues raised by the attacks of 11 September 2001. These are discussed further in later chapters.

Conclusions

The U.S. Federal Energy Regulatory Commission (FERC) has transformed its regulation of the wholesale electricity and natural gas markets. The shift has been from monopoly regulation to regulation that fosters competition in wholesale transactions. The key development underlying this change is the FERC's creation of non-discriminatory open access transmission with Order Nos. 888 and 889 in the electricity sector, and Order No. 636 in natural gas. Through these Orders, the FERC mandated transmission-owning utilities and pipelines to unbundle sales of electricity and natural gas from transmission and transportation services. Both the electricity and natural gas industries have undergone substantial restructuring in the wake of these Orders: new market players and institutions, and hence new interests, have emerged; the role of existing players has been modified; and the parties to, and the path of, wholesale transactions have been altered dramatically. This chapter has also shown some elements of inter-regime dynamics, in that a number of the original changes were carried out for environmental and conservation reasons but then led to further sectoral deregulation for economic reasons. It has also given an initial glimpse into the links between competition and energy regulation, both in the actual design of markets but also in how various aspects of mergers and potential market power were dealt with as the new markets took hold.

The potential impact of these changes on Canada depends on a number of factors. Where American reform has preceded developments in Canadian regulation, as in the electricity sector, pressure to adopt similar reforms in Canada has been strong. This is particularly true where Canadian electricity exporters are concerned about the FERC's reciprocity condition. But while differences between the Canadian and American regulatory frameworks may serve to mobilize domestic interests in Canada to pressure Canadian regulators for change (or for maintenance of the status quo), the ultimate impact is likely to be conditioned in greater measure by federal-provincial and interprovincial relations. Where export markets are at stake, American developments may provide the necessary impetus to achieve federal-provincial and interprovincial agreement on such issues as interprovincial wheeling. Regulation in the United States also serves as a source of ideas that may become the basis of workable solutions to existing roadblocks to Canadian agreements on energy regulation. But we leave to later chapters a consideration of the implications of the California electricity crisis, as well as of the Bush energy plan and its implications for energy security and the new regulatory dynamics of northern natural gas pipelines.

PART 2

ENERGY REGULATORY INSTITUTIONS AND INTER-REGIME CHANGE

4 The National Energy Board

The National Energy Board (NEB) in the early years of the twenty-first century is facing a regulatory context which quite quickly has taken on a new shape and urgency. The events of 11 September 2001 have brought a renewed focus on pipeline security and safety, including provisions in Bill C-46 which require renewed vigilance by the NEB in concert with other federal departments and agencies. The U.S. Bush administration's National Energy Policy, coupled with other underlying changes in North American energy markets, has led to renewed interest in new pipelines to bring northern natural gas to southern Canadian and U.S. markets, especially the latter. The Bush administration's plan, coupled with its weaker alternative to the Kyoto Protocol, also raises new concerns about Canada's long-term energy supply and how much it will serve Canadian versus continental demand. The rapid development of a North American electricity market and international power lines and grids has meant that the NEB's role in the electricity sector has been increased. And underlying all these pressures and changes is a concurrent concern with environmental impacts and with sustainable development.

This recent burst of change contrasts partly with the NEB's decade-long evolution in the 1990s, when it literally 'moved out' and 'moved on' from its regulatory roots. It 'moved out' and away from Ottawa to the oil patch heartland of Calgary in 1991, a movement of considerable distance geographically but arguably even greater in terms of its impact on organizational culture. It 'moved on' as well not only in its full acceptance of deregulated commodity markets and flexible market-sensitive regulatory approaches but also in its institutional tilt towards enhanced environmental and health and safety roles. In the terminology of this book, it is still at its core a sectoral regulatory body because energy facilities still exhibit significant (though reduced) monopoly features, but the NEB has also taken on framework or horizontal regime regulatory functions both regarding the environment and safety and regarding competition. Indeed, there may be pressures building that it become by statute a sustainable development regulator.

While transformation is the dominant picture to be portrayed in this chapter there are also underpinnings of stability and of a return to the way in which the NEB was viewed in its earliest days from 1959 on, but which was badly disrupted in the conflictual 'energy-crisis' years of the late 1970s to 1984. First, it has had leadership stability during the period from 1985 to the late 1990s in the person of Roland Priddle, a consummate non-political energy expert and professional. The emphasis on non-political energy expertise has continued under the tenure of Kenneth Vollman, the present chairman of the NEB. Vollman is an engineer and NEB career official with a strong bent for ensuring that the NEB is a practical results-oriented regulatory body. Second, the NEB is seen, in the relative political calm of deregulated oil and gas markets, as a regulator of technical competence and minimal politics. And third, its status as the main centre of energy expertise in the federal government in many respects has been restored, not only by its own competence but also by the major downsizing in the mid-1990s of the lead federal energy department, National Resources Canada (Doern 1995b).

The focus in this chapter is more on the NEB as a regulatory body itself, including changes in its basic organizational culture, the nature of its core regulatory processes, and its acquisition of newer framework regulatory roles in the environmental and safety fields. The chapter is organized into four parts. First, we relate the origins of the NEB to the larger historical portrait of energy policy presented in chapter 1. Second, we highlight the key features of the current NEB mandate and its organizational transformation prior to and after its move to Calgary, but also into the early 2000s. Third, we examine the NEB's reinvented incentive-based regulation in operation, mainly through a look at how the core monopoly aspects of energy regulation in the pipeline sector have been changed through the adoption of a more flexible negotiated 'settlement process,' but also through a brief discussion of how the export review function has been liberalized and market-tested. Fourth, we look at key features of the NEB's environmental mandate and its safety mandate. Conclusions then follow.

Origins of the NEB

The broad evolution of the National Energy Board must be seen in relation to the three basic periods of energy development traced in chapter 1: 1947 to 1973; 1974 to 1984; and 1985 to the present. As has been indicated, these periods correspond roughly to different levels of reliance on markets versus state intervention to influence the pace and nature of energy and resource development. The first and last periods have been very market-oriented, while the middle period, influenced greatly by the two world oil crises of 1973 and 1979–80, witnessed a surge of government intervention, regulatory and otherwise. Each period also saw the emergence of a new 'ascending' or dominant energy source (from coal and hydro, to oil and nuclear, to natural gas). But, cumulatively, a situation has evolved in which there are now more economic opportunities for inter-fuel substitution in industrial production and consumer use.

The NEB was established in 1959 largely to advise the government on broad energy matters (there was no federal energy department as such at that time) and to regulate oil and gas pipelines and the export of oil, gas, and electricity. Nuclear power was regulated by the Atomic Energy Control Board (now the Canadian Nuclear Safety Commission). The NEB also emerged as the energy industry was becoming more national in nature in that west to east pipelines were being planned or built, though with inevitable Canada-U.S. issues and markets involved simultaneously. Thus, as a sectoral regulator, the NEB was concerned with public interest regulation of monopoly pipeline carriers, but also with the level of exports (and imports) of oil and gas in the longer-term national interest (Lucas 1977, 1978).

Thus national energy regulation, almost from the outset, was multi-functional in that it had to both police a monopoly pipeline sector and plan energy expansion. Indeed, by the time there was an acknowledged need for a National Energy Board, energy issues had become highly politicized as a result of a series of conflicts arising from federal-provincial and Canada-U.S. relationships, particularly regarding the building of the trans-Canada pipeline. In particular, industry-wide issues such as long- and short-term domestic supply and foreign exports, rather than firm specific actions, were the primary concern.

The NEB's primary function from the outset was to be a sectoral planner that would use its powers to regulate interprovincial pipeline construction and especially the levels of exports of oil, natural gas, and electricity in order to protect Canada's long-term energy needs. The Board, because of the limited policy guidance in its authorizing statute, was expected to become the primary framer of Canadian energy policy. Underscoring this responsibility, and establishing the precedent that would shortly be followed in the transportation and broadcasting sectors, the NEB was made the federal government's primary policy adviser. It was mandated to monitor the current and future supply of, and demand for, Canada's major energy commodities and to recommend to its minister such measures that it considered necessary or advisable in the public interest for the control, supervision, conservation, use, marketing, and development of energy and sources of energy.

Within a few years of its creation in 1959, the NEB emerged as a powerful independent regulatory body. In the words of its second chairman, the NEB was perceived to be 'the smallest shop with the biggest clout in town' (quoted in Dewar 1980: 30). In only its first decade of operation the NEB appeared to have successfully carved out an exclusive policy and regulatory space, an outcome that reflected both its power and technical competence to make regulatory decisions and its role as the primary policy adviser to the federal government on energy issues. One measure of its power was the fact that it quickly developed as a closed regulatory shop that 'decided energy issues almost exclusively in response to the representations of the provincial governments and private companies which participated in its proceedings' (Doern and Toner 1985: 83). Other interested parties had greater difficulty gaining effective access, and the federal government appeared to be content with both how the NEB operated and the quality of its policy advice.

Although the ramifications did not appear to be appreciated at the time, the decline of the NEB as the primary regulatory and policy actor within the federal government can be dated from 1966, for it was in this year that a bureaucratic rival emerged. The rival was the Department of Energy, Mines and Resources (EMR), a department which brought together a number of technical units within Ottawa, but more importantly was assigned a policy adviser role to its minister on energy issues. In the first five years of its existence, EMR did not appear to pose much of a challenge to the dominance of the NEB, in part because of its limited policy expertise. One sign of potential conflict emerged in the early 1970s, however, when the Department began to lobby the government to restrict funds for the NEB for policy advisory personnel on the grounds that this was unnecessary duplication (Doern and Toner 1985).

Within a decade, however, the NEB had been displaced as the primary bureaucratic agent in many regulatory and policy sectors. One factor was the growing concern, played upon by officials within EMR, that the NEB was too close to the industry and consequently Ottawa was too dependent on industry information which was channelled through the NEB (Doern and Toner 1985: 85). Another was that the quality and, indeed, accuracy of the NEB's advice and information were suspect. The energy crises, international and intergovernmental, that ensued after the 1973 oil embargo brought the dissatisfaction with the NEB to a head.

Within less than five years, not only had the Department of Energy, Mines and Resources displaced the NEB as primary policy adviser, but the government assumed some of the NEB's regulatory functions for itself and hived off other responsibilities for other agencies (Doern and Toner 1985: Ch. 11). In addition, rather than delegating new responsibilities to the NEB as a consequence of the energy conflicts, the federal government opted to create new regulatory instruments. In 1973, for example, using its power to approve NEB regulations, the Cabinet transferred the power to issue export permits from the NEB to the Cabinet itself, but with the Board still required to advise on the level of export price for gas and oil. In 1975, Parliament passed the Petroleum Administration Act, which gave Cabinet, not the NEB, the power to regulate oil and gas prices. The same year saw the creation of a state-owned oil company, Petro-Canada, which was the result of governmental dissatisfaction with its existing 'windows' on the industry, especially the NEB, which now appeared to be, if not captured, then at least far too sympathetic to the industry.

The displacement of the National Energy Board as primary regulatory agency and policy adviser was completed in 1980 with the announcement of the National Energy Policy (NEP). Although the NEB had lost its monopoly status as policy adviser, throughout the 1970s it retained some status and role in the policy process. In 1980, however, it was completely isolated and excluded from the development of the NEP. Neither its chairman, nor its Board members, nor its staff were consulted by the political and bureaucratic officials in the drafting of the NEP, despite the fact that this was the most comprehensive set of regulatory initiatives in Canadian energy history.

It was only with the demise of the NEP, and the deregulation of oil and gas under the Mulroney Conservative government from 1984 on, that the NEB re-established itself at the heart of the Canadian energy regulatory regime.

The NEB Mandate and Key Changes since 1985

The NEB is an independent federal regulatory tribunal which reports to Parliament through the minister of natural resources. The up to nine-member Board (currently seven) functions as a court of record and thus has powers regarding attendance at hearings, the swearing in and examination of witnesses, the production and inspection of documents, and the enforcement of its orders. The NEB's regulatory decisions and the reasons for them are issued as public documents. Under the National Energy Board Act, the NEB grants authorizations for:

- the construction and operation of interprovincial and international oil and gas and commodity pipelines, international power lines and designated interprovincial power lines;
- the setting of tolls and tariffs for oil and gas pipelines under its jurisdiction;
- the export of oil, natural gas and electricity;
- the import of natural gas. (NEB 1994a)

The NEB also acquired powers regarding the regulation of oil and gas exploration and production activities on Canada's federally owned frontier lands (the Canada Oil and Gas Operations Act) outside of areas subject to federal-provincial accords. The Board also has a duty to monitor the current and future supply of, and demand for, Canada's major energy commodities. Finally, the NEB acts in an advisory function, and may, on its own initiative, hold inquiries, conduct studies, and prepare reports on specific energy matters for the information of Parliament, the federal government, and the general public.

At the core of its business are the NEB's approximately 750 applications annually from energy firms. The great majority of these seek routine orders for export licences, pipeline tolls, and certificates for construction of new facilities. But larger pipeline expansions are also included. Larger projects typically involve an oral public hearing, but the majority of projects are governed by internal processes of examination or written public proceedings (NEB 1996a).

By the mid-1990s, the NEB described itself in ways that reflect the new realities of economic deregulation, expanded social regulation, budgetary cutbacks, and internationalization and globalization. For example, in early 1995 it described itself as:

- 'a leader in the implementation of policies which now provide a comprehensive framework for the free functioning of oil and gas markets, nationally and internationally';
- an efficient and economical regulator whose staff has 'declined from about 550 (in 1985) to 282' (in 1994) and whose expenditures have been reduced by about 14 per cent in the same period;
- a regulator that distinguishes between the 'deregulation of markets for energy and proper regulation of energy facilities' ... in the latter case involving 'considerations of the natural environment [and] human safety';
- a regulator which in 1994 carried out 'environmental assessments of more than 160 projects';
- a regulator which has improved its ability and authority to take 'immediate action when the safety of company employees and the public is at risk' (this includes the designation of its own officers as designated inspection officers);
- a regulator committed to the introduction of electronic filing for its key regulatory activities, with expected further savings and efficiency for the NEB and for the firms involved;
- a regulator whose approximately $34 million costs of operation is now 85 per cent paid for by cost recovery charges from industry, whereas previously its work had been entirely paid for from budgetary appropriations. (NEB 1994a: 1–5)

In Calgary the NEB has functioned in a close daily interaction with the heart of the Canadian oil and gas industry. International and regional energy regulation has also been altered by the provisions of the Canada-U.S. Free Trade Agreement and NAFTA. The essence of the free trade deals was that they made it more difficult for federal energy authorities to interfere with the free flow of energy commodities across the Canada-U.S. border as had been done during the energy crisis era, especially from 1980 to 1984 under the federal Liberals' interventionist NEP (Doern and Tomlin 1991).

By 2001 the NEB's description of its mandate, goals, and vision reveals a shift in emphasis, or at least a change in order of ranking. It stated to Parliament that it seeks to 'promote safety, environmental protection and economic efficiency in the Canadian public interest while respecting individuals' rights and within the mandate set by Parliament in the regulation of pipelines, energy development and trade. In fulfilling this purpose, our vision is to be a respected leader in safety, environmental and economic regulation' (NEB 2001: 1). More specifically, the NEB reports on performance in relation to four strategic goals, as follows:

- NEB-regulated facilities are safe and perceived to be safe.
- NEB-regulated facilities are built and operated in a manner that pro-tects the environment and respects individuals' rights.
- Canadians derive the benefits of economic efficiency.
- The NEB meets the evolving needs of the public to engage in NEB matters. (NEB 2001: 1)

A brief discussion of each of the features inherent in these two evolving statements of its mandate will reveal the contrast to the NEB's earlier phases of operation as a regulator.

First, in 1985 the policy and regulatory approach was changed to facilitate the deregulation of gas. The changes allowed more direct buy-sell relationships between gas producers and gas users, with the conse-quent weakening of some of the previous monopoly powers of the pipelines and distribution companies. Gas deregulation eventually ex-tended to the ending of the NEB-administered rule which had required surplus reserve tests for exports. These provisions had required a 25 to 30 year domestic supply cushion before exports were allowed (Lucas 1978; Doern and Toner 1985; Canada 1988).

As the NEB issues its export licences and orders, it must take into account section 118 of the National Energy Board Act, which requires that the Board satisfy itself that the quantity of gas or oil to be exported does not exceed the surplus remaining after due allowance has been made for the reasonably foreseeable requirements for use in Canada. As mentioned above, export licences and orders are a key part of the NEB's business, and thus there is little doubt that this aspect of its work has been deregulated relative to its earlier history (Watkins 1991).

With respect to overall regulatory efficiency, there is no doubt that the NEB is a leaner institution both in its staff composition and in its approach to other regulatory matters and procedures. Its staff had been cut in half in the mid to late 1980s and in the mid-1990s stood at about 260 full-time staff. The number of Board members was reduced from thirteen to the current maximum of nine. Following a discussion of 'industrial irritants' in 1987, the NEB gradually moved towards a process of 'negotiated settlements' for resolving disputes over tolls between pipeline companies and their customers (see more below). The number of economists employed by the Board has been significantly reduced, in part because there is less need for 'benefit-cost' analysis of export applications. Indeed, there was concern that the mere fact that such analysis was being done would be evidence that the NEB was not practising proper free market approaches.

Both the relocation of the NEB to Calgary in 1991 and the funding of the Board through cost recovery were seen by many in the Board and in the industry as positive pro-market steps. An NEB staff member in Calgary is likely to have lunch with an energy businessperson rather than (as was most likely the case in Ottawa) another bureaucrat. Cost recovery funding has resulted in the need for annual discussions concerning the level of charges, and because of the kinds of information shared, this has resulted in a more in-depth appreciation by both regulator and business of each other's practical world.

There is also a partial link between the Calgary move and the eventual 1996 restructuring of the internal organization of the NEB from ten functional branches to five 'process-based business units' (NEB 1997c). When the move to Calgary occurred, the NEB was being reduced in size, but it also lost a large number of staff who decided not to move. This cadre of staff was replaced by largely Alberta-based persons, who brought with them more of the business-oriented culture of the Calgary milieu. When the senior management of the NEB decided in 1994 to review the NEB's organization and strategic objectives, it faced a barrage of criticism about the organization's style of management. The 1994 review was conducted on a broad participative basis through the ranks of the staff, and it brought out a strong call for a different, less hierarchical way of doing things. Other organizational modes of operating were canvassed, and ranged from awareness of the general 'reinvented government' modes of restructuring service delivery to practical examples of change being put in place in some U.S. state energy regulatory bodies as well as in the Alberta government.

The resulting change is centred around a leadership-team approach, which includes, in addition to the chairman, vice-chairman, and executive director, five 'business leaders' for corporate services, information management, commodities, applications, and operations (including environment and safety areas of the mandate). What this means in practical terms is that knowledge experts such as economists, environmental experts, engineers, and financial staff are no longer lodged in separate functional branches, but rather are dispersed throughout the organization in teams. Some of the teams then focus on key regulated firms. For example, there are teams for TransCanada Pipelines (by far the largest regulated gas pipeline) and for other large pipelines. We discuss the environmental aspects of this team approach below, but in the meantime it is simply important to note that the NEB was changed by its move to Alberta and by related developments.

The flip side of this deregulatory picture is found in the evident addition to the NEB of new framework or social regulatory tasks in both the environmental and occupational health and safety fields (see more below). Indeed, in the jargon of the new NEB 'business plans,' this is seen as one of the NEB's growing 'lines of business,' and the above quoted 2001 statement of its mandate and performance goals shows this emphasis very directly.

In the 1970s and 1980s, the NEB was not known as a bastion of pro-environmentalism (Bregha 1980). It had always been concerned with the safety of energy facilities, but, along with other energy players, it had also fought environmentalists tooth and nail in some extremely high-profile projects, both in southern Canada and in the frontier areas of the North (Bregha 1980; Doern and Toner 1985).

The NEB As Incentive Regulator: Negotiated Pipeline-Toll Incentive Settlements and Export Review Processes

The NEB has gradually moved its system of overall regulation towards an incentive-based system and also towards the use of a negotiated settlement process. The latter process is one used beyond the pipeline-toll area of regulation and, in general, is intended to provide an alternative to the adversarial process that otherwise flows from the NEB's statutory provisions and role as a court of record. An adversarial public hearing process was commonly used until the mid-1980s. In the pipeline monopoly sector, the traditional mode of regulation was a 'cost of service' concept, which is similar to 'rate of return' regulation. The process required the submission of elaborate cost information to the NEB and expensive hearing procedures. Under such a system there was little incentive for pipeline companies to economize on costs because cost savings were passed on to shippers. Under incentive regulation achieved through negotiated settlements (which typically are for four or five years' duration) there are incentives to be more efficient, with the gains shared between the pipeline company and shippers.

Much depends then on the nature of the settlement process and on the role of the NEB. In 1988 the NEB issued guidelines on the settlement process which provided that all interested parties had to be involved in the settlement negotiation and that the agreed settlement had to be unanimous. The concern of the NEB was that the settlement process should not usurp the NEB's overall public interest role. The process did not involve any provision for mediation by NEB staff or outside mediators. NEB staff were present at a couple of the first settlement processes, but the NEB felt that the practice had to stop in case there were later court challenges to an agreement, or a failure to get an agreement, and later action was needed by the Board.

The early steps to incentive regulation took time and reflected the evolution of thinking in the Board, and within the industry (Rochefort 1997). A 1987–8 consultation occurred on the NEB's public hearing process in which the issue of negotiated settlements was raised as an alternative to traditional regulation. Bilateral task forces composed of pipeline companies and their shippers were also meeting and were functioning in such a way that they were reducing the number of tariff issues that had to be dealt with at NEB hearings. A January 1993 workshop on incentive regulation was held and led, among other things, to a generic cost of capital hearing, which also led to greater regulatory efficiency and flexibility.

By 1994 the NEB was able to publish an updated set of guidelines regarding what constituted an acceptable settlement. These criteria are that

1) all parties having an interest should have a fair opportunity to participate;
2) the Board's ability and discretion to take into account any public interest considerations which may extend beyond the immediate concerns of the negotiating parties must not be fettered;
3) the settlement process must produce adequate information on the public record for the Board to understand the basis for the agreement and to assess its reasonableness;
4) Board staff may attend task force meetings upon invitation and solely for the purposes of information exchange and discussion of procedural matters; and

5) the Board will not accept a settlement which contains provisions which
are illegal, or contrary to the NEB Act. (Rochefort 1997: 3)

Several negotiated incentive settlements have been successfully concluded which Board staff argue have met the initial tests of producing
lower toll rates, more efficiency incentives, and better agreement and
consensus. Multi-year agreements have been negotiated and approved
for Interprovincial Pipeline in 1995 and, in 1996, for TransCanada Pipelines, Trans Mountain Pipe Line Company, and Trans-Northern Pipelines. For most of the last five years, nearly all the pipelines under the
NEB's jurisdiction were operating under negotiated incentive settlements with their shippers, and, as a result, the Board had no major toll
hearings. In the early 2000s, however, these agreements will have to be
negotiated and there may also be new toll hearings.

Overall, the NEB quite credibly claims in its performance reports that
'pipeline companies and shipper representatives are satisfied with the
environment and processes created by the Board in which issues concerning traffic, tolls and tariffs are resolved' (NEB 2001:19). It notes
further that 'this streamlined process has resulted in cost savings to all
parties involved by reducing the number of costly and confrontational
public hearings' and that the 'process has been very successful, with
only the most difficult-to-resolve toll and tariff issues coming before the
Board for arbitration' (NEB 2001: 19).

The analysis in this chapter does not deal with other issues that
might be raised about the settlement process. For example, once agreements have been reached and approved, the NEB cannot easily track
whether the agreement is fully implemented, in part because it no
longer has a post-agreement informational trail. In addition, the views
of shippers are hard to discern. Groups of shippers may sign agreements and thus indicate support, but smaller shippers may feel that the
bilateral settlement process gives them no more de facto choice or
influence than the earlier system of regulation. Nonetheless, the NEB's
performance reports indicate that even where such dissatisfaction may
exist (such as in the 2000–1 renegotiation of the TransCanada Pipelines
[TCPL] settlement), 'this dissatisfaction did not result in a complaint to
the Board' (NEB 2001: 19).

While all of the above regulatory re-invention was occurring, the
NEB was still dealing with a pipeline sector that was largely a monopoly. However, in the latter half of the 1990s, proposals began emerging which would convert parts of the energy pipeline market into more

genuinely competitive markets. These would establish competitors for existing pipelines. Thus the NEB has approved Express Pipeline, an oil export pipeline, whose shareholders 'will bear the risk of under-utilization' (NEB 1996a: 2). As more new pipelines are built, the more one will see in the energy sector incumbents resisting new entrants, in much the same way that Bell Canada was able to do in the telecom sector, albeit only for a few years.

Thus the continuing restructuring of the pipeline industry is also influencing the NEB's traditional paradigm of 'cost of service' monopoly pipeline regulation. The commencement of operations in 2000 of the Alliance and the Vector pipelines 'is providing natural gas producers and buyers with an alternative transport route to the TransCanada Pipelines Limited system, which previously was the only means of moving gas from western Canada to eastern Canadian markets' (NEB 2001: 6).

While the focus in this section is on the settlement process in pipeline regulation, brief mention must also be made of the processes for re-viewing and approving energy exports, especially natural gas. The NEB Act requires the NEB to ensure that long-term exports of natural gas are surplus to reasonably foreseeable Canadian requirements. Oil exports are not a problem in this respect because crude oil is only bought and sold on a short-term basis. As mentioned earlier, the politi-cal concern about security of supply was so sensitive that prior to 1987 this aspect of the NEB's mandate was backed by the legal requirement to ensure that there were proven reserves for twenty-five years. There were several reasons for the elimination of this provision, but among them was the view in Western Canada that this was a subsidy cost paid by Western producers to support Eastern consumers and industrial users of gas.

With the Mulroney government's agreement, the NEB in 1987 moved to a market-test and review process to ensure long-term supply (called the 'Market-Based Procedure'). It is important to stress that this export approval function is still anchored by the NEB's own estimating and monitoring of Canada's energy reserves. But the export licence process is now a far simpler two-step process involving assessment (in effect, the monitoring function noted above) and a challenge process. When proposed export contracts are filed publicly with the NEB, any Cana-dian industrial user can use the challenge process if it believes, and can show in a public hearing, that it cannot obtain the gas from a supplier on similar terms and conditions. This mechanism has not been used, and thus the NEB is satisfied after fifteen years of gas deregulation that the market-based approach is working and is more efficient than the pre-1987 export regime (NEB 1997a; 2001: 17). The Board's report in 2000 on natural gas market dynamics and pricing concluded 'that the natural gas market had been functioning so that Canadian require-ments for natural gas were being satisfied at fair market prices' (NEB 2001: 20), with fairness being judged by equivalence or convergence in domestic versus export prices.

The relatively routine and quiet operation of this monitoring func-tion may change under the impetus of the Bush administration's desire to be able to rely even more than at present on Canadian natural gas supplies and eventually on sources such as the vast Alberta tar sands. This is because Canadians may become more politically aware again of longer-term supply issues. Thus far, private producers and users in Canada are satisfied with the market-based monitoring process, but some provincial governments in Atlantic Canada, such as that of New Brunswick, have been raising concerns about whether they will get economic access to Sable Island gas. Moreover, the NEB's own forecast-ing review studies are now having to take into account more complex multiple scenarios, including a maximum Bush NEP scenario in which U.S. demand is forecast at very high projected levels. It would not be surprising if these scenarios, when published, required quite elaborate hearings by the NEB.

The NEB As Joint Environmental and Safety Regulator

As highlighted above, one of the key transformations of the NEB is its assumption of a greater, and more integrated, role in environmental regulation. The NEB had been considering environmental matters re-lated to its activities prior to 1995, but in that year the Canadian Envi-ronmental Assessment Act (CEAA) took effect and provided a further legal imperative for the NEB's role (Sato 1997). The environmental assessment process of the federal government as a whole had itself been transformed, largely by court rulings which had determined that the federal 'guidelines' previously in existence were in fact law-like in their nature (Doern and Conway 1994). As a result of the CEAA, the NEB (as a 'responsible authority' under the CEAA) has to work closely with Environment Canada's Canadian Environmental Assessment Agency to ensure that their joint required processes are efficient and avoid duplication, but at the same time are effective regarding environ-mental assessment.

The NEB's process operates in three phases: first, an evaluation of potential environmental effects of proposed projects; second, the monitoring and enforcement of terms and conditions attached to the project approval; and third, continuous longer-term monitoring of operations. The NEB's application process can involve different types and levels of review depending on the level of public interest and the size of the project. These include a public hearing, a written hearing, or an internal Board process with or without public involvement. A further dimension of the environmental assessment process is found in the provisions of the CEAA itself, which set out four types of assessment process: screening, comprehensive study, mediation, and panel review. Given this array of potential processes, there has been a considerable learning curve for the NEB, affected companies, and intervenors.

One of the generic institutional issues centres on the differences between quasi-judicial versus administrative approaches to regulatory decision-making (Ratushny 1987). The NEB is by statute anchored to a quasi-judicial role, whereas the CEAA processes and the approaches of other departments which might be involved in a joint process are more administrative. As we have already seen above in the discussion of the toll 'settlement process,' the NEB has evolved its own more flexible approaches, but it must always be conscious of the quasi-judicial aspects of its statute, including the fact that its decisions may be appealed to the courts.

Since 1995 the NEB has had several proposals which required a CEAA comprehensive study report. One was subsequently suspended, but three projects (the Express Pipeline project, the Sable Island project, and the Alliance Pipeline project) have proceeded in a variety of ways through to the review panel. While considerable cooperation has taken place between the NEB and Environment Canada, there are bound to be differences of view as to how to proceed in different case situations. For example, in the Express project, the NEB requested that, to avoid duplication, the CEAA provisions for 'substitution' be used. The minister of the environment 'decided that a joint panel would be more appropriate' (Sato 1997: 5) rather than a single NEB process.

Given that there are now several new pipelines being proposed, it is clear that the NEB will experience more environmental business. The Board members have typically been engineers and technically trained persons, but one of the newer appointees to the Board has more direct environmental experience as an academic and consultant. But all Board members are becoming more familiar with their environmental mandate, in part because of the simple length of hearings in the above cases. For example, the Express hearing involved 34 hearing days, including 11 on environmental aspects, and its panel (two Board members and two environmental scientists) made 39 recommendations (Sato 1997: 5).

Another key pressure on the NEB is whether it is a practitioner of *sustainable development* in its regulatory role. As previous chapters have shown, Natural Resources Canada (NRCan) has a statutory mandate (see also chapter 8) regarding sustainable development. The NEB reports to Parliament through the minister of natural resources but is not a part of NRCan as a department. The NEB thus stresses that it has not formally defined sustainable development in the context of its operations. But the NEB does argue that it 'promotes sustainable development, on the basis of the generally accepted principle that sustainable development means "meeting the needs of the present without compromising the ability of future generations to meet their own needs" and that this in turn requires integrating environmental, economic and social considerations' (NEB 2001: 24). The Board then goes on to cite some of its practices and statutory provisions, including its 'public interest' clauses, its duty to ensure that the pipeline will be required 'by the present and future public convenience and necessity.' It also cites its processes and criteria regarding the export of oil and gas, whereby its statute directs the Board to 'satisfy itself that the quantity of oil and gas to be exported does not exceed the surplus remaining after due allowance has been made for the reasonably foreseeable requirements in Canada' (NEB 2001: 25). It then stresses that properly functioning markets are the best assurance of the latter provisions being realized.

These claimed links with the practice of sustainable development are partially but not fully plausible. For example, they do not deal frontally with climate change and reduction of greenhouse gas emissions, reductions which many environmentalists would see as the acid test of the practice of sustainable development in the energy sector. And there is little doubt that the NEB's approach would be different and more difficult if it had an explicit statutory obligation to promote sustainable development. In fairness to the NEB, however, it is perfectly understandable why it prefers to leave this issue to the larger political negotiations going on regarding climate change and Kyoto (see chapter 8). But pressure to make the NEB a sustainable development regulator by statute is likely to increase.

Some of these issues of basic environmental policy and sustainable development, combined with Canadian and North American gas markets and renewed concerns about energy security, will undoubtedly arise in the possible applications for a new northern frontier pipeline for natural gas. The regulatory process will be much more complex than in the earlier Berger era of pipeline debates and processes. Several federal, territorial, and First Nations authorities will be involved. The NEB cannot take a position on any particular route for a pipeline, but it has responsibilities as a lead regulator to ensure that the multiple-board processes function efficiently and effectively. An initial manifestation of this need was shown when the several boards involved released in January 2002 their joint cooperation plan for public comment.

A further type of environmental mandate pressure has already begun to emerge with the increased number of applications to build more international (and interprovincial) electrical power lines. The general impetus here is that the more lines that are built, the more environmental problems occur and have to be managed. In 2000 the Federal Court of Appeal reversed an NEB decision on a power line which the NEB had deemed to be environmentally satisfactory. The court argued that the NEB did not have proper environmental evidence for this view. There are also potential problems in the new competitive electricity supply markets. This is because new supply is generated from many sources, but new electricity marketers will not know where it originates, nor will they even care.

Also arising out of the California electricity crisis and out of the emergence of more international and interprovincial electricity trade are concerns about who regulates and operates the national or Canadian electricity grid. This question will undoubtedly involve debates about the role of the NEB and provincial regulators, as well as the FERC. Grid integrity is inevitably a joint economic, environmental, and security aspect of regulation, in which complex networks are at the core of the system.

A final aspect of the environmental mandate of the NEB deserves emphasis in terms of regulatory organizational culture. The restructuring of the NEB into its 'business-leader' and team model of organization has resulted in the dispersal of its environmental professionals throughout other team groups. Rather than being concentrated in one functional staff advisory group, they are now a part of all other business groups. But there is one 'professional leader–environment' official whose job is to maintain, enhance, and mentor environmental expertise across the Board's business-leader teams. We do not judge the efficacy of this approach here, but there is one note of symmetry about it that deserves some emphasis. In the larger debate on environmental and sustainable development regulation, the case has often been made that for environmental policy to succeed, all federal departments have to become their own regulators. In short, environmental issues have to be every department's business. In a broad sense, that is what the CEAA is all about with respect to its intended impact across the government. And the dispersal of the environmental professionals across the NEB business teams is the attempted institutionalization of the same concept within the NEB.

The focus above has been on environmental regulatory roles, but mention must also be made of the NEB's growing safety regulation mandate. The NEB regulates approximately 40,000 kilometres of pipelines, many of which are aging. Issues regarding stress corrosion cracking are among the problems that have had to be examined in recent years, with further regulatory vigilance needed to ensure the 'integrity of existing pipeline infrastructure' (NEB 1996a: 4). As discussed above, the issue of pipeline safety now gets first priority in the NEB's set of four stated performance goals. In the wake of the September 11th terrorist attacks in the United States, the safety of pipelines takes on an even larger dimension and meaning, and may need further resource requirements. The earliest impacts of these new security concerns have centred around a series of government-wide meetings that the NEB has been involved in concerning critical infrastructure, and also numerous meetings with the U.S. and FERC regulators because of U.S. concern that Canadian pipelines may be targeted to disrupt U.S. supply. Another impact is that the NEB library has had key kinds of information about pipelines removed or made secret because of heightened security concerns.

Conclusions

Between 1959 and the mid-1970s, the National Energy Board was a classic sectoral public utility regulator known for its technical competence and relatively non-political nature. From the late 1970s to 1984, it became institutionally marginalized in political, policy, and regulatory terms, mainly by the ill-fated juggernaut known as the Liberal National Energy Policy. From 1985 to 2000, the NEB has in one sense gone 'back to the future' by reasserting its dominance as the main core of energy regulatory expertise in the federal government.

In the main period examined since 1985, this chapter has shown the ways in which the NEB has indeed 'moved out' and 'moved on.' The move to Calgary had important effects in terms of organizational culture and milieu, but of course it alone does not explain the reinvented nature of the NEB as a regulatory institution. The pressures to deregulate after 1984 came from a supportive Mulroney government. The NEB has also moved to incentive-based regulation because of real concerns by the industry about competitive costs, but also because of the demonstration effect of reinvented regulation among some U.S. energy regulators and receptivity within the NEB to the core ideas of both reinvented government and incentive-based regulation. The recourse to incentive-based approaches and negotiated settlements undoubtedly has merit in that some efficiency gains have been made.

As for its acquisition of greater environmental and safety roles, the causes are also mixed. In part, they are the result of environmental politics in the early 1990s, which, unexpectedly, sent the issue of environmental assessment into the courts, then into new federal law, and finally onto the lap of the NEB. In part, expanded safety roles are a product of the aging of the pipeline system. Regardless of the exact mix of causes, the NEB is now both an economic and environmental regulator in a way that it was not during its earlier history.

Indeed, as we have seen, statements by the NEB in early 2000s tend to put the safety and environmental aspects of its mandate first. At the same time, the Board is conscious of pressure for it to increasingly become a sustainable development regulator. It has no statutory obligation to foster sustainable development, nor does it appear to seek such a role. In the new northern pipeline debate, and in the context of competing proposals, it has its work cut out for it just to manage the complex multi-regulator processes, all of which are functioning in a much more complex energy and environmental (and competitive) regulatory governance system.

The NEB's role in the early 2000s is also likely to change as potential concerns about the long-term supply of oil and gas are raised anew in the wake of the Bush administration's desire to see Canada's supplies as a crucial part of U.S. energy security. Unlike the last debate on Canadian energy security during the 1960s, 1970s, and early 1980s, the next one will have added to it the very big factor of the climate change debate and other related problems of how to balance or reconfigure complex regimes of energy regulatory governance.

5 The Ontario Energy Board

Compared to the National Energy Board (NEB), the Ontario Energy Board (OEB) experienced much less even change across the entire period since 1985. The OEB's transformation is centrally linked to the radical changes in the electricity industry during the late 1990s that produced a more competitive electricity structure, a transformation that had several knock-on effects on energy regulation more broadly. The OEB is now a regulatory agency with an expanded role in electricity as well as gas regulation, and with a mandate informed by performance and incentive-based regulation rather than the earlier utility-cum-adjudicative system. The larger regulatory system in Ontario consists of such other players as the Ontario Cabinet, the new Ontario Hydro successor companies, the Independent Market Operator (IMO), and the federal Competition Bureau. Because of this concentrated and very recent kind of change, this chapter is structured differently than our account of the NEB, though our analytical concerns are broadly similar, namely to focus on how a sectoral regulatory body has been changed and to examine the horizontal regulatory regime pressures.

Each regulatory board is different and functions within its own immediate constellation of political and economic change. For example, environmental and safety issues for electricity in Ontario are multi-faceted, but they fundamentally include nuclear power, Ontario's main source of electricity production. Nuclear safety issues are a federal responsibility, but the new Ontario regime, including the OEB and IMO, will certainly affect the economics and transparency of the nuclear aspects of power generation. New sources of electricity generation and supply offered by the private sector or Ontario Power Generation Inc. will be assessed on technical and economic grounds by the IMO and the OEB (see more below), but nuclear safety is a crucial part of the inter-regime pressures and choices.

We begin the chapter by giving a brief profile of the larger competitive energy and electricity regime put in place by the Harris Conservative government. The second section looks more closely at key institutional features of the new OEB mandate and how it differs from the old pre-1998 OEB (the OEB that had existed since 1960). The third section examines the OEB as an incentive regulator, and the fourth assesses the changing links with horizontal energy regulators, mainly in the environment/safety realms. Conclusions follow.

The OEB and the New Competitive Ontario Regime

Our historical account in chapter 1 and chapter 2's analysis of U.S. influences have already examined the larger impetus for Ontario's quite radical changes in electricity markets. But the OEB needs to be understood first in terms of the new set of institutions established by the Harris government. During the 1997–9 period, the Harris Conservatives replaced the Power Corporation Act (repealed as of 1 April 1999) with new legislation, the Energy Competition Act, which reorganized Ontario Hydro into three separate corporations: the Independent Market Operator (IMO) and two commercial companies, Ontario Power Generation Inc. (OPG) and Ontario Hydro Services (later Hydro One). The former takes ownership of Ontario Hydro's generation assets and has a mandate to maximize their value for the taxpayers. The latter is a holding company with a number of businesses, including transmission, distribution, retail, and operating contracts. It is required to keep its monopoly and competitive businesses separate from each other through an appropriate structure of subsidiary companies. Both companies have been 'corporatized' and are required to operate on a business-like basis; they do not have any oversight role in relation to the approximately 250 local distribution utilities.[1] The oversight responsibility has been as-

---

1 A key decision made by the Harris government was not to totally privatize Ontario Hydro into several companies. This was also the recommendation of the Macdonald Committee. This chapter does not explore this part of regime choice. There are many potential reasons for, or causes of, this crucial choice. Among them are the following: (a) Ontario Hydro exhibited its great political power; (b) the Harris government wanted a better market value for Ontario Hydro assets, lest it be charged with a cheap sell-off, and this required restructuring first (see Minister Wilson's statement to this effect, Ontario Legislature, *Hansard*, 17 June 1998, p. 1554); (c) privatization was simply

signed to the Ontario Energy Board, which reports to the Legislature through the minister (Ontario Ministry of Energy, Science and Technology 1997, 2001). Late in 2001, the Harris government announced that it would privatize Hydro One, a privatization that would be the largest in Canadian history (Vieira 2001). The committment to privatize Hydro One was overturned in 2003, when Premier Ernie Eves succeeded Premier Harris and ran into serious political difficulties over both Hydro One and soaring electricity prices.

The Ontario reforms also created the Ontario Hydro Financial Corporation (which retains the Ontario Hydro name). It is to be the entity which deals with the thorny problem of Ontario Hydro's $30 billion debt and, in particular, its 'stranded debt,' estimated to be between $15 and $20 billion.[2] Stranded debt is debt that could not be serviced as a commercial entity in a competitive market. Hiving this debt off and finding ways to pay it were crucial steps in making the new successor hydro companies viable. Since major parts of this stranded debt were seen to have originated in the nuclear plants, it is a key part of the political-economic equation for the nuclear industry as well (Ontario 1996).

The Independent Market Operator (IMO) has been established as a key part of the sectoral regulatory regime. It is a not-for-profit entity which is responsible for managing the bulk power system and maintaining its secure and reliable operation. Specifically its job is to reconcile physical transactions, dispatch resources in real time to match supply and demand within security constraints, and, as required, declare system emergency conditions and direct all system resources in response to emergencies. It is responsible for collecting offers from competing suppliers and bids from purchasers, and manages market

---

unpopular among the electorate and among Tory MPPs. But the Harris government left the door open for privatization of the non-nuclear, non-Niagara parts, and the Market Mitigation agreement made some form of decontrol mandatory. One of the initial rationales for keeping public ownership, at least temporarily, was that the Ontario government needed the large-scale company to play in the North American market. But this argument does not seem to have withstood the desire to privatize some facilities to gain the benefits of competition. For various interpretations or for further background about the privatization option in Canada and elsewhere, see Wells 1999; Ontario 1996; and Hunt and Shuttleworth 1996.

2 One account says that Genco owes $3.4 billion of the debt, Servco owes $4.8 billion, and the province will service $8.9 billion, leaving $20.9 billion (of the total $38.1 billion debt) to be serviced as stranded debt (Wells 1999).

trading in electricity and related products. It also settles associated accounts, monitors compliance with market rules, and reconciles the performance of market participants. In addition, it forecasts and advises on adequacy and helps to ensure that competition develops quickly and without abuse of market power.

The Harris government regarded the IMO and a strong Ontario Energy Board as 'the most important defences against potential conflicts of interest' (Ministry of Energy, Science and Technology 1997: 18). But the OEB also licenses the IMO and has other joint duties with the IMO, largely because the latter can itself be a source of anti-competitive behaviour unless accountable and transparent systems are fully in place and enforced.

A strengthened OEB is also mandated to regulate investments in the expansion of the transmission grid. In this regard, it is to work with the IMO to ensure that adequate transmission capacity is developed both to maintain reliability and to promote the growth of competition. The OEB now regulates the province's local wires business and all local distribution companies, and is responsible for ensuring that the distribution companies fulfil their obligation to connect and serve their customers. The Board has a key role in ensuring that market participants do not abuse market power or engage in anti-competitive pricing or other monopolistic practices, a duty it shares with the federal Competition Bureau under the Competition Act (Competition Bureau 1996, 1998). A key element here are the required provisions for transfer of effective control of electricity output from OPG to other suppliers of power over a phased ten-year schedule.[3] The OEB has responsibility for ensuring the licensing of all agents, brokers, marketers, and generators participating in the market. Both the IMO and the OEB have duties to advise the Ontario government on how well the market is performing, and to alert the government to any problems arising from the generation company's dominant market position.

The OEB is thus now an expanded independent, quasi-judicial tribunal which reports to the Legislature through the minister of energy, science and technology. The Board operates independently from the ministry and all other government departments. All costs incurred by the Board in its operations are recovered through a cost assessment from the business organizations subject to licensing or regulation by the

---

3 See Ontario, *Transitional Generation License Issued to Ontario Power Generation Inc,* 1 May 1999, pp. 17–20.

Board. The Board now regulates all market participants in both the natural gas and electricity industries in the province, and also provides advice on energy matters referred to it by the minister of energy, science and technology and the minister of natural resources.

The 1998 Mandate Change and the New OEB

The Ontario Energy Board has been markedly changed by the forces and factors outlined above and by the specific provisions and mandate set out in the 1998 *Ontario Energy Board Act*. Table 2 provides a basic portrait of the nature of the changes between the pre-1998 or old OEB (whose history dates to 1960 legislation, and to earlier laws as well) and the new OEB. Table 2 also highlights the changes in mission and objectives, responsibilities, legislation, and membership. Each of these is profiled and examined further below.

The *mission and objectives* are in one sense unchanged in that the OEB's broad public interest role is still paramount. But in most other respects, the OEB's objectives are far broader, as well as more multi-purpose and explicit. It has a mandate to facilitate competition and to provide non-discriminatory access. Its consumer protection role is now explicit and extended to include *quality* of service. As well, the OEB must simultaneously facilitate the availability of financing for the gas and electrical industries, promote economic efficiency, and facilitate energy efficiency.

A brief look at the OEB's explicit *responsibilities* shows a parallel listing of tasks that are common to both the old regime and the new. Thus rate approvals, the approval of ownership changes, pipeline and construction approvals, etc., are similar. So also are responsibilities to conduct references when requested by the Cabinet and generic hearings. These are a form of policy advisory and consultation function. Undoubtedly, the key point of departure between the two periods is the addition of all of the above for electricity, including its extended range of market participants. From previously 'reviewing' Hydro bulk power rates, the OEB will now approve the transmission and distribution monopoly business of the Ontario Hydro successor companies. In short, the OEB has become a truer 'energy' regulator.

In Table 2 the list of statutes that the OEB is governed by, and has responsibilities under, again shows a similar pattern between the old and new regimes. The key statute added is the Energy Competition Act, within which is the Electricity Act and the Ontario Energy Board Act.

Table 2
The Ontario Energy Board before and after 1998 reforms

Institutional element	Pre-1998	Post-1998 reforms
Mission and objectives	The Board's primary objective is to ensure that the public interest is served and protected. – to balance the competing interests of consumers, investors, and the environment – to ensure that rates for gas are just and reasonable for both cus-tomer and share-holder	The Board's primary objective is to ensure that the public interest is upheld. – to facilitate competition in the generation and sale of electricity – to provide generators, retailers, and consumers with non-discriminatory access to transmission and distribution systems in Ontario – to protect the interests of consumers with respect to prices and the reliability and quality of electricity service – to promote economic efficiency – to facilitate the maintenance of a financially viable electricity industry – to facilitate energy efficiency – plus similar objectives for gas
Responsibilities	*Natural gas:* – Approving: rates ownership changes transmission pipeline construction franchise agreements certificates of public convenience and necessity storage facilities *Electricity:* – Reviewing Ontario Hydro bulk rates *Advisory:* – References and generic hearings – Advice to government on energy matters	*Natural gas:* – Approving: rates ownership changes transmission pipeline construction franchise agreements certificates of public convenience and necessity storage facilities – Licensing gas marketers *Electricity:* – Issuing retail electricity licences – Issuing electricity distribution licences and rate orders – Approving Ontario Hydro Services Company Inc. (OHSC) rates

Table 2
The Ontario Energy Board before and after 1998 reforms

Institutional element	Pre-1998	Post-1998 reforms
		– Issuing licences to IMO and transmission/generation wholesalers
		– Licensing all distributors and market participants
		– Market surveillance role
		– Approving IMO budgets and fees
		– consumer service and quality
		– implementor of government policy
		Advisory:
		– References and generic hearings
Legislation	– Ontario Energy Board Act	– Energy Competition Act
	– Municipal Franchises Act	– Electricity Act
	– Petroleum Resources Act	– Ontario Energy Board Act
	– Public Utilities Act	– Municipal Franchises Act
	– Assessment Act	– Oil, Salt and Gas Resources Act
	– Toronto District Heating Corporation Act	– Public Utilities Act
		– Assessment Act
		– Toronto District Heating Corporation Act
Membership	– Up to 8 full-time members including Chair and Vice-Chair, plus several part-time members	– Same

The *membership* of the OEB stays the same. There is no statutory limit on the number of members, but policy has put the limit at about eight members appointed by the lieutenant governor in council (Cabinet). Though board members are appointed by Cabinet there has been a considerable effort made over the years to ensure their political independence. OEB chairs and members have generally been drawn from the legal and financial professions, or the civil service, and they have never been particularly well known to the public at large. Of perhaps crucial interest in the latest regime change of 1998–9 is the fact that the

Chair of the OEB is Floyd Laughren, the former NDP government's finance minister. Not only was the political judgment made by the Harris government that a political heavyweight was needed, but also that there was value during the transition period in such a person coming from an opposition party.

The OEB As Incentive Regulator

Like the NEB, the OEB has moved from a world of basic utility (rate of return) and adjudicatory regulation to incentive- and performance-based regulation. Table 3 shows some of the features inherent in this transformation, linked inextricably to the overall approach, the changed structure of interests and financing, as well as to other interacting characteristics of the mandate changes discussed above. Interestingly, the core of these changes towards incentive regulation is not found directly in the statutes, but rather comes largely from the broader policy of the Ontario government (and indeed, as we have seen, from the reinvented regulatory governance policies of most Canadian and Western governments in energy and other regulatory sectors). Some of the recent changes began to evolve within the OEB in the early 1990s, but they had been constrained because they were being developed within the contours of an earlier statute that was very traditional in its legal provisions.

The new regulatory approach contains a broader regulatory tool kit that allows the OEB a more varied multi-functional role. These tools include greater discretion procedurally; the express power to forbear from regulating if the OEB judges that competition is effectively in place; and the far greater use of regulatory instruments such as codes and standards developed with, and effectively enforced by, industry-consumer processes and associations. None of this means that the former regime's adjudicative rate-setting functions do not remain crucial, but there is little doubt that the OEB must transform itself to be able to give concrete meaning to these changes in regulatory philosophy.

Such changes are also mirrored in the now inherently more complex structure of key interest groups and interests with which the OEB must interact. Despite the avowed goal in the statute and in policy of treating gas and electricity sectors equally (the level playing field concept), it is already evident how uneven the interest group politics will likely be, especially in the immediate transition period of the early 2000s. The old OEB was essentially a gas regulator dealing with three (now two) gas

Table 3
The Ontario Energy Board as incentive regulator

Institutional element	Pre-1998	Post-1998 reforms
Regulatory approach	– A classic adjudicative tribunal, functioning mainly through public hearings; conducted in a court-like manner – A gradual greater use of some more informal approaches in the 1990s, but without statutory change – Movement to competition in gas in mid-1980s – Fairly limited and very prescriptive regulatory tool kit	– Given an incentive-based and performance-based regulatory philosophy – Still important adjudicative role and procedures – Licensing role on electricity – More procedural discretion – Power to forbear from regulating where appropriate – Greater ability to use industry-based codes and other more flexible instruments – A wider-ranging regulatory tool kit – Some assymetries of powers between electricity and gas
Key interests and interest groups	– Essentially focused on 3 (now 2) large monopoly gas companies – Some gas-marketing and retail interests – Gas consumer interests in intervenor process (funded through cost award) – Consumer and environmental interests – Ontario Hydro, but only periodic relations when Hydro bulk power rates 'reviewed' (not regulated)	– Much more complex and diverse array of interests; with electricity interests being far more diffuse and complex than gas interests – Ontario Power Generation – Ontario Hydro Services – IMO – Over 250 municipal hydros – Association of Major Power Consumers in Ontario – Consumer and environmental interests – Independent Power Producers Society of Ontario – New smaller retail marketing and wholesale interests – Plus existing gas interests
Structure, finances, and personnel	– Small staff of 38 with legal and gas industry expertise – Financed initially through taxation, but evolved to 100% cost recovery financing	– Appeals require structural separation of staff advising the Board versus the director of licensing – Wider range of expertise needed – Staff has doubled (more than 90)

utility companies. There was therefore a fairly simple, even cosy, regulatory interest group realm. The addition of complex electricity interests means a massively different regulatory-political world, which now embraces not only the two still huge Ontario Hydro successor companies, the IMO, and the new market participants, but also the 250 municipal hydros, the latter enmeshed in Ontario local government, indeed in the historical politics that early in the century led to the formation of Ontario Hydro as a then populist, provincially run institution (Armstrong and Nelles 1986; Freeman 1995).

The marriage of issues inherent in the incentive-based system to some features of adjudication is manifest in other changes in the internal structure and personnel of the OEB. One of the key internal structural changes is that the new OEB has a statutory director of licensing. The board will thus have to deal with appeals by firms to his or her decisions, and this necessitates changes in the internal independence of this role and in how other staff of the OEB advise (a) the board and (b) the director of licensing. Separate realms must be carved out to ensure both the reality and appearance of regulatory fairness. Another change is that the OEB staff (about 38 professional and support staff in 1997) has more than doubled (to 90) and will increase further over the next few years, but then be reduced somewhat as the system matures and reaches a new equilibrium state.

The financing of the OEB remains the same. Cost assessed user charges or fees cover all of the Board's operations. The revenues actually go to the Ontario treasury rather than to the OEB itself, with the Board still having to justify its budget to the treasury on efficiency and other grounds. But the fee amounts are sufficient to pay for the costs of the OEB, and thus there is no taxpayer burden.

In an overall sense, it is evident that the OEB now has a much broader mix of governing functions and tools available to it. As we have seen, it is now much more explicitly an adjudicative, rule-making, policy advising, educative, and monitoring body across the entire energy sector in Ontario (except for nuclear safety). In this sense, the Board is now more *political*. By political we do not refer to partisan politics; rather, we mean 'small-*p*' politics, in the sense of greater discretionary power. A broader tool kit, and the ability to choose among tools and to mix and match them, imply greater political roles. This does not say anything about how well this enhanced political power will be exercised. But the days of being only a passive adjudicative Board are gone. The OEB must still be independent, but it will be more political in the above sense of the word. This also means that its internal culture and standard operating rhythms of behaviour will change, and indeed are changing.

The central regulatory mode for the new Ontario competitive electricity system is still regulation by board or commission. It is likely, however, that relations among OEB members will change and indeed that new kinds of board members may have to be appointed. Board members will still have duties in traditional adjudicative hearings, where two members can often fulfil board tasks. But the board members are likely to have to think and behave more often as a full collective board. This is because its de facto policy-making or policy-advising roles (reflected in generic hearings, the greater use of codes, general advice, and transition steps) are now expanded. Fiscal restraint is such that the Ontario government is unlikely to increase the size of the board, and thus the board will have to ratchet up its collective processes in some important ways. If changes have to occur in relations among board members, it means that relations between OEB staff and board members also have to change, and indeed *among* OEB staff.

In another sense, it is important to stress that in fact the regulatory *mode* is now not simply coincident with the single Board. One almost immediately has to think about the larger *sectoral energy regulatory regime* that has been put in place. The IMO is also a regulator-operator in that technical operation (and therefore the sub-rules) are within its domain. It, too, is a collectively governed, non-profit body, but, as we have suggested, it can be the source of predatory market power unless it too is regulated (see chapter 7 on competition regulation). For the OEB, the IMO is both regulatee and senior partner in regulatory governance.

As mentioned above, the appointment by the Harris government in March 1998 of Floyd Laughren as head of the OEB signalled that a heavier weight of political leadership is inherent and needed in the new OEB. All regulatory heads (especially those who head a collective board) are hedged in by competing interests, time and budgetary constraints, and legal provisions. Above all, a regulatory head knows that, when push comes to shove, the industry has assymetrical power based on knowledge. The industry being regulated simply knows more about its business than the regulator ever can.

For the leadership of the new OEB, one fact is clearly different. The old OEB's mandate was much more passive and dealt mainly with gas. The head of the OEB did not have to take too many initiatives of his or her own. The new OEB has more room for risk-taking and leadership.

This flows from the point made earlier about its greater 'small-*p*' political nature. Thus, there is more room for choice as to just how aggressive or active the Chair will be on competition and access issues (particularly the potential predatory practices of the Ontario Hydro successor companies). There is also considerably greater room for an educative or persuasive leadership role, such as on how the 250 municipal hydros might evolve. To be sure there are always limits on these roles, given that the Board must still adjudicate, but there is without doubt much more room for an activist role by the head of the OEB as compared to the older system.[4]

We have already noted that the new OEB will need a planned doubling of its staff. But there are also the potentially even more crucial issues of qualitative capacity to deal with. This is tied as well to changing the culture of the Board. The OEB is likely to need a greater economic and technical, as opposed to legal and financial, competence to correspond to its new combined roles of both traditional adjudicator and competition promoter, consumer advocate and energy efficiency promoter. It will need more expertise in economic sub-fields such as competition policy (analysing anti-competitive predatory activity) and in new forms of information and compliance-performance monitoring and auditing.

It is a very small step to go from a discussion of the OEB's quantitative and qualitative staff and resources to that of the new approaches to compliance inherent in the new regime. This is because approaches to compliance intrinsically raise the question of who actually *works for* the Board in direct ways and who *works with* the Board and carries out activities in the name of the Board or facilitates Board activity through their own self-interested behaviour.

Incentive- and performance-based regulation, including financial and qualitative service performance, means that private players take on ever greater public roles. Industrial interest groups and associations become, in effect, mini-surrogate governments which not only complement the state's activities but become increasingly the de facto front-line regulatory vehicle for compliance. In the transition period to

---

4 Part of the new politics of regulatory leadership can be found in the range of interests Floyd Laughren has touched upon since becoming the Chair of the OEB. His speeches have been broad and conciliatory as the transition period progresses, and reflect a crafted kind of leadership by someone who knows Ontario's politics rather than just its energy interests. See Laughren 1998a, 1998b, 1999.

electricity competition, this has been most clearly reflected in the development of a series of codes. There are many good reasons for pushing these tasks further into the industrial and public interest group domain. It can enhance effectiveness and a sense of responsibility, and it can avoid slower more ponderous direct regulation and micro-management by the regulatory Board itself. But its weak point, its capacity gap, if you like, is whether it can be carried out within a credible system of accountability and transparency to the public and to democratically elected representatives.

These are relatively early days for the new OEB and its compliance partners in this respect, but such aspects of its new evolving role will be critical. Ultimately, its credibility will turn partly on what kind of monitoring information is produced and developed. Performance 'league tables' or report cards will have to be produced on individual utility companies regarding both licence compliance and quality of service. Regardless of how dressed up the new competitive regime is, the Board's jurisdiction and the functioning of the larger regime are still centred on a utility service that is an *essential public service* to citizens and voters, not just to disembodied 'customers.'

Some of these latent political and economic concerns surfaced during 2000–2 when the Ontario government delayed its opening of the new competitive energy market for two years until May 2002 (Laughren 2001; Ontario Ministry of Energy, Science and Technology 2001). Part of the delay was the result of natural teething problems, but a larger political imperative came from the well-publicized traumas of the California electricity crisis of 2000–1 with its spiralling prices and blackouts, and also some of the concerns about price spikes and volatility in Alberta's system of competitive electricity markets (Jaccard 2002). We discuss the California crisis in chapter 7 and Alberta's difficulties in chapter 6, but there can be little doubt overall that these developments caused Ontario and its new energy regulators to be more cautious and to be more concerned about the exact shape of the Ontario market design, its transition measures regarding prices to various consumers, and the nature of the Ontario electricity grid and its links to the larger North American electricity grid.

A considerable amount of political nervousness in Ontario was also evident in 2002 regarding the privatization of Hydro One. The Harris government had announced that it would be privatized, but when Premier Mike Harris was replaced by Ernie Eves as the Conservative premier of Ontario in the spring of 2002, suggestions were made by the premier that privatization was not the only way to restructure this other key part of the former Ontario Hydro. Long-term leases were also a possibility (Moore 2002). But eventually, early in 2003, Premier Eves announced that Hydro One would stay under public ownership. With hindsight, it is quite remarkable how the overall electricity restructuring in Ontario was initially achieved without major political controversy. But the Hydro One aspects were always bound to elicit a potentially different response. The first reason was the media coverage of the California issue, which simply raised some doubts about relying on markets to an excessive degree. The second reason is that Hydro One had close links with the more local elements of the industry network, which have strong populist roots going back to the formation of Ontario Hydro. The third reason is that the opposition parties in Ontario saw this as a good issue to take up against an Eves Conservative government that was politically vulnerable.

Some of the growing pains, and possibly the permanent pains, of restructured electricity markets were experienced in the fall of 2002. Electricity bills for Ontario customers increased markedly, in part because of an unusually hot summer, but also because electricity supply was inadequate. Supply did not meet demand because nuclear plants had not been restored to use, and also because the Eves government's handling of Hydro One had prompted investors in power supply to doubt the Ontario Tories' commitment to market-based pricing. Ontario ministers were openly talking about the need for rebates for consumers, as had occurred in Alberta. In short, they favoured markets when prices were going down or were stable, but not when prices were too high, too fast. The Eves government also began to publicly blame the Ontario Energy Board for not watching the new market carefully and ordered a review of the OEB's mandate and resources. But the opposition parties blamed the Eves regime for not funding the OEB properly to do its now much more difficult and comprehensive job (Mackie 2002).

The OEB and Horizontal Environmental Regulation

Environmental regulation involves not only the new duties of the OEB but also Ontario, and potentially federal, environmental bodies that share part of the task or whose hearings, rules, and appeal processes have to be coordinated or taken into account. These duties are inter-regime in nature in that key economy-wide or horizontal rules regarding the environment (or indeed 'sustainable development') increasingly intersect with more particular industrial sectors such as gas and electricity. These interactions link to concerns with how environmental regulation both within Ontario and federally affects the degree to which all competing energy sources (oil, gas, hydro electricity, nuclear) are forced to 'internalize' their environmental costs. We look at this in an overall way first, and then with respect to nuclear reactor safety and long-term waste management, where the lead regulator is the federal Canadian Nuclear Regulatory Safety Commission. Nuclear safety is a crucial feature for Ontario because, as we have seen, the largest part of its electricity generation is provided by CANDU reactors, though now nuclear energy is challenged by the competitive presence of other newer technologies for cheaper gas-fired electricity generation.

The degree of required internalization of environmental costs is supposed to produce the proverbial 'level playing fields' of real fully costed energy prices and markets. But the political reality is that hydrocarbon energy source and user industries have far more political clout in Ontario and Canada generally than nuclear interests have. The nuclear industry is simply weak by comparison, and will probably become weaker if Ontario adopts, as it is likely to do, an inherently more neutral position concerning energy sources than was the case in the 1960s, 1970s, and 1980s, when nuclear was its preferred source. Energy playing fields may well eventually become level (to the degree to which they internalize environmental costs), but in the meantime they have a decided political tilt to them that does not favour nuclear.

The breadth of horizontal regulatory politics and trade-offs is such that they embrace the Kyoto negotiations. For example, late in 1999 Canada made a proposal that would have rewarded countries that export nuclear reactors with emissions credits against their greenhouse gas emissions (because nuclear plants emit no greenhouse gases). This was strongly opposed by the German government. The German government included Green Party coalition members, and its opposition was premised on its view that such projects were incompatible with sustainable development and with its view of the Kyoto process. The German government also announced in 2000 that it was phasing out its nuclear reactors over a twenty-year period. The point of this example is to stress that the macro regulatory politics of these trade-offs are complex, and involve mixtures of both principled and tactical bargaining, in this case on the part of both the German and Canadian governments. They and dozens of other countries will find it difficult, not surprisingly, to balance the risk of catastrophic accidents (the main political Achilles heel of nuclear power) against the risks of slow change and deterioration in the planet's climate caused by the burning of fossil fuels (the political Achilles heel of nuclear energy's main competitor energy source). Other aspects of Kyoto are examined in chapter 8.

But within the Ontario government, the OEB is influenced by the pressures emerging through its links to the provincial environment ministry. Environmental regulations have a significant effect on the cost of competing power, principally power derived from fossil fuels. Dewees points out that 'since 1994 Ontario Hydro has been limited to the emission of 175,000 tonnes of sulphur dioxide per year and the sum of sulphur dioxide and nitrogen oxide emissions have been limited to 215,000 tonnes per year' (Dewees 2001: 159). It had also agreed voluntarily with the government to limit nitrogen oxide emissions to 38,000 tonnes per year by the year 2000 and to stabilize its emissions of carbon dioxide at 1990 levels by the year 2000; and to reduce them by 10 per cent by the year 2010. These agreements apply only to Ontario Hydro and not to any other generator in the province. Accordingly, in the discussions leading to the new restructured electricity system in Ontario, the Ontario government was urged by the system designers to ensure that air emissions were regulated at least as strictly for the restructured market as they have been for Ontario Hydro, but to date this has not materialized. As Dewees points out, 'ideally, one would like to know the change in the marginal cost of generation from each existing OPG thermal plant that would result from varying levels of control of each pollutant, as well as the anticipated utilization of those plants, as well as the same information for new generation units that might be constructed in the foreseeable future' (Dewees 2001: 160.). However, there were larger forces at play in the Ontario environmental regulatory equation. Under the Harris Conservative government in the late 1990s, Ontario's Environment Ministry suffered severe resource cuts and a simple lack of zeal for enforcement (Krajnc 2000). Ontario's neo-Conservative agenda was focused on other priorities, such as tax cuts. The Walkerton Inquiry further brought out the realities of this environmental regulatory deficit.

Another key regulatory and policy uncertainty here is the cost of controlling carbon dioxide emissions, which of course is tied to the extent of the reductions. As mentioned in chapter 2, Canada's Kyoto commitment is to reduce its greenhouse gas emissions to 6 per cent below 1990 levels during 2008–12, which will require reductions of at least 26 per cent below the business-as-usual scenario for 2008–12. If such large costs are to be imposed on the electricity sector, then in theory they would also apply to other fuel sources, and, moreover, equally tough limits should be placed on all other sectors generating greenhouse gases, including transportation, industry, and domestic fossil fuel consumption. But Ontario's inter-regime energy regulatory politics, not to mention national energy politics, is unlikely to produce such elegant solutions in the near future.

When we focus on nuclear safety per se, it is first important to note that the word *nuclear* is scarcely mentioned in the statutes or guidelines of the OEB. Nuclear power is, however, a part of the story of the expansion of Ontario Hydro and its debt burden. Nuclear power is also a part of an earlier story of efficient power generation before the recent decline of reactor performance. Perhaps the underlying rationale for the new energy regulatory regime, however, is its endorsement of new sources of power generation and competing technologies for such generation, especially through smaller scale generation facilities and add-ons.

Moreover, the fact that institutionally the OEB will become a more economics-oriented board means that the economics of all forms of generation, nuclear and otherwise, will receive more systematic public exposure and analysis by the OEB in combination with the IMO. It is in this overall and often indirect sense that nuclear power will be governed by a provincial socio-economic regulatory regime to complement its federal health and safety regulation by the Canadian Nuclear Safety Commission (Jackson and de la Mothe 2001).

The nuclear industry has accepted the responsibility of managing its wastes and isolating them from the biosphere throughout their life cycle, a very long-term commitment. It has also largely internalized its waste management costs. In short, the costs are borne by the consumers. Few other industries have taken on such long-term commitments, in addition to the difficult burden of trying to prove their safety over thousands of years. For many industries, large volumes of wastes have traditionally been discharged directly into the environment, where they were no longer seen as the responsibility of the producers. The health and environmental costs were, and in many cases still are, borne by society at large or by future generations, representing a significant subsidy to current consumers.

But the nuclear industry has not dealt yet with all of its long-term waste management issues, and thus the public is not convinced by expert reassurances, nor by scientific and technical arguments alone, that such safety can be guaranteed (Brown and Letourneau 2001). Public mistrust on this aspect of nuclear waste management goes beyond issues of expertise in that it is simply difficult, if not impossible, to clearly envisage institutions which are inter-generational, and indeed extend to sequences of decisions and processes of accountability which extend outwards to one hundred years or more. Moreover, solutions to waste management problems will probably require processes that involve the interested publics, not only as receivers of information, but as active participants in the key decisions about siting and establishing waste management facilities, and perhaps in the operational management process as well.

Conclusions

The major changes in the Ontario energy regulatory governance system constitute a 'power switch' in three different senses. As the analysis has shown, it has brought changes in the sources and costs of energy and electricity generation through competition. It reflects changes in political power among and within institutions and interests in Ontario and elsewhere. It also has brought changes in the capacity of the OEB and other players in the sectoral and horizontal energy regulatory regimes to actually regulate in the public interest.

This chapter has assessed the nature of the OEB as a transformed regulatory body set in a larger competitive energy and electricity market and regulatory regime. Through a basic framework of institutional elements, it has also assessed, and raised questions regarding, the OEB's *likely* regulatory capacity to fulfil its new tasks. Where appropriate, it has also drawn out some impacts of the new regulatory system for environmental regulation overall, and nuclear power safety per se. Four main concluding points deserve emphasis.

First, there is little doubt that Ontario's new competitive energy-electricity regulatory governance as a whole constitutes a major change, albeit still a half-way world between the old regime of Ontario Hydro dominance and the lack of independent regulation and the new world of a partially broken-up but not fully privatized Ontario Hydro regulated more transparently. If power switches and competition were analogous to traffic lights, the new regime could be cast as living in a yellow-light district of managed competition rather than a green-light district. The new regime is one intended to ensure *managed* competition in a networked *essential service* political-economic industry.

Second, this chapter in the context of analysis in earlier chapters, shows that the causes of regime change are genuinely multi-faceted and complex rather than simplistically ideological. The political-economic forces of change, built up gradually over two decades, have produced changes in many jurisdictions, such as the United Kingdom and United States, that are similar in many ways. The causal factors thus include overbuilding and overcapacity, leading to excessive and unsustainable debt and higher energy prices than necessary; bloated and unaccountable public enterprise and private hydros; significant technological change, the efficacy of which has increasingly been demonstrated, especially for alternative sources of electricity generation; political pressures for choice in public services; the availability of alternative institutional examples in other countries; and the need to keep Ontario energy prices competitive with U.S. prices to enable Ontario industry to compete in the U.S. market, a market on which Ontario has become ever more dependent in the free trade era.

Third, the new Ontario Energy Board is situated in the larger inter-regime regulatory world and can only be fully understood in the context of such complexity. The OEB is becoming a very different kind of regulator as it switches from the relatively quiet life of a gas utility, adjudicator-style regulator to a multi-functional performance-based regulator now extended into the far more complex world of Ontario electricity politics at the point of transition into a quasi-competitive world. The OEB's new mandate and range of instruments make it a more 'small-*p*' political regulator because its opportunities for exercising discretion are greatly enhanced. Its compliance roles are significantly more partnered with industrial, consumer, and environmental players and hence will raise new issues of accountability and shared governance.

In all of the above, environmental regulation and specific nuclear power issues are a part of the seamless background of change. The regulatory pressure is in the direction of ensuring that all sources of energy internalize their environmental costs, but the complex regulatory regime politics, within Ontario, nationally, and globally, does not even come close to guaranteeing such desired level playing fields. Regarding nuclear safety, the word *nuclear* scarcely appears in Ontario regime reform plans, laws, and institutional changes as such. Nuclear reactors were a part of the 'overbuilding' chapter of the story of the forces of change in Ontario. They are probably a part of the untold story of why Ontario Hydro was not privatized or broken up into still more separate companies. But the new OEB is likely to become the de facto economic regulator of nuclear power, if not directly, then certainly as an arena through which more transparency and debate about the economics of nuclear power generation will occur in the next few years.

6 The Alberta Energy and Utilities Board

The Alberta Energy and Utilities Board (AEUB) is an independent, quasi-judicial agency of the government of Alberta. Established on 15 February 1995 by the Alberta Energy and Utilities Board Act, the AEUB is the amalgamation of two previously separate energy regulators, the Energy Resources Conservation Board (ERCB) and the Public Utilities Board (PUB). On 1 April 1996 the Alberta Geological Survey (AGS) also joined the organization. As a newly created agency, the AEUB is still in its infancy, but it is far from a fledging regulator. Cumulatively, the lives of the Energy Resources Conservation Board, the Public Utilities Board, and the Alberta Geological Survey span a more than 85-year time period (Breen 1993). With the establishment of the Board of Public Utility Commissioners (the predecessor organization to the Public Utilities Board) dating back to 1915, the youthful AEUB is ironically the oldest regulatory agency in the province of Alberta.

This chapter examines key changes in the structure, functioning, and regulatory approach of the AEUB over the past decade. In the first section, we examine the organizational mandate and key changes in the agency's external and internal environment. In its external environment, the AEUB has had to address the challenges of an aging provincial energy infrastructure, the changing profile of the energy industry, Alberta's declining reserves of conventional crude oil and natural gas, heightened landowner-industry conflict, and growing public expectations for active involvement in energy development. Internally, the AEUB has undergone a number of transformations, most notably its own organizational birth, but also two major reorganizations. In the second segment of the chapter, we take a closer look at the AEUB's internal environment, exploring agency leadership, board representation, and organizational culture. Given the breadth of the AEUB's mandate, judicious selection of the organization's Chair and board members is crucial. Culturally, the agency is predominantly a technical establishment, with a core culture of integrity, public service, and technical competence.

The chapter's third section examines changes in the AEUB's regulatory approach in the areas of incentive regulation and service-oriented regulatory governance, with a focus on negotiated settlement processes. In the fourth section, we look at the influences of the environmental regime on Alberta's energy regulator, influences which have had powerful impacts on the AEUB, prompting the organization to adopt new regulatory functions and to modify existing processes (a discussion of competition regulatory regime impacts is left until chapter 7). In the conclusion, we identify three broad shifts characterizing the AEUB's evolving role and functioning: from adjudicator to facilitator, from stand-alone regulator to networked regulator, and from sectoral to framework regulator.

Mandate and Key Changes during the Last Decade

The Alberta Energy and Utilities Board is responsible for the 'safe, responsible, and efficient development of Alberta's energy resources,' oil, natural gas, oil sands, coal, and electrical energy (AEUB 2000a: 2). The Board is also responsible for the pipelines and transmission lines that move energy resources to market, and regulates investor-owned gas, electric, and water utilities with a view to safe and reliable service at just and reasonable rates. The mission of the AEUB is 'to ensure that the discovery, development, and delivery of Alberta's resources take place in a manner that is fair, responsible, and in the public interest' (AEUB 2000a: 2).

Perhaps ironically, one of the key changes at the AEUB during the last decade is its own organizational birth. The Alberta Energy and Utilities Board Act, proclaimed in force on 15 February 1995, created the agency by merging the Energy Resources Conservation Board and the Public Utilities Board. Sections 2 and 3(1)(a)(b) of the AEUB Act read, 'The Alberta Energy and Utilities Board is established as a corporation consisting of its members. The Board shall consist of (a) the members of the ERCB and, (b) the members of the PUB.' But the AEUB was clearly intended to be more than a holding company for the PUB and the ERCB. Through the AEUB Act, the new regulator's jurisdiction and its 'powers, rights and privileges' encompass the combined jurisdiction, powers, rights, and privileges of the ERCB and the PUB (sections 8[1] and 10[1]). The lion's share of the AEUB mandate originates from the ERCB, which had regulatory authority over virtually all aspects of energy resource development, with the exception of utility rate regulation, which was the primary responsibility of the PUB. Given the broader jurisdiction of the ERCB, this organization was also the larger of the AEUB's two predecessor units, with a staff complement of roughly 600 employees, versus the PUB' s less than 100 workers.

In the AEUB's first full year of operation, fiscal year 1995–6, the Calgary-based organization addressed issues related to the merger, including the 'proud' launch of the new agency's corporate identity. While this was perhaps the most visible sign of the merger process, other important milestones in the first year included the establishment of a single employee policy, common salary administration for all employees, and the use of mixed work teams for several hearings and initiatives. In this first year of activity, the Alberta Geological Survey (AGS) also joined the Board. On 1 April 1996 the AGS was transferred to the AEUB from the Department of Resource Development (also part of the provincial energy portfolio). The affiliation with the AEUB was meant to establish 'closer links between two important groups involved in geoscience within the Alberta government, and to strengthen the province's geoscience activities and products in the energy sector' (AEUB 1996: 2). The operations of the Alberta Geological Survey have remained fairly independent from the AEUB, however, with AGS staff continuing to work out of Edmonton and the organization maintaining a separate web site and information service from the AEUB.

To respond to its new organizational reality, the Board restructured its internal operations in its inaugural year. In June 1995, four months after the proclamation of the AEUB Act, the agency began a restructuring of existing ERCB and PUB departments on a scale that had not been seen in either parent organization since the 1970s. The reorganization grouped PUB and ERCB staff into four divisions sharing common regulatory and operational processes: Facilities, Resources, Utilities, and Corporate Services. The Facilities Division regulated wells, pipelines, batteries, and plants, and in 1996–7 it also became responsible for regulating waste facilities (when regulatory authority over upstream oilfield waste was transferred to the Board from Alberta Environmental Protection). The Resources Division regulated the development of subsurface reservoirs and surface and subsurface coal and oil sands;

regulation of the electricity supply industry resided with the Utilities Division; and the Corporate Services Division supplied service and support functions to the organization (accounting, information systems and technology, communications, human resources, legal services, and administrative services).

The new regulator also formalized its approach to planning in its inaugural year of activity to 'guide short-term priority-setting and operations, and to set a framework for anticipating long-term, future needs' (AEUB 1996: 2). As part of this new planning approach, the AEUB identified its 'core processes' and grouped them into four areas: adjudication and regulation, applications, surveillance and enforcement, and information and knowledge. Of these, the AEUB clearly views adjudication and regulation as the priority process. Its self-described 'raison-d'être' is 'to adjudicate issues related to the operation of designated utilities within Alberta and to ensure that the development, transportation, and monitoring of the province's energy resources is in the public interest.'[1] The Board's regulatory processes are governed by more than forty pieces of legislation regulating the province's energy resource and utility sectors. The application process consists of handling, processing, and ruling on applications for energy and utility activities and for amendments to existing approvals. Surveillance and enforcement involves reviewing industry data and records, inspections of operations, and monitoring compliance with industry regulations and standards. The core process of information and knowledge refers to the Board's collection, storage, analysis, appraisal, and dissemination of information, and its efforts to ensure the integrity and accountability of data collected by and submitted to the Board.

The initial organizational structure adopted by the Board (i.e., Facilities, Resources, Utilities, and Corporate Services) gave way to a new alignment of activities in 1999, when the Board undertook another reorganization 'in order to better achieve its strategic directions, and to put in place a structural realignment that will better serve our stakeholders' (AEUB 1999c: 1). Whereas the prior organization was based to a great extent on industrial segments (i.e., facilities, resources, and utilities), the nine branches of the new organizational structure are more reflective of AEUB core processes. This is intended to provide 'a clearer view of where to go in order to conduct business with, or obtain information from the EUB' (AEUB 1999c: 1).

---

1 AEUB web site: http://www.eub.gov.ab.ca/bbs/eubinfo/mission.htm.

The nine AEUB Branches are Regulatory Support, Applications, Corporate Enforcement and Surveillance, Information and Systems Services, Utilities, Resources, Finance, Human Resources, and Law. Regulatory Support coordinates new regulatory policy and the AEUB hearings process; the Applications Branch handles all application processes for resource development; conservation projects, and facility development, and Corporate Enforcement and Surveillance deals with all high-level enforcement and compliance actions. Information and Systems Services is responsible for AEUB data collection and dissemination, and includes AEUB Communications; the Utilities Branch continues to regulate the electricity supply industry, while the Resources Branch is responsible for energy and mineral resource appraisal. The Finance, Human Resources, and Law Branches provide corporate services to the organization in each of their respective functional areas.

The merger of the ERCB and the PUB helped to resolve one of the problems arising from the former division of regulatory authority between the two boards. In utilities regulation, the ERCB was responsible for new facilities approval, while the PUB was responsible for utility rate regulation. This division of regulatory authority presented difficulties when, for example, the ERCB approved a new facility proposal while the PUB refused to include the new facility in the utility's rate base (Keeping 1993). By combining the two regulators' jurisdictions, the merger permitted a more coordinated approach to utilities regulation.

But while the merger helped to address one of the existing problems in Alberta's energy regulatory governance, it introduced other challenges. First, by creating an organization with a much wider regulatory ambit, it made it more difficult to find board members or chairpersons with experience across the full range of the agency's jurisdiction. Second, and related to the first, at the same time as the Board's regulatory authority was expanding, the size of its board was contracting. The inaugural board had fewer members than the combined boards of the former ERCB and PUB. Third, the integration of the two formerly separate regulators involved a fair degree of cultural adjustment for staff members – particularly those of the PUB, the much smaller of the two organizations. We discuss these challenges in more depth in the following section of the chapter.

Amidst this organizational change, the AEUB also faced significant change in its external environment. Among the numerous forces and tensions with which the AEUB has had to contend, five changes stand out as particularly salient:[2] the maturation of the province's energy infrastructure, depletion of Alberta's conventional crude oil and sweet gas reserves, the changing profile of the petroleum industry, the growth in landowner-industry conflict, and the emergence of the public as a powerful AEUB stakeholder. Indeed, in the ERCB's 1991 annual review of Alberta's energy resources, the feature article, entitled, 'Shaping the ERCB's Future,' identified all of these issues as challenges to the ERCB (Alberta Energy Resources Conservation Board 1992). While the substance and impact of these changes will be addressed in greater detail in subsequent sections of this chapter, we examine each of them briefly here.

The maturation of Alberta's energy infrastructure presents new regulatory issues for the provincial regulator. Until the 1970s, the ERCB focus was on the 'front-end' of energy developments, that is, approvals of new energy proposals, but by the early 1990s, the focus broadened to include Alberta's growing infrastructure of 'suspended, aging, and changing energy facilities' (Alberta Energy Resources Conservation Board 1992) . As Alberta's wells, pipelines, batteries, and other facilities age, they require greater regulatory attention, particularly in the area of compliance and enforcement. Older producing oil and gas facilities need increased monitoring and inspection, orphan wells and other orphan facilities require proper abandonment, and the public and environmental concerns of inactive wells call for regulatory attention. In response, Alberta's energy regulator has had to increase the attention it pays to these issues, including heightened monitoring of aging facilities, increased requirements for proper orphan well abandonment, and new requirements to bring down the level of inactive wells.

Another key change in Alberta's energy regulatory environment is the decline in reserves of conventional crude oil and sweet natural gas. The province's conventional crude oil reserves have been declining at a rate of 6 per cent per year since the mid-1980s. This has spurred the development of new techniques to improve oil recovery from conventional reserves, and has fuelled public and private interest in developing the province's rich oil sands. Where new oil recovery techniques exhibit different production characteristics, the AEUB has had to modify

---

2 While the development of the environmental and competition regulatory regimes are also key challenges, we reserve discussion of these issues to the chapter's section on inter-regime influences.

conventional means of regulating oil development (e.g., changing well-spacing requirements and allowable production rates for horizontal drilling). Oil sands development requires even greater regulatory change, as the production techniques are not only fundamentally different from conventional oil projects, but are also frequently experimental. The declining reserves of sweet natural gas in Alberta have prompted a key change with which the provincial regulatory has had to contend. The expansion of sour gas drilling in the face of declining sweet gas reserves presents distinctive environmental concerns. Sour gas developments generate tremendous public concern over the potential risks of sour gas leaks to human, animal, and environmental safety. Beginning in the mid-1980s, the then ERCB began studying in earnest the behaviour of sour gas in accidents and the safest alternatives for the public in the event of sour gas emergencies; it also began consulting the public regarding sour gas safety and risk (Alberta Energy Resources Conservation Board 1994: 19).

The profile of the petroleum industry has also transformed dramatically in recent years both in size and in character. The number of companies in the industry has exploded, from less than 100 companies in the early 1970s to some 1,300 in the late 1990s. In contrast to the situation in the previous decades, when the lion's share of companies were large and highly knowledgeable about (and compliant with) energy regulation, the vast majority of newer operators are small, unfamiliar with regulatory requirements, and lacking the financial resources to dedicate to regulatory compliance. In some cases, small operators even perceive regulation as inimical to the profitability of their operations. For the AEUB, the changing face of the petroleum industry has required an increased emphasis on compliance and enforcement, not only in terms of surveillance, but in terms of educating the newer players as well. This has been no small task, particularly given the difficulty of communicating with such a large number of firms, many of whom are not members of an industry association. These first three challenges can be summed up in the words of the ERCB in the early 1990s: '... among the many influences shaping today's energy regulation, the maturing of Alberta's petroleum sector is one of the most significant' (Alberta Energy Resources Conservation Board 1994: 19).

In addition to the challenges of an aging provincial infrastructure, declining reserves, and changes in the petroleum industry's profile, the AEUB has also had to address the rising incidence of landowner-industry conflict. While land-use conflict is a tension inherent in energy resource development at any time, throughout the past decade landowner-industry conflicts have grown in both number and intensity. This is in part related to the changes identified above, for example, where landowners have concerns about orphan wells, abandoned facilities, and sour gas developments, or where landowners are dealing with numerous operators (some of whom have been known to renege on commitments to landowners). But conflict is also rising because of the changing socio-demographic profile of landowners. A growing proportion of landowners are financially established professionals (many of them retired petroleum industry executives themselves) who have no financial requirement for the income resource development can provide. They tend to be far less compromising in their opposition to energy developments in their environs. In addition to these factors, a number of dramatic conflict situations, for example, industrial sabotage in northwestern Alberta and the shooting of an oilfield executive, have increased public and media attention to landowner-industry issues. As we will discuss, in response to the growth in landowner-industry conflict, the provincial regulator has developed a rigorous set of public consultation guidelines for industry and has designed an 'Appropriate Dispute Resolution' system.

Throughout the past decade, the AEUB has also had to come to grips with growing demands from the broader public (not just landowners) for active involvement in energy resource development decision-making. While the Board has long regulated in 'the public interest,' which it defined as 'maximizing benefits to the Alberta public and minimizing negative effects on the environment, social values and Albertans' way of life' (Alberta Energy Resources Conservation Board 1993a: 5), the organization has now had to learn to regulate *with* the public – not as a nebulous 'public interest,' but as real individuals with real concerns about specific issues. Throughout the 1990s, the public has emerged as a powerful AEUB customer, client, and stakeholder. This change has prompted the AEUB to include the public in multi-stakeholder policy development processes, to produce public education documents for those who seek active involvement, and to revisit (and in some cases revise) Board decisions sparking public concern.

Leadership, Representation, and Core Culture

The AEUB is led by its board, consisting of a Chair and board members appointed by the provincial government for varying terms. These appointments are not partisan, but rather are based on the individual experience and expertise of candidates in the energy industry. The Board's role is to 'protect the public interest in energy resource development and public utility regulation' (AEUB 2000c: 6), while the Chair has responsibility for 'directing and coordinating the EUB's regulatory mandate' (AEUB 2000c: 6). This delineation of duties is reflected in the AEUB's organizational structure, in which branches have an operational reporting relationship to the Chair and a regulatory reporting relationship to the board (i.e., communication on regulatory and adjudicative matters). Given the strong leadership role of the Chair, we begin by examining this role and the individuals who have filled this post at the AEUB. We then discuss the board as a whole, focusing on key changes in board composition and representation in recent times.

Two individuals have chaired the AEUB since its inception: Celine Belanger and Neil McCrank. Belanger, a native of Alberta and member of the National Energy Board between 1990 and 1995, was the inaugural Chair of the AEUB. As Chair, she followed through on the organizational restructuring recommendations prepared under former ERCB vice-chairmen Frank Mink and Phil Prince. She hired a chief executive to manage the agency's day-to-day operations, and appointed four division leaders for each of the newly created divisions, Resources, Facilities, Utilities, and Corporate Services. The term of the Chair is normally five years, but Belanger served only half of this period, leaving abruptly in 1998. Although the minister of energy provided no explanation for her unexpected departure, insiders suggested a number of factors may have contributed: the lag between AEUB hearings and the issuing of final decisions; the inability of the Board to retain staff; increasingly strained relations between the AEUB and oil sands producers; and the then upcoming deregulation of electricity generation (Byfield and Hope 1998).

Belanger's successor, Neil McCrank, placed second behind Belanger in the 1995 competition for Chair. Appointed on 31 July 1998, McCrank is an electrical engineer with close to twenty years' senior level experience in the Alberta government. Prior to joining the Board, he was deputy minister of the Alberta Department of Justice for almost ten years. As the new Chair, McCrank undertook his own restructuring of the agency. He did not retain Belanger's chief executive, preferring instead to work directly with the organization's four division leaders. Within a year of his appointment, he reorganized the AEUB into its present nine branches (as previously discussed, Regulatory Support,

Applications, Corporate Enforcement and Surveillance, Information and Systems Services, Utilities, Resources, Finance, Human Resources, and Law). To enable himself to focus more on the long-term strategic direction of the organization, McCrank also reintroduced an executive position to handle the AEUB's day-to-day operations, appointing a chief operating officer in January 2000 (AEUB 2000c).

Since the creation of the AEUB, there have been a number of new faces on its board, and a number of significant departures. Although the AEUB Act stated that the board of the AEUB would consist of the board members of the ERCB and the PUB (Section 3[1]), some board members of the ERCB and PUB did not continue to serve on the inaugural board of the AEUB (three of these owing to retirement). With the increased workload brought on by the new regulator's expanded authority and rising levels of industry activity, the inaugural board faced a daunting challenge: an expanded workload both in size and scope, and a reduced board capacity not only in terms of sheer numbers but also in terms of experience with the full range of the new regulator's mandate.

To address this challenge, many hearings in the first few years of the AEUB's existence relied on acting board members to furnish the requisite expertise and manpower (division leaders at the AUEB are all acting board members). In addition, three new board members have been appointed since the AEUB's creation, two in 1998[3] and another in 1999. The 1998 appointments brought individuals to the board with political and administrative experience in rural municipal government, and senior-level management experience in the oil and gas industry (AEUB 1998c). The 1999 appointment sought to enhance the board's capacity to address utility deregulation by adding a member with senior management experience in the deregulated electricity and natural gas markets (AEUB 1999a). Despite these additions, however, the number of board members is still roughly the same because the board has lost several members since 1995. Some of these departures were significant losses to the board's corporate memory and experience, perhaps most notably two members whose appointments dated back to 1987 (one passed away and the other left to head the Canadian Energy Research Institute).

---

3 There were actually three appointments in October 1998, but one was to reappoint a member who had left to work in industry for a year following close to ten years as a board member.

The present board consists of eight board members and the Chair. Collectively, they bring a wealth of technical experience to the board in the engineering, scientific, and legal disciplines. In addition, they possess combined practical experience at both the senior management and operational levels in virtually all sectors, stages, and dimensions of energy development. Board members not only have industry backgrounds but also have worked in the public, academic, and political spheres. The board includes former senior managers from Alberta's oil, gas, and electricity sectors, a previous long-time staff member of the AEUB, and a former municipal employee and past mayor. In addition, the board includes a member with professional experience in environmental, health, and safety issues, as well as a former dairy and beef farm operator. This group represents a mixture of new and old members, with the longest-standing members' appointments predating the creation of the AEUB (one member had served the ERCB since 1989, and another was appointed to the PUB in 1991). To provide additional support and expertise at hearings, eight new acting board members were recently appointed. These appointments not only include senior level AEUB staff members but also, for the first time, appointments from industry as well.

The challenges of the merger and the increased workload have been felt not only at the board level but throughout the organization as a whole. Integration of ERCB and PUB staff has been a gradual process, with cultural differences predominantly resolved through the PUB staff's adaptation to the culture of the larger organization with which they now work. Initially, the majority of PUB's staff and board members remained in Edmonton and used video-conferencing when necessary, but now almost all staff are working out of Calgary, the long-time home of the ERCB. The one remaining Edmonton-based PUB board member commutes to Calgary for hearings, rather than video-conferencing as in the past. In addition, staff handling utility regulation at the former ERCB and PUB are progressively merging their operations. While the high level of restructuring activity has no doubt had an impact on morale, the major factor impacting employee satisfaction at the Board is the steadily increasing workload. The Board has taken steps to bring AEUB remuneration levels closer to industry rates and to expand recruitment efforts, but in the interim many staff work long hours to meet the demands of the AEUB workload.

This commitment reflects the core culture of the agency. The fundamental tenet of the organization is to 'do the right thing.' This means spending the time to learn the issues, following through on commit-ments made, and acting at all times with integrity. Staff are delegated relatively greater authority levels than in provincial government de-partments and identify very strongly with the agency's mission of serving the public interest. AEUB employees typically have technical degrees and/or industry experience, and the organization views itself as first and foremost a technical agency. This can be seen in the former ERCB's self-description: 'The ERCB is a largely technical organization made up of professionally qualified and experienced support people' (Alberta Energy Resources Conservation Board) 1994: 30). Given the important role the AEUB plays in handling public concerns at the field level, field staff are now recruited not only for their technical back-grounds but also for their ability to communicate and deal with the public. Nonetheless, technical competence remains the core character-istic of the AEUB workforce.

Incentive Regulation: Negotiated Settlement Processes

Over the past decade, Alberta's chief energy regulators, the ERCB, the PUB, and now the AEUB, have increasingly adopted incentive-based approaches to rule-making and greater service-orientation in agency operations, policy development, and regulation. This organizational reinvention has sought primarily to reduce the number of public hear-ings and to respond to growing demands for public involvement in energy regulation. In addition, the budget constraints of government-wide deficit reduction have propelled the search for less expenditure-intensive means of regulating. With regards to public involvement, the number of landowners, interest groups, and other community mem-bers insisting on having a say in energy resource development has multiplied, and their demands risen in intensity, not only because of broad-based trends towards greater citizen involvement in policy-making, but also because of the proliferation of sour gas development in Alberta and the maturation of the province's energy infrastructure. As to budget constraints, from the mid-1980s to the early 1990s, the ERCB alone had to contend with a 20 per cent reduction in its staff complement, from some 820 employees in the mid-1980s to less than 675 at the beginning of the following decade.

In addition to these pressures, the agency's external environment has also been marked by broader shifts in thinking about regulation and management, including the rise of incentive regulation and new public management. As a result of these various pressures, energy regulation in Alberta has taken on a new character, marked by a shift from traditional command and control regulation to greater use of negotiated forms of rule-making and service-oriented regulatory governance. This shift spans a range of regulatory processes, including policy development, adjudication and regulation, and compliance and enforcement, and is exemplified by the AEUB's development of negotiated settlement processes, public consultation and appropriate dispute resolution systems, and multi-stakeholder policy development initiatives. We focus here only on negotiated settlement processes.

The AEUB developed a negotiated settlement process for utility rate determination as part of its objective of increasing regulatory efficiency and effectiveness. The organization describes the process and its benefits as follows: '... in a negotiated settlement process, a utility engages in direct negotiations with its customers to establish tolls, tariff, and terms and conditions of service. This encourages concerned parties to understand issues and reach agreement in a less adversarial and costly environment, free of legal procedures and without a hearing' (Alberta Ministry of Energy 1998: 31.) Since the mid-1990s, the Board has been encouraging the utility industry and utility industry stakeholders to enter into negotiated settlements and has been monitoring negotiations where they occur, but the Board did not develop and release guidelines for negotiations until the latter half of the decade. In 1998 the AEUB released Informational Letter IL 98–04: 'Negotiated Settlement Guidelines: Tolls, Tariffs, and Terms and Conditions of Service.' The negotiated settlement process by this point came to be viewed not only as a substitute for adjudication, but also as a *complement* to AEUB hearings: '... negotiated settlement is a process that is alternative or complementary to the traditional hearing process in dealing with utility related issues such as tolls, tariffs, and terms and conditions of service' (AEUB 1998a: 2).

IL 98–04 outlined the principles, procedures, and AEUB expectations respecting the negotiated settlement process. Underlying the process are a number of key principles: that parties participate in good faith; that the negotiation process be open and fair, confidential, and flexible enough to address individual circumstances; and that sufficient information be available to further participants' understanding of the issues being negotiated. Participation in negotiations is voluntary, and the guidelines stipulate that all parties with an interest in the negotiation must have the opportunity to take part. When parties initiate and reach a negotiated settlement, they include a copy of the settlement agreement and related documentation (e.g., details of unresolved issues, rates and terms and conditions of service that will result from the agreement, description of issues for which agreement is not unanimous, etc.) with their AEUB application. When the application comes before the Board, the Board determines the acceptability of the agreement using traditional regulatory decision-making criteria; for example, whether the agreement is in the public interest, is reasonable and fair, and conforms with existing law and Board policies. If the Board takes issue with all or part of a negotiated agreement, it gives the parties the opportunity to return to negotiations to address and resolve any concerns. If the parties cannot resolve outstanding issues, the application then proceeds to a hearing. While the Board has not made mandatory the negotiated settlement process, it 'encourages' utility companies and stakeholders to use the negotiated settlement guidelines. The process is still relatively new, but in 1998/99, the AEUB was aware of at least five negotiated settlement processes (Alberta Ministry of Energy 1999: 40).

The shift to incentive and service-oriented regulation at the AEUB is also visible in the Board's development of public consultation guidelines and an appropriate dispute resolution system. While the negotiated settlement guidelines discussed above represent a substantial shift in responsibility for decision-making – from the AEUB to regulated industries and their customers – the AEUB's initiatives on public consultation and appropriate dispute resolution mark an equally significant release of decision-making authority to regulated companies and their stakeholders. The Board's intent with these initiatives has been to develop a framework within which energy developers and the public can resolve their concerns, differences, and conflicts in direct interaction with one another, rather than in adjudication at AEUB hearings.

Inter-regime Influences: Environmental Regulation

Over the past decade, the AEUB has increasingly been influenced by the environmental and competition regulatory regimes. In an energy producing province, the AEUB is no stranger to integrating environmental considerations into energy resource development, and with Alberta as one of the first Canadian provinces to deregulate its electricity industry, the AEUB has had to address new regulatory issues emerging from competition as well. In this section, we examine the main inter-regime influences on the AEUB emanating from environmental regulation. Competition aspects are examined in chapter 7.

Resource conservation has always been at the core of energy regulation in Alberta. Indeed, it was concerns over oil and gas wastage in the early development of the province's Turner Valley oilfield that provided the initial stimulus to create an energy regulator. 'The tremendous glow generated from flared gas was sufficient in the 1930s to keep the Turner Valley oil field almost in a state of perpetual daylight. It was this waste, combined with the realization that the excessive gas production was having a damaging effect on the reservoir, that brought the question of oil and gas conservation to public debate and eventually brought forth legislation designed to curb such a practice' (Breen 1993: xix). But while the Board has a long tradition of environmental conservation, environmental protection is a relatively new concept in the Board's regulation of provincial energy developments.

These broader environmental issues began to rise rapidly in the consciousness of Alberta's energy regulator in recent times. In the early 1990s, for example, the then ERCB stated that in addition to the maturation of petroleum exploration in the province and more modest expectations for world oil prices, environmental considerations in energy resource development and growing public expectations for environmental protection were altering its corporate strategy (Alberta Energy Resources Conservation Board 1993a). Similarly, the feature article in the ERCB's 1991 annual review of the province's energy resources (Alberta Energy Resources Conservation Board 1992) stated that the world of energy was changing rapidly and identified 'concerns for the environment' as one of the key shifts. The review included a separate section dedicated to the environment, 'Energy Resources and the Environment,' and discussed some of the pressures on the regulator emanating from sustainable approaches to development. The Alberta Clean Air Strategy recommended that both the ERCB and the Natural Resources Conservation Board (the latter responsible for review of non-energy resource development projects in the province) adopt a 'full cost' approach to regulation, that is, one including social and environmental costs in regulatory decision-making. Pressures to incorporate environmental considerations into AEUB decision-making have continued unabated throughout the 1990s.

For the AEUB, one of the central challenges of integrating the environment into energy resource regulation takes place at the inter-organizational level. The Board has addressed this challenge by seeking to clarify, at both the legislative and inter-organizational levels, its jurisdiction and role vis-à-vis other organizations with environmental mandates. Legislatively, for example, when the Alberta Environmental Protection and Enhancement Act was proclaimed in 1993, amendments were made to the Energy Resources Conservation Act to affirm the then ERCB's environmental jurisdiction. 'The amendment confirmed the Board's view that its longstanding responsibility to protect the public interest includes environmental matters associated with energy projects' (Alberta Energy Resources Conservation Board 1994: 26). This amendment not only confirmed the regulator's existing environmental jurisdiction, but expanded it as well. Whereas the Board's consideration of environmental matters was previously confined to local environmental impacts, the Environmental Protection and Enhancement Act defined environmental considerations more broadly (Keeping 1993).

Inter-organizationally, the AEUB signs memoranda of understandings (MOUs) with other government agencies, most notably Alberta Environment (AE), to clarify roles and responsibilities. These understandings seek to clarify, coordinate, and harmonize the two agencies' respective roles in energy development regulation. AEUB/AE MOUs exist in areas including waste management, release notification requirements, and oil sands developments.

Notwithstanding MOUs, jurisdictional borders between agencies can still be difficult to navigate, not only for the government agencies involved but for industry and the public as well. Where possible, the AEUB strives to provide a 'single window' for industry and the public as well as to develop joint guidelines and approval processes with other agencies. The ERCB, for example, developed a single window for coal industry applications in 1992, so that industry could submit one application to the ERCB, who would then coordinate the application's review by as many as a dozen government departments (Alberta Energy Resources Conservation Board 1993a). And the ERCB released joint public consultation guidelines in 1989 with Alberta Environment. The AEUB has also conducted a number of joint hearings with the Canadian Environmental Assessment Agency on coal development in the latter half of the 1990s and collaborates with other agencies to research, monitor, and store resource materials related to the environment.

Another crucial influence on the AEUB of the environmental agenda is the rise of the public as a powerful AEUB 'customer' and stakeholder. Both landowners and environmental groups are now integral members of the energy regulatory community, members to which the AEUB has had to respond. For example, the AEUB launched five major initiatives on petroleum resource development and the environment during fiscal year 1999–2000 in response to landowner concerns. These projects were substantial undertakings and included the previously mentioned Alternative Dispute Resolution initiative, the implementation and clarification of flaring requirements, and a large multi-stakeholder process to review public safety requirements for sour gas.

The emergence of the public as a potent energy regulatory stakeholder is visible when the Board reopens, revisits, or revises its decisions in response to public dissatisfaction with them. In 1993, for example, environmental group reaction to the then ERCB's updated requirements for deep well injection and disposal prompted the regulator to reopen the process. More recently, in 1999, public concerns over a sour gas pipeline permit granted by the AEUB induced the Board to revoke the permit and hold a hearing. Environmental groups have even challenged the Board's jurisdiction. In 1993 an advocacy group legally contested the then ERCB's authority to decide on an application made by Syncrude to amend its commercial approval, claiming that Syncrude had not complied with the Alberta Environmental Protection and Enhancement Act. While, in instances such as these, the public has not always been successful in its attempts to alter or influence regulatory decisions (e.g., the Board decided to reinstate the pipeline permit following the hearing), the public has become, nonetheless, an actively engaged member of the AEUB's regulatory milieu.

In addition to addressing jurisdictional issues and the new pressures of an active public, the AEUB has also adopted new functions and adapted existing ones in response to the environmental regulatory regime. In some cases, new and/or modified functions are the product of inter-organizational agreements. For example, based on an agreement with Alberta Environmental Protection (AEP), the AEUB now has sole regulatory authority over upstream oilfield waste (before September 1993, this industry sector was regulated jointly by the then ERCB and the AEP). Similarly, through inter-organizational agreement, the AEUB adapted its application processes for oil sands developments by integrating its application review processes with AEP.

In other cases, new and/or adapted AEUB functions are a consequence of new regulatory issues arising from increased concerns for the environment. AEUB initiatives on climate change fall into this latter category. In 1991, for example, the then ERCB included forecasts of greenhouse gas emissions in its provincial energy requirements report for the first time. AEUB initiatives on flaring have also been prompted by the climate change agenda. Alberta's Clean Air Strategic Alliance (CASA) recommended that the AEUB reduce the volume of solution gas flared in the province. While solution gas conservation has always been part of the regulator's mandate, the AEUB developed new flaring requirements (not just for solution gas but for flaring in general) largely as a result of CASA recommendations (AEUB 2000b). The AEUB describes the relationship between AEUB objectives, the CASA recommendations, and its new flaring requirements as follows: '... the Board believes that CASA's recommended goal and management framework for eliminating routine solution gas flaring, while recommended in the context of solution gas management, are consistent with the AEUB's overall intent to optimize resource conservation and ensure appropriate levels of environmental protection. Accordingly, the AEUB has adopted them to encompass flaring in general' (AEUB 1999d: 1). This passage reflects not only the influence of the CASA recommendations on the Board's decision-making, but the Board's adoption of environmental protection as a new function. This marks quite a change from the beginning of the decade, when, as mentioned above, the regulator listed public expectations for environmental protection as one of the factors altering its corporate strategy. Now, along with its traditional conservation mandate, environmental protection has become a key component of the Board's 'overall intent.'

Conclusions

Throughout this chapter, we have examined key changes in the external and internal environment of the Alberta Energy and Utilities Board. The organization has had to confront and adapt to tremendous change in its external environment, including the changing profile of the province's energy industry, growing expectations for active public participation in energy developments, and the rise of the environmental and competition regulatory frameworks. Internally, the AEUB has been transformed by its own organizational birth and subsequent reorganizations, and has altered its fundamental regulatory approach by adopting incentive regulation, enhancing its service orientation, and redesigning its compliance and enforcement processes. Over the past decade, we can discern a number of shifts underlying the AEUB's evolving role and functioning: from adjudicator to facilitator, from stand-alone regulator to networked regulator, and from sectoral to framework regulator. While these shifts are inter-related and not easily separated from one another, we discuss each of them below, noting some ways in which they relate and reinforce one another.

Although adjudication remains the 'raison-d'être' of the AEUB, many of the key changes of the organization in the past decade reveal that the regulator's role as facilitator, rather than adjudicator, is growing. The AEUB's negotiated settlement processes for utility rate determination and its appropriate dispute resolution initiative for landowner-industry conflicts are examples of this shift. In both the negotiated settlement and ADR processes, the AEUB does not seek to impose solutions on energy industry stakeholders, but rather to provide the parties with the guidelines and framework that enable them to reach decisions without 'command and control'-style government intervention.

This decentralization of the locus of decision-making is also apparent in the agency's shift from stand-alone regulator to networked regulator. The ascendance of the environmental (and competition) regulatory regimes has 'de-insulated' the AEUB in its regulatory decision-making. As a sectoral regulator, it had been accustomed to a relatively impermeable decision-making sphere; that is, energy regulation was its responsibility, and it discharged this responsibility with a fair degree of independence. As horizontal issues, most notably the environment, have appeared on the regulatory landscape, the boundaries of the AEUB's decision-making environment have become far more porous. In response to this new regulatory milieu, not only has the organization sought greater jurisdictional clarity between itself and other environmentally mandated organizations, but increasingly it has had to integrate and coordinate its activities with other public agencies. In this sense, the once 'stand-alone' AEUB is becoming an evermore 'networked' regulator.

In sum, the Alberta Energy and Utilities Board is rapidly transforming in response to multiple and varied forces. Over the past decade, the agency has adapted and reinvented itself as its regulatory milieu has evolved. This pace of change and need for adaptation is not likely to abate. In the coming years, the AEUB will need to rely on its adaptive capacity to adjust and transform to meet the challenges of its evolving regulatory environment.

7 Energy and Competition Regulation: Towards Workable Competition

Key aspects of the sectoral energy regulatory regime have been brought out in the previous three chapters on the NEB, OEB, and AEUB. With a sectoral focus, they have shown how energy regulation has changed over the last fifteen years, but always in the context of the particular influences and shaping events and interests in each jurisdiction, one federal and two provincial. These sectoral energy board–level analyses have also shown the presence of horizontal regulatory regime influences and institutional arrangements, particularly regarding expanded environmental roles. But we have by no means come close to capturing the two horizontal aspects of energy regulation previewed in chapter 2, namely, competition regulation and environmental regulation (including sustainable development and climate change). In short, we need to deal more frontally with the institutional implications of whether the energy regime is best seen as a 'competitive order' or as a system of managed workable competition, and also (in chapter 8) with how energy is now regulated in environmental and sustainable development terms. Some insights into these issues were provided in the analysis in chapter 3 of U.S. developments led by the FERC, where inter-regime issues of market design and competition and merger issues were brought out but not fully discussed.

In this chapter, we examine the competition aspects of these horizontal influences. This cross-cutting incursion into the energy regulatory world is discussed in four sections. First, we sketch out the core features of competition and competition regulation in Canada (with some further comparative references, as well). Second, we highlight the role and preferred positions of the federal Competition Bureau in its approach to sectoral regulators as a whole, as the latter increasingly regulate industries which are becoming more competitive. Third, we look at how this impacts institutionally on the structure of regulation in the energy sector, with particular attention to electricity but with some reference also to natural gas. Many of these developments involving the sharing of regulatory space between the competition authority and the energy sectoral regulator are of quite recent vintage and involve the Competition Bureau's view of gradual experiments with electricity competition in Alberta, where competition is under way, in Ontario, where it began on 1 May 2002, and in Nova Scotia, where it is being contemplated. The fourth section draws out some problematic issues about what the interactions of intersecting regimes might mean as energy regulation evolves further in the coming decade or so. This begins with a brief discussion of whether the California electricity crisis has any lessons for Canadian electricity restructuring as well as issues regarding regulatory accountability in complex inter-regime institutional contexts. Conclusions then follow.

Competition and the Regulation of Competition

Competition policy and regulation consists of those rules and actions of the state intended to prevent certain restraints of trade by private firms (Janisch 1999). Stated more positively, it is intended to promote rivalry among firms, buyers, and sellers through actions in areas of activity such as mergers, abuse of dominance, cartels, conspiracies in restraint of trade, misleading advertising, and related criminal and economic offences that are held to be anti-competitive. For mainstream economists, the overall purpose of competition policy and regulation is to protect and expand competition as a means of allocating scarce resources in an efficient manner and maximizing choice for consumers through the supply of a variety of products and services or goods of good or acceptable quality. The competition policy regulatory and decision process pursues these goals through interactions, lobbying, and pressure among interests and institutions which lead to the formulation of the main statements and statutes of competition policy and the deciding of individual case decisions by competition regulatory authorities such as the federal Competition Bureau (Conklin 2001; Doern, 1995; Doern and Wilks 1996).

But competition and competition regulation are not the same thing. However, understanding the former is crucial, and this starts with economics and economists. Understanding the regulation of competition means dealing with politics, and with how states and regulatory institutions arrange and carve up the competition regulatory space or terrain.

Competitive markets are the idealized end product of competition policy (Helm and Jenkinson 1998; Burke, Genn-Bash, and Haines 1991). Whether cast as free markets or simply as competition, they require the existence of the following features:

- consumers who are able to choose and purchase the good or service, and the provider of the good or service;
- producers of goods and services who are able to attract customers by producing what the latter want and by adjusting quality and price;
- the availability of enough information on the price, quality, and availability of the goods or services to enable the market to function;
- a sufficiently large number of producers and consumers for both to be able to choose, and for no one individual consumer or producer to determine the price. This latter condition may mean that there is free entry into, and exit from, the industry.

While economists concede the textbook nature of these characteristics, they also see them functioning in practice and hence as endowing economic and political life with many desirable features. Competition may also arise because of the presence of 'contestable markets.' Unlike perfect competition, a contestable market can consist of one or a few firms which may still be efficient. This is because firms in the industry will maintain prices close to the competitive level because of the threat posed by potential entrants (Baumol, Panzar, and Willig 1988).

However crucial these economic starting points are, they are not enough because competition regulation depends also on what different elements of the state actually do at several levels of action and inaction. The actual competition regulatory regime involves (a) core elements in normal descriptive terms (e.g., what exactly is abuse of dominant position?); (b) core elements expressed in laws and statutes (e.g., qualifying phrases such as 'unduly' or 'significant lessening' or 'fair competition' or competition 'in the public interest'); (c) competition as reflected through exempt or partially exempt sectors (e.g., regulated sectors; banks), by which is meant *exempt* in some way from general horizontal economy-wide competition rules; and (d) other laws and policy fields with impacts on competition (trade law, intellectual property law).

Of crucial importance in the last decade is trade policy and regulation itself (Trebilcock and Howse 1999). The Canada-U.S. Free Trade Agreement, and then NAFTA and the WTO Uruguay agreements, were also free trade or liberalized trade agreements. Indeed, a good case can be made that the most significant *competition* policy change in Canada over the last fifteen years has been free trade, rather than anything done in the name of competition law itself.

It is also quite essential to stress that in a federal state such as Canada, competition policy is also a de facto provincial concern. The Competition Act is a federal law under fairly secure federal powers, but the provinces have political and some legal room to manoeuvre. Thus it has been evident historically in the energy field that Alberta has strong views about how oil and gas distribution within Alberta is to occur and be politically managed (Pratt and Richards 1980). Similarly, Ontario and Quebec have aggressive positions about just how much competition might be allowed/managed in electricity.

The Competition Bureau and Industry Sectoral Regulators

As indicated above, competition regulation or anti-trust law and policy is a complex regulatory field itself, and hence this section can only sketch out its core features in the briefest of ways (Janisch 1999; Doern 1995a, Doern and Wilks 1996). We outline the core statutory mandate and the role of the Competition Bureau with regard to its relations with sectoral or industry regulators.

Under the Competition Act, the commissioner of competition (before 1999, known as the director of investigation and research or DIR) has overall responsibility for administering the various elements of the law. These elements range from bid rigging and price fixing (which are criminal offences) right through to civil or economic offences related to anti-competitive behaviour in areas such as mergers, misleading advertising, and predatory behaviour. The office that supports the commissioner is the Competition Bureau, which is a part of the 'ministry' of Industry Canada, but independent of it and its minister for operational decisions. The commissioner of competition and the Competition Bureau also have a competition advocacy and advisory role under the legislation, which has been exercised through presentations and testimony before sectoral regulators and in other forums (see more below regarding such interventions in the electricity restructuring process).

Table 4
Competition Bureau's principles for promoting competition in sectoral regulation

- Competitive markets should be put in place as soon as possible.
- Sectoral regulators should have an explicit (statutory) mandate to promote competition.
- There should be regulatory control of market power held by market incumbents.
- Regulatory control is required when there are *essential facilities* in an industry, access to which is needed in order to compete in a market.
- Competition law (i.e., the DIR as regulator) should be relied upon to prevent other anti-competitive business practices.
- Sectoral regulatory law should contain mechanisms in law for 'removing regulation when its costs outweigh its benefits,' such as sunset provisions and provisions for regulatory forbearance.
- Mechanisms should be provided for coordinating the roles and responsibilities of sectoral regulators and the Competition Bureau to minimize overlap and duplication.

As various sectoral regulatory realms, such as telecommunications and energy, have undergone competitive transformations arising from both technological and ideological change, the Competition Bureau has set out a fairly consistent set of overall principles concerning what it would like to see happen with sectoral regulators and the division of their roles (Competition Bureau 1996, 1997, 1998b, 2001). Table 4 lists the Competition Bureau's principles, which are then discussed briefly below.

The first principle is that competitive markets should be put in place as soon as possible on the grounds that 'effective and efficient competition, where it can be implemented, is really the best mechanism for achieving the low-cost and innovative supply of products' (Lafond 1999: 3). As a second principle, the Competition Bureau argues that sectoral regulators should have an explicit (statutory) role to promote competition. This is to ensure that an onus is placed on sectoral regulators to minimize restrictions on competition, but also to provide them the necessary legal authority to order pro-competitive restructuring or deregulation.

Because of important issues in the transition to competitive markets, a third principle emerges in which the Bureau argues that there should be regulatory control over excessive pricing arising from market power held by market incumbents (e.g., the market power of Ontario Power Generation in Ontario's electricity system restructuring, as discussed in chapter 5).

A fourth principle does not relate to transition per se. Regulatory control is considered necessary by the Bureau when there are *essential facilities* in an industry, access to which is needed in order to compete in a market, which are not subject to effective competition, and for which 'the cost of replication would raise an excessive barrier to entry' (Lafond 1999: 5). The Bureau argues that this is an issue on which the sectoral regulator should take the lead role because such market access issues often involve complex technical and pricing matters concerning which the sectoral regulator will have the most expertise, and therefore be best able to take timely action. Thus the location and institutional build-up of expert knowledge is a key factor in inter-regime design and inertia (Doern 1998).

The fifth principle then shifts to the Competition Bureau's own role per se. Competition law (i.e., the commissioner of competition as regulator) should be relied upon to prevent other anti-competitive business practices. Such practices refer to those which prevent or lessen competition unduly in a market: for example, mergers giving the merged company substantial control over prices, price fixing, or long-term contracts by a dominant company which prevent competition.

Again, because of transition and on-going change, the Competition Bureau has also advocated the creation of mechanisms in law for 're-moving regulation when its costs outweigh its benefits' (Lafond 1999: 6). One such mechanism is a sunset provision setting a specific time for the ending of the rule. Another is the use of *regulatory forbearance* provisions, which require the regulator not to intervene when an activity in the market is shown to be subject to sufficient competition to protect the public interest. Such forbearance provisions should be statutory in the Bureau's view, and the sectoral regulator's statute ought to supply a clear indication that competition law applies in areas in which the regulator is forbearing.

The seventh and final principle advocated by the Competition Bureau is that beyond the above dictums, there will undoubtedly be a need for other mechanisms for coordinating the roles and responsibilities of sectoral regulators and the Competition Bureau to minimize overlap and duplication. Such mechanisms could include periodic meetings of officials to alert each other to common problems or to cases which pose jurisdictional problems. Again this is important, but it leaves out the issue of how coordination problems may be triggered, and perhaps resolved, through the actions of firms and interveners taking regulators to court or simply deciding which of the dual regulators to appeal to first, depending on their own strategies, political and economic.

The seven principles enunciated above show that the scope or horizontal stretch of competition regulation is expanding into other, heretofore more purely sectoral realms. It is also evident that competition is expanding, but also that competition regulation confers different qualifying meanings as the two realms of regulation converge, collide, and seek accommodation with each other.

Joint Competition Regulation in Energy

How have these concepts of competition and the competition regulator's principles of inter-regime relations functioned in the case of energy as a sector? This is an overall question that can be asked for a number of countries and jurisdictions, for example, the European Union (Cameron 2001; Bailey 1999; Joskow 2000; Farrell and Forshay 1994). The answers to this question in Canada must be expressed with caution because the first real test of these relations is in the electricity sector and the restructuring of electricity is still very much 'in transition.' Indeed, in a very real sense, regulatory realms are always in transition. Hence, we need to rely on the stated views of the Competition Bureau, and on some of the responses and actions of the provinces, as restructured electricity markets and regulatory systems are being debated, are being put in place, or are beginning their operations in the new context. We do not yet have a set of significant cases or litigation regarding anti-competitive behaviour which might test, in real situations, the boundary lines between the two regimes.

Although we will focus here on these new electricity-centred developments, it is important to note that competition in oil and gas markets has always been politically 'managed' in some overall sense. Oil markets are driven by world supply and demand, and hence are competitive in a fuller sense, but they too can be influenced at the margins of pricing by the OPEC cartel (Nakicenovic, Grubler, and McDonald 1998; Morse and Richard 2002). Moreover, it must be reiterated (see chapter 1), that historically in Canada oil markets were once partitioned. The National Oil Policy of 1960 formally divided the national market so that from the Ottawa River Valley west, consumers were served by Alberta oil at higher than world prices, while those to the east of that line were supplied by cheaper imported oil. This was done as a way of promoting the development of the Alberta energy industry (McDougall 1982; Doern and Toner 1985). There was no overt action against this by the then existing competition authorities, whose legal mandate was, in any event, much weaker than the current Competition Act.

The federal competition authorities were engaged, albeit symbolically, in investigating the oil companies during the first and second energy crises of the early 1970s and 1980s, when oil and gas prices soared (Doern and Toner 1985). And they have investigated gasoline pricing at the pump in regions where anti-competitive behaviour was alleged by local consumers and/or politicians as the cause of higher local prices than most other geographic locations. The typical outcome of such examinations was that no collusion on pricing was found or could be proven. Later in the chapter, we will bring in natural gas competition, especially in the context of Nova Scotia's review of its electricity energy restructuring, but, in the main, we are focusing in this chapter on the electricity sector. In the context of inter-regime changes, we proceed first with a discussion of Ontario, then Alberta, which was in fact the first province to restructure, and finally Nova Scotia. Discussion and debate has also occurred in British Columbia and New Brunswick, which we do not explore here (New Brunswick 2001; Competition Bureau 1997).

Ontario

The Competition Bureau provided its views of Ontario's electricity (and gas) restructuring first at the stage when Ontario's Electricity Market Design Committee was doing its work and later when Ontario's Energy Competition Act was tabled in 1998. Chapter 5 has already set out the core institutional features of the new competitive regime in Ontario, but the focus in chapter 5 was largely on the OEB. Institutionally, the other key agency with a competition regulatory role is the Independent Market Operator (IMO), and its role, in turn, requires a closer look with respect to distinctions between electricity as a *product* versus a *service*.

Ontario energy officials stress that electricity as a commodity is a relatively new concept in the Ontario economy:

> Electricity is often perceived as a service. But, in the restructured industry the lines between 'commodity' and 'service' are sharply drawn. Much as there is a service component to virtually any good that we purchase on a day-to-day basis, and the same with electricity. The final price of the commodity will have many other non-commodity elements.

This view of electricity as a commodity is a key concept in reforming this industry. A commodity is a generic, undifferentiated product, that can be produced readily and sold easily to a large number of customers in a standardized quantity. Electrical energy, a collection of electrons, fits the commodity description well. For many years we have combined the electrons with a whole bunch of other services (voltage regulation, reactive power, operating and standby reserves) that, although essential for the delivery of power or the reliability of a transmission system, are not commodities. Consumers bought a whole lot of other 'things' when they paid the electricity bill. Separating the commodity from the services allows buyers and sellers to establish a market place with a focus on producing power at the lowest possible cost. Prices, specifically the prices of electric power, become a very important signal for both sides of the market. (Jennings and Chute 2001: 133)

In this product market, existing generators will be able to sell electricity products in a way that trades off the costs of operating against the risks of not selling power. So will other potential generators. Customers, too, will be able to make decisions to buy electricity products based on a knowledge of production technologies and flexibility.

However, there remain the natural monopoly or *service* elements for which regulation must be the substitute for competition. Services such as transmission and distribution require a *fair market* regulator to enforce service standards and establish compensation levels for the costs incurred. Thus, 'the IMO will be an independent market maker and transmission system operator that will ensure open access to the transmission system and fair market procedures for buyers and sellers. These fair market practices will facilitate the maximum participation in the IMO-run wholesale spot market, contributing to efficient price discovery and transparency in the commercial buying and selling of electricity' (Jennings and Chute 2001: 134). The IMO's role is also crucial in maintaining the reliability of the electricity system, and for defining and enforcing the minimum standards for connecting to the transmission network. To ensure that these standards are reasonable and do not themselves restrict market participation, the IMO is accountable to electricity market participants through its board of directors and will be liable for its actions. It is also regulated by the OEB.

The Competition Bureau broadly supported the Ontario restructuring effort, largely on the grounds that 'it will promote the most efficient use of energy resources in the province and will lead to the development of new electricity supply options tailored to meet the full benefits of competition' (Competition Bureau 1998a: i). Moreover, it supported 'the rapid adoption of [its key elements] to help ensure an orderly transition to open and effective competition' (Competition Bureau 1998b: i). In addition to supporting the basic powers given to the OEB and IMO, it also supported the development of provisions requiring the OEB to forbear from regulation in any case in which competition is sufficient to protect the public interest. It also endorsed the requirement for distributors to structurally separate their regulated distribution activities from their other activities, and the establishment of charges and fees on government-owned electricity sector companies equal to the taxes and fees they would pay as private sector companies.

However, the Competition Bureau argued that the Ontario restructuring does not deal with 'with the underlying source of the generation market power concerns, the concentration of generation assets within Ontario Hydro' (Competition Bureau 1998a: ii). Structural remedies such as the divestiture of generation facilities were seen by the Competition Bureau as crucial to ensuring competition. Some of this was in fact a part of the market design process, but not to the extent that the Competition Bureau saw as needed or desirable.

Ontario Power Generation (OPG), the successor generation company to Ontario Hydro, is bound by the Market Power Mitigation Agreement (MPMA). This agreement is the result of detailed negotiations between the Market Design Committee and OPG to deal with the fact that the generation sector in Ontario is dominated by OPG, which has over 80 per cent of provincial generating capacity. The MPMA is a very detailed agreement, but at its core are provisions for OPG to gradually withdraw generating capacity from the market on a fixed schedule.

While these large market power concerns were naturally crucial to the design of the Ontario system, so also were other aspects of day to market fairness or competition as a fair market process. The introduction of new gas and electricity retailers meant that the Ontario Energy Board had to regulate the conduct of such market players. First, all such players had to be licensed by the OEB. Second, they had to abide by a code of conduct which applies to these companies and their sales people when selling to consumers. Third, a dispute resolution system was put into place to mediate disputes (OEB 2001). In April 2002, just prior to the May 1st launch date of the new electricity system, the OEB announced that it had issued its first penalties against two electricity retailers for misleading or inappropriate sales practices.

Alberta

In Alberta, the Electric Utilities Act of 1995 sketched the broad framework for the future of Alberta's electricity industry, an industry which, unlike in other Canadian provinces, was privately owned. The main purposes of the Act were to establish a competitive market for electricity generation; ensure that the costs and benefits of existing generators be shared equitably among electricity customers; assure that investment in new generating capacity be based on market signals; and, where regulation was still required, minimize the costs and provide efficiency incentives (Alberta 1999: 5). This initial move towards deregulation and restructuring was followed in 1998 by the Electric Utilities Amendment Act, which further laid the groundwork for restructuring of the province's electricity industry. Under this latter Act, electricity transmission and distribution were to be regulated, while competition was introduced into retail electricity supply, beginning 1 January 2001.

Electricity restructuring has altered the AEUB's regulatory role in electricity in a number of respects. First, while the regulator continues to review applications for new generating capacity, it no longer examines whether proposed plants are necessary to meet future electricity requirements. When applications come before the AEUB, the Board's review is focused solely on whether the proposal meets environmental and siting requirements. Second, the AEUB is no longer responsible for regulating electricity rates but, instead, regulates system access tariffs.

In the new industry, the market price for electricity is established by the Power Pool, an organization that matches demand with lowest cost supply on an hourly basis. The open, fair, and efficient operation of the Power Pool is the responsibility of the Power Pool Council, an organization representing all market participants. The transmission administrator oversees the system to ensure rates are fair, access to the system is non-discriminatory, and the system operates safely and reliably. System access tariffs are established by the transmission administrator and are subject to AEUB approval.

The AEUB also acquired a new 'oversight' function in the deregulated electricity market. In 1998, for example, when a rotating power outage impacted a number of areas in southern Alberta, the minister of energy requested that the AEUB coordinate an investigation into the cause of the problem. While the Board found no evidence that the outage was caused by improper behaviour of market participants, its report resulted in the creation of an industry-government task force to identify ways to reduce the risk of outages in the future. Similarly, the AEUB initiated a review of the province's wholesale electricity market to determine 'whether the market is functioning to produce reliable electricity supply at competitive prices during Alberta's transition to electricity deregulation.' (AEUB 2001b). The organization conducted this review in conjunction with the market surveillance administrator, a member of the Power Pool Council responsible for monitoring the effectiveness of the market.

Overall, the competition regulatory requirement has refocused and reoriented the AEUB's role and function in electricity regulation. Electricity deregulation and restructuring has largely carved out the agency's traditional sectoral regulatory role of rate regulation, replacing it with framework regulatory functions such as market oversight.

The federal Competition Bureau presented its preferred views to the Alberta government as the latter's restructuring debate and process occurred. In most respects, the Bureau's key concerns were met. One of the different features of the Alberta system is that the Power Pool Council is more a private non-profit entity than a governmentally established body.

The issues of fair and workable competition have other manifestations in Alberta at the day to day consumer level. Starting in April 2002, Alberta natural gas consumers will have their rates set on a monthly basis, rather than twice a year. This decision flows from the core notion of unbundling services, which produces more varied or changing prices, but it also confronts the fact that most individual consumers want stable or orderly pricing. The AEUB saw the move as being economically sensible, but also as a way of showing a higher degree of transparency for consumers.

Nova Scotia

Early in 2001, the government of Nova Scotia also launched a review of the role of energy in the province's future, initially via a discussion paper, *Powering Nova Scotia's Economy* (Nova Scotia 2001a), and then a later energy strategy paper (Nova Scotia 2001b). Among the questions being examined is the provision of more competition. At present, the provincially owned utility, Nova Scotia Power Inc (NSPI), is a vertically integrated monopoly which owns and operates 97 per cent of the generation, 99 per cent of transmission, and 95 per cent of the distribution systems in Nova Scotia. It is regulated by the Nova Scotia Utility and Review Board (UARB). The relatively recent introduction of natural gas is the main source of competitive pressure on NSPI.

Competition policy issues had already emerged in NSPI's reaction to competition from natural gas. It sought the ability to 'provide Load Retention Rates (LRRs) to industrial customers, and to seek approval from the UARB for a process for rapid approval of Energy Solutions Packages (ESPs) ... a key focus of these options would be to prevent customers from switching to gas for space and water heating purposes' (Competition Bureau 2001: 3). The Competition Bureau had intervened in the hearings over these measures and expressed its usual concerns about anti-competitive behaviour.

Unlike the situation in Ontario, where rapidly increasing electricity prices in the early 1990s (see chapter 1) and helped trigger the steps to competitive restructuring, Nova Scotia's prices were stable and competitive for most of the 1990s. The Competition Bureau and the Nova Scotia review process were thus naturally inclined to ask the obvious question: why, then, should more competition be contemplated or be needed?

The Competition Bureau's advice was that there were several good reasons for 'pro-competitive restructuring' even in 'an electricity system performing as well as Nova Scotia's has over the past several years' (Competition Bureau 2001: 5). The first reason given was to maximize the benefits of natural gas for consumers and businesses in the province. The second reason for restructuring was the fact that restructuring is occurring in neighbouring jurisdictions. New Brunswick is intending to introduce wholesale electricity competition by 2003 and is exploring changes needed to give NB Power greater access to U.S. markets. This is important in itself, but it ultimately becomes a third reason: for Nova Scotia to attract investment from globally and continentally mobile firms, its supply of electricity and energy as a whole has to be competitive and innovative.

The Competition Bureau's advice to the Nova Scotia review was that the province should adopt an 'evolutionary approach.' The Bureau's choice of advisory language for Nova Scotia was somewhat more precautionary than it had been for Ontario. In part, this was because Nova

Scotia's situation in terms of energy markets was different, but also there was a necessary sense of caution arising from the cumulative experience with electricity restructuring in Alberta and Ontario, and from the intense media coverage given to the California electricity crisis of 2000–1 (Jaccard 2002).

The Competition Bureau's suggested evolutionary approach was drawn from a report prepared for the Bureau by Dr Larry Ruff, an American energy expert who had been involved in virtually every restructuring process around the world over the previous decade, including California's (Ruff 2001). The approach consisted of four phases: (a) an initial process of carefully analysing options, which would involve both key stakeholders and independent experts; (b) a second stage which would involve a restructuring of NSPI's rates to give efficient price signals to consumers considering energy options; (c) a third stage which would centre on the internal restructuring of NSPI to promote some of the potential benefits from competition, and doing this without the break-up of the NSPI; and (d) a fourth phase which would restructure the system to create more open competition, but with the caveat that even divestiture of NSPI assets would only be done to the extent that it 'promotes workable and efficient competition in Nova Scotia' (Competition Bureau 2001: 7).

There is not much doubt that there is greater caution in the advice given Nova Scotia. This is actually best captured in Ruff's report and is all the more authoritative because it comes from an expert who has been engaged in most of the electricity restructuring experiences and experiments. His summary view is worth quoting in full:

> International experience in the 1990s indicates that the ISO/spot market model pioneered in the UK has become the generally accepted way to create real competition in electricity, and that a carefully designed and implemented market based on this model can be successful, in the sense of maintaining reliability, stimulating adequate investments, reducing political and regulatory interference in the market, and producing fair and efficient prices for consumers and producers alike. This experience also suggests that nobody gets everything right the first time, and that markets with design and/or implementation flaws can create – or at least fail to prevent – reliability problems and high prices. But it took California to demonstrate just how badly a competitive market could be designed, how bad the effects could be, and how much worse the effects could be made by the political reaction. (Ruff 2001: B-4)

Inter-regime Accountability: The California Crisis and Transitional Imperatives

Competition regulation and energy regulation each have separate regime characteristics and institutional modes of evolution, but they are now entering each other's regulatory space. They both imply a level of regulatory knowledge and coordination, but they have not been designed by one government functioning as a single purposeful actor. Rather, they are the resultant outcome of separate political processes and even separate time scales of policy and political thinking and action. In purely democratic terms, they raise issues about accountability or, more accurately, accountabilities (Flinders 2002). We examine these inter-regime accountability issues, first through a look at the California electricity crisis referred to above, but then in a more Canadian institutional context.

The California electricity crisis is a necessary reference point largely because of its size and linked consequences. It is important to ask whether there are lessons to be learned from it, but equally its roots in a quite different U.S. (and Californian) political system also warrant caution in lesson-drawing. As chapter 3 has shown, four years of planning and political negotiation led to the start-up of the California competitive electricity market in 1998. Two features of the market design proved pivotal in the later crises of soaring prices and rolling blackouts. The first was that a form of 'market separation' was designed (negotiated) into the wholesale market. The wholesale market was centred on an Independent System Operator (ISO) and a separate Power Exchange (PX) for day-ahead trading, but 'only in California was the ISO prevented from operating an efficient spot market' because the PX and other scheduling coordinators were to operate 'day ahead and perhaps shorter-term markets to determine trading schedules that would be delivered to the ISO an hour or so before real time' (Ruff 2001: B-5). The ISO would then implement these schedules.

The second feature of the California design was that the retail market was centred on the notion that the investor-owned utilities (IOUs) would not enter into hedging contracts on behalf of final customers 'but would simply deliver electricity to all consumers or their designated competitive retailers at the average PX price, which could vary widely over time' (Ruff 2001: B-5). There was a logic to this, but unfortunately last minute political negotiations resulted in the IOUs 'agreeing to cap retail prices at 10 percent below pre-market prices until they had recovered all their stranded costs or, if sooner, 2002, without changing the no-IOU hedging part of the original deal' (Ruff 2001: B-5).

The market-separation feature of the wholesale market caused continuing problems to which the ISO had to respond in an ad hoc fashion. But problems reached the point that the U.S. federal regulator, FERC, ordered a major overhaul of the system's fundamental flaws. The price-capping feature did not produce substantial problems for the first two years because PX prices stayed low and the IOUs could thus pay down stranded costs (Jaccard 2002). However, early in 2000, demand for electricity increased rapidly, though supply did not, and hence average PX prices increased tenfold between May 1999 and January 2001. The system was also frequently operating under critical 'stage 3' emergency conditions, with some rolling blackouts across northern California. Meanwhile, during this period, retail customers were still paying low prices. The difference in price, of anywhere from 10 to 35 cents per kWh, was coming from the IOUs and was then being paid by the State of California. Early in 2001, the cumulative gap between wholesale costs and retail revenues was estimated to be as high as U.S. $20 billion.

The knock-on effects have been of true crisis proportions. Key companies such as Pacific Gas and Electric and Southern California Edison are virtually bankrupt. Several banks have also become overextended in their loans to energy companies, with related concerns about effects in other parts of banking policy and confidence in financial markets. The State of California's previously healthy budgetary surplus of $10 billion is fast disappearing through the need to buy spot energy to keep California supplied with power. A new state-owned entity, the California Power Authority (CPA), has been established to manage the assets and contracts from these emergency measures.

Moreover, because California has to buy 'out of state power' to fill the supply gap, there are strong pressures to ensure that California consumers should not be subject to 'price-gouging' by these out-of-state suppliers. These include BC Hydro's Powerex, which was 'named' as one of the 'gougers' in a California report (Stueck 2001). Later, in May 2002, the U.S. Federal Energy Regulatory Commission (FERC) ordered 150 companies selling energy or related services to California in 2000 and/or 2001 to supply information and documentation related to their trading strategies (Stueck 2002; Duane 2002). In addition to Powerex, this order applied to such Canadian energy companies as TransAlta, Enmax, and TransCanada Pipelines. Central to the FERC inquiry were the trading practices of Enron, the giant energy trader which had gone bankrupt and whose practices in the California market were being examined in several ways. The California case also shows that Canadian companies can be examined by American regulators concerned about possible anti-competitive behaviour. Following these developments, the cry in California is for California prices to be set at rates that are 'just and reasonable' as determined by the FERC, a regulatory value which resonates with the earlier pre-competitive regulatory age.

The analyses of the California crisis also point to system problems on the supply side of the equation (Joskow 2000; Jaccard 2002; Duane 2002). The fact that no new power plants had come on line in California for over ten years has been attributed partly to strong environmental pressures and rules. While this is a key contributing factor, and a quintessentially regulatory inter-regime one, it raises the question of even earlier cumulative effects. Thus Ruff concludes that 'the lack of new capacity coming on line now is largely due to the lack of starts in the ten years *before* the market began operating in 1998. This investment hiatus was due to excess capacity resulting from regulatory mistakes of the 1980s and five years of uncertainty in the early 1990s surrounding the restructuring itself' (Ruff 2001: B-8). New supply capacity has entered the planning and construction stage since 1998, but it will be some time before it will be operational.

In his overall conclusions about the California crisis, Ruff does ask, 'if competitive electricity markets are inherently susceptible to disaster whenever supplies become tight and spot prices increase,' whether 'it may be better not even to try to create such markets' (Ruff 2001: B-8). His own answer to this question is that competitive markets are still worth pursuing because the California situation 'can largely be explained by one simple and obvious mistake: the IOUs were buying short to sell long. This is the same mistake that caused the collapse of the U.S. savings and loan (S&L) industry in the 1980s ... But it is a mistake that has been recognized as such and avoided in virtually every other jurisdiction that has created a competitive electricity market' (Ruff 2001: B-8).

Similar cautionary advice has been tendered by experienced Canadian analysts such as Mark Jaccard. After analysing both the California experience and some of Alberta's early problems, Jaccard offers three conclusions about the design and functioning of competitive electricity markets, a reform which he favours but with conditions:

1) Until we have a great deal of experience to the contrary, we should assume that, in the absence of specific mechanisms, competitive electricity markets will experience a cyclical pattern of overinvestment and underinvestment, with the latter leading to periods of inadequate reserve margins and diminished reliability.
2) We should assume that, in tight market conditions, suppliers will be able to influence the spot market price.
3) We should incorporate mechanisms that enable demand-side response that can cost-effectively dampen spot market price volatility while recognizing that any mechanism will be insufficient to eliminate all such volatility. (Jaccard 2002: 24)

There is little doubt that Ruff and Jaccard are correct about the core problems in the California debacle, but there is also little doubt that these are more than just technical problems of market design. Markets and versions of competition are always politically mediated and designed to some degree, which is precisely why notions of workable and ordered competition are central to the merging of the two regimes. In the United States, this sense of negotiated markets, even in a political culture that is more market oriented than Canada's, is also a product of the 'separation of powers' within state and national governing institutions. The fact that there was extensive private ownership of electricity utilities also meant that there were more realms of commercial self-interest to negotiate with, through, and around (Duane 2002). Thus, in some respects, California may not be a case that Canadian planners need worry about, since it may well be quite literally a case beyond the norm.

Nonetheless, it would appear that some planners and advocates of electricity restructuring in Canada have observed the California situation carefully and that it has been one of the factors in the slower than planned start-up for Ontario's restructuring (2002 versus the initially planned date in 2000) and for the evolutionary approach (and the use of the word *evolution*) in the Nova Scotia debate. Alberta's review of its electricity market problems also has a form of California-induced caution about it, in a province whose political system is more free market–oriented than the Canadian norm, and which already had privately owned electric utilities.

But beyond the immediate issue of the California comparator, there are quite genuine issues about political accountability or the lack of it in these complex interacting regulatory regimes. This dense regulatory complexity, as regimes merge and meld into each other, produces a lack of accountability and potentially greater disrespect for democratic political institutions. If there is no overall discipline in policy thinking and implementation about the overall regulatory governance system, then not only is there simply bad or ineffective policy but there is also a significant loss of basic democratic accountability. However, the difficulty is that accountability in such complex networked systems must be understood at several levels.

For example, consider accountability in Cabinet-Parliamentary government in Canada. Accountability in its broadest form under Westminster-based systems of Cabinet-Parliamentary government involves a set of processes whereby elected ministers are held accountable to Parliament and officials are accountable to ministers. The Cabinet and its ministers are responsible for all policy, and, in addition, ministers are accountable for all decisions made within the ambit of such policies. Accountability for individual decisions is supposed to apply even though officials have been the de facto decision-makers in many individual situations. Thus, in theory, ministers would resign over major errors of omission or commission.

Accountability in the above system tends to centre on the notion of 'answerability' or having to account for what is being done. The occasions for giving an account are numerous and can include Parliamentary question period; scrutiny before Parliamentary committees; supplying information to national auditing bodies; internal reporting to the central fiscal and political agencies of the government; and specialized reporting on matters such as human rights and privacy. Ultimately, however, these systems of accountability are underpinned by the larger dual imperative of the potential for a government to be defeated if it does not command the confidence of the House of Commons.

But, in itself, this central Parliamentary aspect of accountability does not answer all the questions that many ask about the concept of accountability, particularly in regulatory realms. These include: accountability by whom? accountability to whom? accountability for what? and accountability over what time frame? The question of accountability by whom can mean accountability by the minister to Parliament, by a sectoral regulator such as the OEB or AEUB to Parliament, by a system operator (e.g., Ontario's IMO to the OEB), and by energy suppliers and pipelines to the regulator (several of them). The issue of *to whom* accountability is owed can be posed in that many players think that there should also be accountability to the citizens or interests most affected by a regulatory policy, as well as to Cabinet and Parliament. For example, in the Ontario electricity restructuring case, key decisions about competition were in fact made by the premier of Ontario and by the minister of energy, science and technology. But the formal accountability regime for competition at the provincial level is a complex and often opaque set of reporting relations (a system of 'watching us– watching you' bodies) such as those between and among the OEB, the IMO, and the minister.

The question of accountability *for what* raises difficult concerns about whether the 'what' refers to precise and measurable performance criteria regarding the price of electricity, fairness among different users, and the like, or other criteria related to democratic processes (e.g., the right to have hearings and be consulted) or to some combination of both performance and process criteria. The issue of the relevant *time frame* is important because accountability occasions can be annual or even monthly, and thus short-term accountability reporting regimes may distort real accountability simply because many policies and regulations are, by their nature, long-term in their consequences (e.g., new sources of power coming on line) and in the time needed to mature (e.g., the handling of sunk costs).

One does not have to ask too many basic questions before it is realized that in practice there are many kinds of accountability within and among a set of sectoral and horizontal regulatory bodies, in this case a set of provincial and federal energy bodies and a competition regulatory authority (Flinders 2001). Any further loss of clarity arising from a failure to consider inter-regulatory relations can only make things worse in terms of any simple notion of democratic accountability. But making accountability clearer is not an easy or self-evidently defined task, and it may not jibe with simplistic efficiency or competition criteria either.

While all of the inter-regime issues are compelling in a globalized economy and in complex national and provincial jurisdictions, they do not produce easy answers, or simple road maps, to the 'simplification' of competition versus sectoral regulatory institutional relations. Nor do they indicate how much of the coordination of the state's regulators can or should be done by the state itself or by private interests and citizens 'coordinating' them through private actions of various kinds. The former option can involve further choices as to which part of the state one is talking about (the executive, legislature, or judiciary), and it raises the issue of whether the state can in fact 'regulate its regulators.' The latter option, on the other hand, can produce many kinds and degrees of private action (legal and political) with vastly varying degrees of transparency and power in the actions taken.

To ask questions about who might 'coordinate' the interacting regulators, let alone interacting regimes of regulators (e.g., energy plus competition plus environment – see chapter 8), is to simultaneously ask questions about political power. And the most elementary aspect about political power in energy politics is that it is continuously contested. The importance of multiple regulatory venues is bound to produce a complicated political game. Both competition regulators and energy sectoral regulators may use each other as a threat to a given industry or firm: that if it does not act appropriately, another authority may decide even more unfavourably. Similarly, affected private interests may play off one regulator against another to obtain favourable action or to postpone it. Obviously, there are limits to such gamesmanship in that there are some mechanisms of real or attempted coordination among competition and sectoral regulators.

Conclusions

Energy regulation has been increasingly influenced by horizontal competition regulation. There is little doubt that the main policy direction over the last fifteen years has been towards more competition. The oil sector has always been centred on world competitive markets and prices, and natural gas has also seen the opening of competitive forces. Electricity markets have been restructured, but in a way which had to distinguish between essential service elements and competitive product elements in an otherwise still essential industry.

The Competition Bureau's principles of engagement with sectoral regulators, in general, and energy regulation, in particular, reflect this careful treading through the shoals of workable competition. The workable competition experiments and/or debates in Alberta, Ontario, and Nova Scotia, with California as a cautionary backdrop tale, are an important change in energy regulation and governance, but one whose outcomes are not wholly predictable. Again, this is because inter-regime accountability and coordination are more complex and opaque, a fact which becomes ever more true when one adds, as we will in chapter 8, the energy and environment regulatory interactions and collisions.

8 Energy and Environmental Regulation: Regulatory 'Stacking' in the Climate Change Era

The second realm of inter-regime energy regulatory change centres on energy regulation in relation to environmental regulation. Chapters 1 and 2 introduced the most basic historical contours of the energy-environment links, including the Berger Commission, the Brundtland report and the emergence of the sustainable development paradigm, and Canada's commitments under the Kyoto Protocol. We have also had some insights into these shifts from our earlier accounts of the NEB, OEB, and AEUB, where, even more clearly than in the competition realms, these sectoral regulators have taken on new environmental regulatory tasks themselves. These chapters have shown how these environmental tasks always had to be taken on in the full knowledge of the ways the environment departments and laws of each jurisdiction were functioning. Indeed, in a very real sense, the environment departments were the main sources of pressure from within the government pushing these traditional regulators to change, pressured in turn, of course, by the even broader environmental lobby and by public opinion (VanNijnatten and Boardman 2002).

The purpose of this chapter is to examine further and more completely the nature of the changes induced by the horizontal expansion of environmental regulation and regulatory institutions into energy regulatory realms (as well as into other related sectors such as forestry, including the key question of forest sinks). The focus in the chapter is on the federal government, mainly Environment Canada and Natural Resources Canada, but many of the same issues are being played out at the provincial level *within* provincial governments, where energy ministries and environmental ministries (variously structured) have to accommodate each other or do battle with each other, institutionally speaking. The chapter provides some very brief illustrative discussion of provincial change. Provincial environment departments have in general embraced concepts of sustainable development, but in some provinces such as Ontario, environment ministries have also suffered from serious resource cuts and serious setbacks in regulatory compliance (Krajnc 2000).

To capture and explain the main contours of inter-regime change over the last fifteen years, the chapter is organized into four sections. First, we briefly trace the continuing importance of traditional environmental regulation or so-called end of pipe regulation or emission and pollution control, often described in terms of 'command and control' regulation. The second section then examines the regulatory institutional change which has accompanied the adoption of the paradigm of sustainable development. As indicated in earlier chapters, the crucial regulatory impact of this paradigm is that it seeks to be preventative by ensuring that environmental damage does not occur in the first place. And, broadly speaking, it tends to imply that regulation becomes more incentive-based and flexible rather than founded on 'command and control' approaches. As will be argued, however, some form of 'command' by the state is always central to the efficacy of incentive-based regulation. The third section then deals with the regulatory and institutional implications of climate change policy and of Canada's commitments under the Kyoto Protocol to reduce greenhouse gases. Not only does the Kyoto Protocol involve the obvious global regulatory dimensions, it is also an energy and environment regulatory challenge which engages both the 'clean-up' and 'preventative' aspects of environmental regulation in a full-scale collision with the carbon-producing elements of the energy sector. Indeed, for many it raises the issue of the extent to which Canada and the world can move towards a low carbon economy (Dunn 2001; Grubb, Vrolijk, and Brack 1999).

The fourth and final section then brings out the central argument of the chapter as a whole, which is that the overall pattern of energy-environmental inter-regime regulation is not that of the replacement of command and control regulation with incentive-based regulation. Rather, the institutional pattern is one of regulatory *stacking* in which regulatory systems are layered on top of each other, but rarely in an orderly fashion. This is partly because of the pressure and demands of interests operating through complex sets of environment and energy regulators within Canada (and globally). But it is also because of the central reality that effective incentive-based environmental regulation demands, and

crucially depends on, some form of 'command' in the setting of reduced pollution levels or levels of sustainability. Thus, at a very basic
level, incentive-based regulation does not replace command and control regulation but rather is crucial for the latter to function in any
effective way. Some detailed 'controls' may disappear under an incentive regime, but some form of command is always present or few of the
incentives are likely to work.

Traditional 'End of Pipe' Environmental Regulation

The era of traditional environmental-energy regulation dates from the
dawn of the formation of environmental departments in Canada at both
levels of government, but especially with the formation of Environment
Canada in 1970. It was dominated by an end-of-pipe 'clean-up' approach
to pollution, involving, in the energy sector and others, a quite confrontational approach between Environment Canada's regulators and regulatory scientists and the business sectors being targeted for regulation and
for emission or effluent controls (Schrecker 1984; Macdonald 1991; Doern
and Conway 1994). These regulatory institutional battles often occurred
over long cycles of tension and foot-dragging as the science was debated,
company investment needs and pay-off periods were accommodated,
and other macro economic situations (recessions, high inflation) were
seen as reasons for postponement.

The typical approach to regulation to control emissions was also one
of using 'best practicable technologies,' which meant that these new
technologies would eventually be installed and used in *new* facilities
and plants, but that the *old* plants and processes would continue to
pollute (Olewiler 1994; Doern 1990). The energy sector, or elements of it,
were embroiled in these scripted regulatory struggles concerning environmental hazards such as lead in gasoline, acid rain, and nitrogen
oxides and volatile organic compounds (NOX-VOCS). These emerged,
in turn, across the 1970s and 1980s, and eventually environmental
progress was made. The task of dealing with these hazards became
increasingly international and global, and also increasingly interactive
among the pollutants (Barrett 1999; Kaul, Grunberg, and Stern 1999;
Lafferty and Meadowcroft 2000). Perhaps the lone energy exception to
this history was in nuclear energy, where the need for regulatory protection in reactor safety was paramount from the beginning. But even in
the nuclear sector there are classic traditional regulatory struggles in
realms such uranium mining and in the battle over the long-term

storage of nuclear wastes (Doern and Morrison 1980; Doern, Dorman, and Morrison, 2001).

Another key realm of energy-environmental regulation was not so much 'end of pipe' as building the pipe in the first place. As chapter 4's account of the NEB has shown, the approval and operations of southern pipelines included a continuing concern about pipeline safety and contiguous environmental effects. The initial Berger Commission debate of the 1970s centred on northern pipelines and of course galvanized environmental NGOs and public opinion, including the emerging strength of Aboriginal peoples in the North (Poelzer 2002; Bregha 1980). The role of the National Energy Board was a factor here because, as we saw in chapter 4, it was seen as being largely unreceptive during this earlier era to environmental concerns. There is also a direct causal line between the Berger debate and the eventual development of federal policies on environmental assessment (Doern and Conway 1994). Federal environmental assessment processes (and their provincial counterparts) were intended to provide a regulatory mechanism for assessing projects (often energy and resource development projects) prior to their start-up, either to prevent them from proceeding or to ensure that remediation steps were put in place in the design of the project or plant so that adverse environmental effects were minimized or eliminated. These regulatory approaches at the federal level were based until 1990 on federal *guidelines* rather than laws. The reason for this was that key parts of the energy lobby, backed by the then Department of Energy, Mines and Resources (EMR), wanted to ensure that there was political discretion available to weaken the effect of these processes. This changed in 1990, not out of any particular change in federal willingness, but rather because federal courts ruled that the guidelines were de facto federal policy and that a federal law should be in place (Doern and Conway 1994).

This account is an all too brief summary of a rather complex history, but it does suggest that the energy and environment regulatory interaction was quite conflictual and always involved the difficult politics of how quickly environmental change should and could occur. But it is important, despite the changes portrayed in the next two sections of this chapter, not to see this as being a regulatory form of the *past*. It is but one part of the regulatory stacking process. There is still traditional regulation of this end-of-pipe kind, which has been present in areas such as sulphur in gas, MMT gas additive, and, of course, ultimately in the Kyoto Protocol and the eventual reduction of carbon emissions (see below).

It is also crucial to mention that energy commodities such as these are not the only areas where environmental-energy regulatory interaction occurs. Energy regulation occurs through the regulation of the auto sector and its technologies for emission control, and also through energy conservation encouraged and facilitated through building codes. The federal Energy Efficiency Act (and regulations) enables the federal government to make rules in areas such as energy performance levels and energy labelling for products that use energy (Natural Resources Canada 2000: 39).

Sustainable Development and the New NRCan–Environment Canada Regulatory Relationship

The origin and central features of the sustainable development paradigm have already been set out in previous chapters. This key paradigm is now a formal part of policy-making in all Western countries, albeit with widely varied degrees and forms of practice and non-practice (Lafferty and Meadowcroft 2000). But federal policy statements have elaborated further on what sustainable development means for the energy economy. It is a policy paradigm which 'requires that Canada's present energy needs be satisfied without compromising the ability of future generations to meet their needs. Sustainable development means that the energy economy performs well economically and environmentally, i.e. that sound economic performance is balanced with appropriate consideration of the environmental effects of producing and consuming energy' (Natural Resources Canada 2000: 29). Furthermore, federal policy asserts that 'in the case of energy, sustainable development does not imply preserving one particular source of energy for another. The challenge of sustainable development is not to guarantee future generations with specific reserve levels for any particular form of energy. Rather the challenge is to provide secure, safe, efficient, reasonably priced and increasingly environmentally friendly access to energy services' (Natural Resources Canada, 2000: 31). At the present stage of energy and sustainable development policy, this is more an aspiration than a reality in that oil and gas are the dominant fuels.

While this chapter provides a basic federal government–focused story, it must be stressed as well that the provincial governments have also been experiencing related but varied versions of the same kinds of inter-regime links and conflicts, as each embraced the concept of sustainable development as part of its policy rhetoric and hoped-for energy-environmental regulatory practice. Each province has had to deal with its own domestic debate about sustainable development and provincial energy-environment issues, including the overall debate about how each province might be affected by climate change commitments, given local-regional energy sources and industries and given local-regional climate change impacts or feared impacts. For example, the general debate about electricity restructuring inherently brings out differences in provincial situations. Each province's current prices and mix of energy types for the generation of electricity are different, and thus the approach of each province to the value of restructuring varies and on the whole is quite cautious. For example, British Columbia's generation is 89 per cent hydro, 5 per cent natural gas, and 5 per cent other, whereas Nova Scotia is 66 per cent coal, 23 per cent oil, and 9 per cent hydro (Jaccard 2002: 20). Residential electricity prices in Britich Columbia are 6.1 cents per kilowatt hour versus 9.4 in Nova Scotia.

To provide some provincial context for energy-environmental regime interactions, we highlight briefly three provinces. We have already seen some of the interactions in Alberta and Ontario in the previous chapters on the AEUB and OEB, so that here we mention illustratively Quebec, New Brunswick, and British Columbia. A major change in Quebec energy policy occurred in 1996 (Quebec 1996). The Parti Québécois government's policy document *Energy at the Service of Quebec: A Sustainable Development Perspective* was still anchored around the central role that Hydro-Québec had played in the Quebec political economy. But the policy acknowledged important changes such as establishing a new relationship with Native peoples (a key issue in large-scale hydro projects), promoting new ways of developing the economy, including industries that were less dependent on intensive hydro power, and ensuring more equity and transparency (Quebec 1996: 10–11). Changes in Quebec also included the establishment of an energy regulatory board as an arms-length regulator. The absence of such a regulator had shown the extent to which Quebec energy policy had been equated with close relationships of power between Hydro-Québec and successive Quebec governments, and functioned without a really independent regulator. Quebec policy also firmly endorses the concept of sustainable development as a policy goal, and Quebec has been strongly supportive of Canada's basic climate change policy.

For its part, New Brunswick energy policy has had to steer a course in which it is not an offshore oil and gas supplier but in which it is clearly embedded in a new North American energy market. Its 2001 *White Paper on New Brunswick Energy Policy* pulled no punches and said in its Introduction that 'there is little option but to become part of what is developing into a fully integrated North American electricity supply and marketing grid. In order to participate and to continue to capture the benefits of a competitive market, New Brunswick must operate by rules and procedures compatible with those established by FERC' (New Brunswick 2001: 1). As chapter 3 has already shown, the U.S. Federal Energy Regulatory Commission has been a key regulatory institutional force in driving the electricity restructuring process in North America.

Meanwhile on the West Coast, British Columbia's energy policy was also responding to new sets of political-economic forces and inter-regime dynamics. British Columbia had thrived on hydro power, and its energy policy had also been influenced by a very strong green lobby, which had been among the key forces in British Columbia's not developing its offshore oil and gas resources, indeed of having a moratorium against such development. A lot of this appears to be changing under the auspices of the new Liberal government. It came to power in 2001 after a decade of economic doldrums and has taken very strong steps to reduce the BC deficit and generate better economic growth. It is increasingly looking at its offshore oil and gas potential as a regional economic engine, especially vis-à-vis the U.S. energy market and also as a source of revenues for the cash-short province.

A Task Force on Energy Policy published its interim report in 2001. The task force, in keeping with the mandate given to it by Premier Gordon Campbell, wants an energy policy 'consistent with exemplary environmental practices,' but its focus is undoubtedly on energy development (British Columbia 2001: i). Its first three elements of a suggested strategic direction are growth, diversification, and competitiveness. And the task force notes that 'if the past can serve as a guide, a comprehensive energy policy can be the early-21st century equivalent of the two-river policy of the latter half of the 20th century' (British Columbia 2001: iii). The two-river policy refers to key hydroelectric investments made on the Peace and Columbia Rivers, especially in the heyday of the W.A.C. Bennett era in BC politics.

Not all of British Columbia's possible new energy policy can focus on offshore oil and gas and diversification away from a 'two-river' hydroelectric policy. The task force takes note of the role of fuel cells as a potential alternative energy source (and industry) whose birth in Canada is with the BC-based Ballard Power Systems Inc and other related BC and Alberta (and national) companies.

While this brief provincial context is important, our concern in this chapter is with how the concept of sustainable development plays out in the core regulatory institutions of the federal government. Sustainable development as an idea also means that there is a broader set of government-wide sustainable development players simply because all federal ministries are expected to develop and implement sustainable development strategies (Toner 2000). We focus here on NRCan and Environment Canada, as core regulatory and policy institutions, and the nexus of relations between the two. It is their joint evolution as institutions that is important in understanding the changing nature of energy regulation, in general, and sustainable development and climate change, in particular.

We have already sketched out in chapter 2 some aspects of NRCan's transformation and will say more below, but we have said little about the nature of Environment Canada as a regulator in the sustainable development era of the last decade or so. Environment Canada as a policy and regulatory department wants 'to see a Canada where people make responsible decisions about the environment; and where the environment is thereby sustained for the benefit of present and future generations.' Its *mandate* is 'to preserve and enhance the quality of the natural environment, including water, air and soil quality; conserve Canada's renewable resources, including migratory birds and other non-domestic flora and fauna; conserve and protect Canada's water resources; carry out meteorology; enforce the rules made by the Canada–United States International Joint Commission relating to boundary waters; and coordinate environmental policies and programs for the federal government.' Its *mission* is 'to make sustainable development a reality in Canada by helping Canadians live and prosper in an environment that needs to be respected, protected and conserved' (http://www.ec.gc.ca/introec/index_e.htm, 16 May 2000).

Environment Canada's statutory authority flows from such major legislation as the Department of Environment Act, Canada Water Act, Canada Wildlife Act, Canadian Environmental Assessment Act, Canadian Environmental Protection Act, and a number of other laws (fourteen Acts in total that are its own responsibility). The department and its minister also formulate policy and regulate jointly with other ministers and departments under the auspices of several other laws, including the Fisheries Act and more recently the Oceans Act. Numerous regulations also flow from parent statutes, and the department's activities are driven as well by an ever growing number of international environmental agreements and protocols.

Environment Canada's current mandate and relations with NRCan must be placed briefly against the historical backdrop of the department and of environmental politics and economics (Brown 1992; Doern and Conway 1994). The pattern here is one of a double dose of 'rise and fall' in political fortunes and levels of basic political saliency in the context of a quite steady long-term growth trajectory in the underlying importance of environmental matters and of concern about sustainable development (Toner 1994). The first dose of 'rise and fall' occurred in the 1970s and 1980s respectively. After its birth, Environment Canada enjoyed a decade of expansion in the 1970s with a heady confidence in its mandate and science, backed by the growth of environmental non-governmental organizations or ENGOs. From the late 1970s until about 1988, a long decline occurred, largely evidenced by a policy of weak regulatory enforcement of many of its 'end of pipe' controls, deference to real or imagined provincial jurisdiction, and opposition within the federal government from economic and resource departments and their allied business interest groups (Harrison 1996; Hoberg 1998; Van Nijnatten 2002).

The duration of the second dose of 'rise and fall' encompassed the last decade. Environment Canada's sense of place in national priorities reached its zenith with the announcement of the $3 billion Green Plan in 1990. This elevated position was underpinned by several contributing forces and ideas, which included: some newsworthy natural disasters in the late 1980s; the ascendancy of evidence and debate about global warming; and the articulation of the philosophy of sustainable development, first by the Brundtland Commission and then its endorsement by G-7 leaders at their 1988 Toronto Summit. A new federal assertiveness was in evidence during this period, backed by opinion polls that strongly supported both the environment as a national priority and federal leadership. Arguably, this period peaked or ended with the Rio Earth Summit in 1992, but included the important acid rain agreement with the United States.

The most recent decline occupies the period since 1992 (Stephanick and Wells 1998). Cuts in the Green Plan began to occur almost immediately, but the dominant impetus for the decline in the environment as a perceived political priority came from the recession of the early 1990s and initiatives to manage the growing federal deficit. These initiatives took the form of a major governmental reorganization in 1993 and the introduction of Program Review in 1994. The cumulative consequences and effects of the latter's multi-year cuts extend right to the present. The net effect of the various phases of Program Review was that Environment Canada absorbed a cut of over 31 per cent in its budget and almost 23 per cent in its personnel (Canada 1996: 4) But meanwhile, the department's mandate had in fact grown, as had its statutory base. These enlarged responsibilities had emerged from the development of legislation such as the Canadian Environmental Protection Act (CEPA) and the Canadian Environmental Assessment Act, as well post-Rio obligations on matters such as global warming and biodiversity (VanNijnatten and Boardman 2002). Parliament has further deepened the mandate through a revised CEPA in the context of continuing resource constraints. The commissioner of the environment and sustainable development drew particular attention in his first report to Parliament to what he called a serious 'implementation gap' (Commissioner of the Environment and Sustainable Development 1999).

David Anderson's tenure as Environment Canada's minister in the third Chrétien mandate has reflected the need to articulate a more comprehensive view of approaches to environmental management. He has argued that

> we are seeing broadly-based momentum toward a new architecture of environmental management. Canadians are more attuned to action moving beyond the symptoms to addressing root causes; and they understand and appreciate approaches which focus on rewarding personal and corporate responsibility up front rather than emphasis on regulations and enforcement after the fact. It is an architecture on which Canada can be a world leader in bringing science and innovation to bear on our challenges. (Anderson 2000)

Anderson has argued much more publicly than his predecessors about the need for green taxes. He has also been influential in gaining the adoption of new spending initiatives when the era of federal surpluses emerged in 2000. The 2000 federal budget speech announced that from 1999–2000 to 2002–3 the federal government would invest $700 million to enable Environment Canada and its partners to address environmental priorities. These initiatives include the Green Municipal Enabling Fund and the Green Municipal Investment Fund as well as one for the Great Lakes basin. They also contain funding in support of the protection of species at risk and, on the tax side of the ledger, an Ecological Gifts Program to allow for a reduction of capital gains tax on donations of ecologically sensitive lands. Other funds have been established to promote innovation and enhance science capacity, including the Sustainable Development Technology Fund and the Canadian Foundation for Climate and Atmospheric Sciences.

These changes all suggest a movement away from the traditional regulatory mode presented in the first section of the chapter, but only partly. The core view of Environment Canada, pressured by NGOs, is that regulation of a fundamental kind is still crucial. It is important institutionally and politically to appreciate in this context that Environment Canada has always had to battle with the anti-environment lobby from within. Other federal departments which have largely industrial clientele or which were seen to be pro-business in their mandates have been considered to be such a lobby in two senses. First, departments such as Industry Canada and Natural Resources Canada had their own interests to pursue in the inevitable internal struggle for political attention, resources, and capacity. They were competitors with Environment Canada. Second, they represented industrial views within the state. As long as Environment Canada was primarily an 'end of pipe' department with ambitions to regulate key industries such as the energy industry, it was in a state of permanent tension and conflict with these departments. This snapshot of early interdepartmental postures does not mean that no discussion or cooperation occurred across departmental lines, but such occurrences were the exception rather than the rule.

In recent years, the core instinct for opposition in principle and in practice has been altered by the shift to the sustainable development paradigm examined above and by some institutionalized forms of learning and change. First, as we have seen, the paradigm of sustainable development has been endorsed at a government-wide level as a part of national policy. Furthermore, in many senses, because it is a preventative approach paradigm, it requires the addition of more nonregulatory instruments of governance (initially at least), and it depends upon a department such as Environment Canada being able to influence the policies and decisions of its fellow departments at much earlier stages in the decision process than had earlier been the case. This does not mean that sustainable development has been practised as such, but it has been institutionalized to some extent. A further impetus to institutionalization emerged in the creation of the position of the commissioner of the environment and sustainable development, whose role as a part of the Office of the Auditor General of Canada is to scrutinize and report on, on a regular basis, the extent to which all departments were developing and implementing sustainable development strategies (and other environmental measures). Again, this institutional presence does not guarantee changed behaviour, but it does exert pressure simply because departments have to continuously report in a more public manner.

If these features in a sense begin to 'open the doors' of interdepartmental policy and regulatory politics, there are at least two other elements of change which suggest that Environment Canada and other pro-green forces may be pushing against interdepartmental doors that are being 'left' more open by the erstwhile lobbies from within. While our concern here is with NRCan, one can also see this in relation to a core economic department such as Industry Canada.

With regard to Industry Canada, the potential for more open doors is centred on the fact that the federal government's lead department of the micro economy has been the chief architect of the need for an innovation policy paradigm rather than old-style industrial policy. It is far more inclined than it once was to see progressive environmental and sustainable development policy as a potential source, and indeed cause, of innovation (Doern and Sharaput 2000). Moreover, from the early 1990s on, Industry Canada could no longer function as if the industry sectors in its policy community were homogeneous vis-à-vis core environmental politics. Its industrial clientele increasingly included, at a minimum, four different kinds of industry-environment clusters. First, it of course did have polluters in industries such as pulp and paper and chemicals, but even these were more conscious than before of the need for change. Second, it had industries such as telecommunications and software that saw themselves as essentially clean and non-polluting. Third, there were new environmental industries (and an Industry Canada branch of the same name), which were seen as innovative and new economy oriented, and some of which thrived on the existence of tough regulation. And finally, though well beyond Industry Canada's own bailiwick, there were financial and insurance industries that were increasingly active in matters of greening because part of their job was to ensure that firms did not have environmental liabilities.

But what have been the 'open door' impulses in NRCan? At first glance, they would not seem to be much more than a crack in the doorway. After all, as we see in the test case of climate change policies and global warming, NRCan's instinct, urged on by Alberta and key energy provinces, is still to defend the oil and gas industry and avoid or slow down precipitous post-Kyoto targets. But in other respects, there are other influences at play. As we saw in chapter 2, NRCan was formed in 1993 to become a hopefully more integrated arena for dealing with *natural resources*. This meant bringing federal forestry policy and services under one roof with sectors such as oil, gas, and mining. While these sectors still have a strong tendency to function as separate fiefdoms within NRCan, one feature of recent thinking has caused change at NRCan. This is the view that too many parts of the rest of the federal government were beginning to lump all of NRCan's industries as being a part of the 'old economy' of Canada's natural resource–dominated past, rather than its 'new economy' centred on knowledge and innovation. Chapter 2 has shown that at the insistence of both its ministerial incumbents and key parts of the resource industries, NRCan has sought to reassert that the natural resource industries have always been innovative (and global). As a result, NRCan's own presentation of its mandate and mission focuses on the innovation paradigm and furthermore links it closely to sustainable development.

Some of this embrace of the new paradigms is also undoubtedly budget related. NRCan also faced heavy cuts in the 1990s, and hence it and other departments needed to seek each other out in more cooperative ways than had been the norm in earlier eras. For example, a memorandum of understanding was reached on science and technology policies and resource strategies for sustainable development among several of the federal science-based natural resource departments.

To repeat, none of the points made above is intended to argue that a new heyday of sustainable development and economy-environment integration has arrived in some perfect form between these two core departments. Far from it. There is still a lobby from within that Environment Canada must deal with and seek to influence. NRCan seeks to be a sustainable development entity but is still dominated by core oil and gas energy interests. But there are shifts in thinking and even in useful rhetoric, and there are forms of institutionalization that have been put in place which have the potential for inducing and requiring further change. And all of this changes the nature of NRCan and Environment Canada as part-regulatory bodies and part-broader policy departments.

Climate Change, the Kyoto Protocol, and Global Regulation

For many, dealing with climate change through the Kyoto Protocol and commitments to reduce greenhouse gas emissions is the ultimate acid test of whether sustainable development policies, rules, and processes can be made real and operational (Houghton 1997; Dunn 2001; Rowlands 1995). For our purposes in this chapter, the key question is to what extent is the Kyoto Protocol regulatory in nature, and if so, which regulatory institutions have produced it and are needed to implement it. If Kyoto is regulatory, then it is undoubtedly regulation at the global level. Nationally, it is rule-making at federal and provincial levels (with great conflict between the federal government and Alberta, in particular), and within the federal government, it has involved some institutional convergence but also considerable conflict between NRCan and Environment Canada. To capture these realities, we need to proceed in this section in two stages. First, we set out a capsule history of the Kyoto process up to and including the July 2001 Bonn (COP6) meetings, which brought all key countries on board except for the United States, and the February 2002 announcement by the Bush administration of its alternative to Kyoto. Next we look at the core institutional processes used at the national federal-provincial and stakeholder level. We leave to the next section the task of exploring further the NRCan–Environment Canada regulatory nexus revealed by Kyoto, thus building on the more general treatment of this relationship in the previous section.

The negotiation of the Kyoto Protocol followed years of policy and economic analysis, as well as decades of scientific research on whether and how human emissions of greenhouse gases are causing climate change (Grubb et al. 1999; Houghton 1997; Dotto 1999). The 1979 World Climate Conference created the World Climate Research Programme to help stimulate research, and in 1988 the Intergovernmental Panel on Climate Change (IPCC) was established. It was the IPCC's successive reports that provided the scientific underpinning first for the UN Framework Convention on Climate Change and then for the 1997 Kyoto Protocol. The IPCC's first assessment report was published in 1990, the second in 1996, and the third in July 2001.

Based on the work of several hundred scientists from around the globe, the IPCC's assessments produced an ever stronger overall scientific consensus, which more and more governments were beginning to accept, though not yet to act upon with firm commitments. In short, even though the Kyoto Protocol had been adopted in 1997 with targets for greenhouse gas emission reductions as indicated in chapter 2, they were not yet implemented and the protocol was not yet ratified. But all parties knew that, at its core, the Kyoto Protocol was regulatory and

Table 5
Typical stages in global green policy and regulation-making

- Early awareness and scientific identification of hazard.
- Global recognition of problem.
- Convening of meetings to develop a convention.
- Development of major ministerial statements of concern.
- Development of convention: actual negotiating sessions; between-negotiations study and lobbying.
- Development of strategy for regulation and control.
- Development of protocols: actual negotiating sessions; between-negotiations study and lobbying.
- Development of control measures.
- Development of funding mechanism.
- Implementation: signature, ratification, entry into force.
- Enforcement.
- Built-in review, feedback, and discovery of links to related or new hazards and pollutants.
- Renegotiation of treaty.

---

rule-based in that targets for reductions were required. Accordingly, some countries, institutions, and interests were already beginning to change their behaviour in anticipation of eventual commitments. But policy solutions as a whole and the character of the policy mix, including its specific regulatory provisions, would only emerge in more detail after protracted negotiations among eventually 178 countries and with enormous pressure coming from national and international NGOs and scientists (Newell 2000; Calamai 2001a, 2001b, 2001c).

Since Kyoto is unambiguously global governance and regulation (plus incentives) through international conventions and protocol-setting, it is useful for our purposes to have a sense of the typical stages which other global green decision processes on other environmental hazards (e.g., acid rain, CFCs and the ozone layer) have gone through. Table 5 suggests the quite typical stages which can emerge (Doern 1993).

Clearly what we think of as regulatory and control measures emerge formally at the middle stages (which, for climate change, is nominally already a ten to twenty year cycle, depending upon when one wants to start the policy-regulatory clock). But, given that climate change solutions were going to eventually involve a fundamental attack on the 'carbon economy,' there is no doubt that regulatory control via agreed reduction requirements was central to the ultimate politics of Kyoto from the very beginning (Rowlands 1995, 1997).

Table 6
Climate change portfolio of actions

- Implementing energy efficiency measures, including removing institutional barriers.
- Phasing out distorting policies ... such as some subsidies and regulations, non-internalizing of environmental costs, and distortions in transport pricing.
- Cost-effective fuel-switching measures ... such as renewables.
- Enhance sinks or reservoirs ... such as improving forest management and land use practices.
- Implementing measures and developing new techniques for reducing ... other greenhouse gas emissions.
- Encouraging forms of international cooperation ... such as coordinated carbon/energy taxes, actions implemented jointly, and tradeable permits.
- Promoting national and international energy efficiency standards.
- Planning and implementation of measures to adapt [to climate change].
- Research aimed at better understanding the causes and impacts of, and adaptation to, climate change.
- Conduct technology research ... [for] minimizing emissions ... and developing commercial non-fossil energy sources.
- Improved institutional arrangements, such as improved insurance arrangements to share the risks of damages.
- Promoting voluntary actions to reduce greenhouse gas emissions.
- Education and training, information, and advisory measures for sustainable development and consumption patterns

---

Source: adapted from Grubb et al. 1999: 16.

But the IPCC and Kyoto processes as a whole also identified all the other possible actions that countries and stakeholders could take, some combination of which would be needed both to deal with the problem and, equally important, to forge a consensus around which a negotiated and enforceable global agreement could emerge. This was because the final complex package not only had to meet the core test of reducing greenhouse gas emissions, but also had to do it in a way that was economically efficient (hence the need for flexible incentive-based regulation and other technological measures) and equitable, especially between developing and developed countries (Rowlands 1997) but also *within* countries (see more below). An IPCC policy-makers' working group had quite early on identified the portfolio of actions (set out in Table 6) which countries could consider. Many of these kinds of action are both significant and difficult, but others were frequently labelled 'no regrets' actions since they would be beneficial and relatively costless no matter what future negotiations might hold.

While such portfolios of action were being thought through and pushed globally, Canada's strategies were proceeding in tandem through newly created domestic institutional processes. Many research and technology oriented activities began in the early 1990s, but after the 1997 Kyoto Protocol was negotiated, Prime Minister Chrétien, the premiers, and other first ministers directed the federal, provincial, and territorial ministers of energy and environment 'to examine the impacts, costs and benefits of implementing the Kyoto Protocol, as well as the options for addressing climate change' (National Climate Change Process 2000: 2). They were to do so under 'a guiding principle that no region should bear an unreasonable burden from implementing the Protocol' (National Climate Change Process 2000: 2). Thus was implanted at the political level the central importance of a guideline rule regarding equity considerations among Canada's regions, analogous to the larger 'equity' debate in the global negotiations among countries. Such a guideline rule was undoubtedly needed in an overall national unity sense, but it was especially imperative for accommodating Alberta. Alberta was already rhetorically casting Kyoto as 'another NEP,' and it knew, of course, that it was the province at the heart of the carbon-producing part (albeit not the core carbon-using part) of the Canadian economy.

This directive from the first ministers resulted in the establishment in 1998 of the National Climate Change Process (the National Process). A National Implementation Strategy (among other initiatives) resulted from an elaborate multi-governmental, multi-stakeholder process involving sixteen issue tables, or working groups, composed of about 450 experts from industry, government, academia, and NGOs. The issue tables reviewed seven key sectors of the economy and eight cross-cutting strategies, and an analysis and modelling group integrated the results into a comprehensive preliminary analysis.

The National Implementation Strategy has been summed up as:

- taking action to reduce risks and to improve our understanding of risks associated with climate change, as well as the costs and consequences of reducing emissions and adapting to a changing environment (see First National Business Plan);
- instituting a national framework that includes individual and joint action, and recognizes jurisdictional flexibility in responding to unique needs, circumstances and opportunities;
- adopting a phased approach, which schedules future decisions and allows progressive action in response to changing domestic and international circumstances and improved knowledge;

- improving our understanding of the functioning of the climate system and the national and regional climate change impacts as they affect Canada, in order to take actions to reduce emissions and adapt to a changing environment;
- understanding the necessary relationship between international and national strategies;
- developing our understanding of the implications of emission reduction targets and major options, including cross-cutting policy approaches such as emissions trading and allocation of responsibility for reducing emissions, before making decisions about targets or moving to the next phase of the strategy. (National Climate Change Process 2000: 3)

These highlighted elements undoubtedly do reflect the complexity of the mix of regulatory and non-regulatory actions eventually needed. Other statements about Kyoto by the federal government also stress more overtly that actions regarding climate change can provide *opportunities* for Canada in that they are already leading to innovative products and services. One such initiative cited often is the Ballard hydrogen-powered fuel cell. Federal policy also draws attention to a number of federal funding programs to promote new technologies and approaches (Natural Resources Canada 2000: 164). These include the $150-million Climate Change Action Fund (CCAP) introduced in 1998, and the Sustainable Development Technology Fund (SDTF) announced in the 2000 federal budget, as well as other initiatives cited earlier.

One further element of Canada's approach to the Kyoto Protocol negotiations and implementation, nationally and internationally, is the issue of carbon sinks. Canada sought, and at Bonn in 2001 eventually obtained, agreement for the crediting of carbon sinks for removing carbon dioxide from the environment. This was based on the fact that plants and trees 'breathe in' and store carbon dioxide from the atmosphere, and thus forests and agricultural soils that absorb and store carbon dioxide are known as 'carbon sinks' under the Kyoto Protocol. Canada wanted credit for enhancing sinks (Canada 2001a, 2001b). The credit-for-carbon-sinks issue became a key negotiating issue on several levels, moral, political, and economic. The EU and many NGOs sought to exclude them on the grounds that they did not constitute a real reduction in greenhouse gas emission, and the claim that they did was based, in the view of some, on dubious or not 'credible science.' Canada and other countries with large forests, such as Australia, Japan, and Russia, supported the inclusion of carbon sinks. In the end, the Bonn 2001 agreement included them under certain conditions.

The carbon sinks element of the Kyoto story is of course complex in its own right, but it is of some import to the domestic regulatory politics of the eventual national position and of the core regulatory bargain. The forest sinks provision simply had to be part of the package or Canada would have had to impose fairly draconian direct emission control targets in a way that would seriously harm national unity in general (as defined by the federal and provincial governments), and would violate the federal-provincial principle of not imposing undue burdens on any one region.

In 2002 the larger politics, symbolism, and practical realities of Kyoto became more starkly apparent as the Chrétien government and the provinces faced the immanent deadline of actually signing on to specific commitments. Several past and current positions converged and collided. The first was that Canada's initial Kyoto commitments had always been partly based on a desire to simply look better than the United States, and thus to convey foreign and green policy virtue to the rest of the world. When the Bush administration abandoned Kyoto in June 2001 and announced its own largely market- and incentive-based alternatives in February 2002 (Bush 2001, 2002), the Chrétien government was in a sense hoisted by its own petard. Not only was the Bush administration saying that it did not really care much about how it *appeared* to the rest of the world, it meant that Canada's Kyoto position now had to be crafted in the light of the fact that its oil and gas industry (mainly Alberta's oil and gas exports) could be put at a comparative disadvantage in its main market, the United States, and that other Canadian industries centred in Ontario might face similar disadvantages if they had to pay higher energy costs than their U.S. competitors. Moreover, the United States was now keenly interested in longer-term Canadian oil and gas supplies (Cordon 2001). Hence, selling oil and natural gas, especially the latter, was a key imperative, all the more so because Chrétien was also initially determined to woo Alberta for the next political-electoral round of Canadian politics (Tupper 2002), especially in the initial context of the weakened political standing of the Canadian Alliance during the brief Stockwell Day era.

The other imperative was that as real decisions were needed in 2002, the specifics of exactly what types of reductions in emissions or the arrangement of credits had to be determined through some kind of specific cost-benefit analysis of regulatory alternatives. During 2002 this resulted in a flurry of studies and leaked studies of what the costs and benefits – but mainly the costs – of action and inaction would be. Competing studies and projections by business lobby groups (both general and petroleum lobby groups) and by Alberta and other producing provinces showed such costs to be very high, with Alberta claiming at times that it would decimate the Alberta and Western Canadian economy (Toulin 2001; Fife 2002; Dunfield 2002). The federal government and some NGOs claimed that these cost projections were highly exaggerated and often ignored the costs of not taking action (Chase 2002; David Suzuki Foundation 2000).

There is little doubt that both sides were playing the tactical game of analytical exaggeration since this often happens when serious regulatory battles reach their point of no return or of actual decision-making and compliance (Jaccard, Nyboer, and Sadownik 2002). For example, such tactical analytical gamesmanship had occurred in the great Canada-U.S. free trade debate during 1987–8 (Doern and Tomlin 1991). There is also little doubt that neither side had perfect information or could know with certainty what kind of final bargain they were actually dealing with, and around which they could model and estimate costs and benefits.

These dynamics, coupled with the availability and demonstrated effect of the Bush administration's alternative to Kyoto, helped sow the seeds of a 'made-in Canada' alternative to Kyoto as well. The Alberta Conservative government began seeking support among the provinces and in Ottawa for a package of initiatives which would reduce and lower emissions, but which would rely more on the development of alternative technologies and which would be calibrated to keep Canadian energy competitive in U.S. markets (Alberta 2002; Moore 2002b). By the autumn of 2002, a larger business coalition, the Canadian Coalition for Responsible Environmental Solutions, had been formed. Though critical of the lack of specifics in the federal approach to Kyoto, neither it nor the Alberta alternative was any more specific.

Splits also began to occur in the Chrétien Cabinet about the wisdom of Canada's signing an agreement, given the new North American energy and environmental context propelled by the very aggressive and determined Bush administration (Mertl 2002). The 2002–3 leadership race to succeed Prime Minister Chrétien as leader of the Liberal party was already making such splits more apparent, all the more so because it is the successor to Jean Chrétien as prime minister who will have to deal with the practical fallout from a detailed national plan, whose contours and details in 2002 are unknown to most Canadians as voters, citizens, and energy consumers.

The Bush anti-Kyoto policy also prompted Canada to add a further caveat to its eventual signing on. This came in the form of a federally suggested Canadian need to get 'clean energy' credits for energy which it exported to the United States, such as natural gas and hydroelectric power, which replaced dirtier U.S. alternative sources of supply from coal and oil-fired energy (Canada 2002). Whether the world agrees with this further condition remains to be seen, but the likelihood of this seems very doubtful.

The above discussion of key international, North American, and national elements of the Kyoto commitments certainly suggests that the protocol is ultimately at its core *regulatory* (given its dependence on targeted emission reductions when it comes into force and is implemented). It is also unambiguously global and horizontal in its reach across energy sectors and the energy economy of producers and users of energy. But the discussion also shows that it is much more than that, and that its approach to energy governance necessarily, in both political and practical terms, involves numerous tax-based, spending, research-based, and voluntary initiatives. However, we need to say more concerning what it reveals about the nature of regulation, including the relations between our two examples of regulatory institutions in this chapter, NRCan and Environment Canada, and between traditional end-of-pipe command and control regulation and incentive-based regulation.

Environment-Energy Regulatory Stacking: Command and Control and Incentive Regulation

The concept of regulatory stacking is a useful one for understanding Canada's now combined environment-energy inter-regime regulatory world. This is because it is a world which now permanently combines ever more tightly *both* command and control regulation of the 'end of pipe' variety with sustainable development modes of regulation of the preventative 'command' and *partly* incentive-based variety. Both kinds of regulation are present and needed, and the core regulatory institutions must negotiate how these are stacked and combined virtually all the time. And the political and policy grease for the negotiating wheel is found, in part, in the larger array of policy instruments or the proffered 'portfolio of actions' discussed above.

Natural Resources Canada and Environment Canada are at the centre of this regulatory stacking relationship within the federal government, but, as we have seen, they are not alone. Some aspects of their relationship have already been noted above. They have both adopted the concept of sustainable development and hence can in principle deal with each other differently than in the earlier days of the EMR–Environment Canada relationship of the 1970s and 1980s. The commissioner of environment and sustainable development pushes and prods from the outside, as do complex pressures from NGOs and traditional business sectoral interest groups.

Some other important forms of institutional learning and cooperation also occurred in the evolving preparations for climate change and Kyoto. Research on climate change occurred quite early on in the 1990s and involved scientists in both departments (Doern and Conway 1994). A Climate Change Secretariat was formed and, though located at NRCan, was jointly chaired by, and managed with, Environment Canada. It became engaged in policy research, and, of course, large numbers of policy and scientific staff then became involved in the larger National Climate Change Process referred to above. All of this overarching preparation and negotiation was run through federal and provincial sets of energy ministers and environment ministers.

There were other, perhaps more subtle, pressures and changes emerging in this now increasingly joined-up institutional melange. The impact of the sustainable development paradigm was not just in the policy goals it contained but also in the way in which it implied a different more catholic approach to stakeholder consultation. Within NRCan, this had a particular resonance because the Canadian Forestry Service, which joined the then new NRCan in 1993, saw itself as having stronger instincts towards a sustainable approach than some of the traditional energy sectors. And, of course, the forestry sector in Canada was itself under heavy global criticism and green-consumer boycotts at the international level (Stanbury 2000). In any event, approaches to policy-making as a whole were changing within NRCan.

Importantly, the climate change file meant without a doubt that policy and regulatory development would be, and would have to be seen to be, massively horizontal across governments, between federal and provincial governments (and, of course, in global negotiations, when national negotiating teams showed up). Indeed, in both the federal-provincial and international arenas, 'environmental' players often found more common ground with their provincial or international counterparts than they did with the 'energy' players in their own government.

This is because at its core the climate change file was still profoundly command-centred, in the sense that greenhouse gas emission reductions and controls (how much, how fast, and exactly how fair and equitable) were at the core of energy-environmental regulatory regime politics. And though we have focused for analytical reasons on the NRCan–Environment Canada interplay, the set of horizontal players was of course not confined to them alone. In the Kyoto process, the negotiations proceeded from the international environmental arena and hence were in one sense led by Environment Canada, but always in concert with the Department of Foreign Affairs and International Trade (DFAIT). And, of course, ultimately it was Prime Minister Jean Chrétien who decided and announced in September 2002 in Johannesburg that Canada would ratify the Kyoto Protocol. But NRCan was the main conduit to the energy industry, and its minister until early 2002, Ralph Goodale, was the Western Canadian politician with the largest array of links to the Alberta-centred energy industry and to the politics of Western Canada.

It must be remembered that for most of the period covered in this book, the Kyoto story for Canada was one of de facto inaction on the core question of actually implementing greenhouse gas emission reductions to match commitments. In this sense the larger energy interests represented partly through NRCan held sway over the nominal environmental interests. This constellation of forces only began to shift in a hard political way when Prime Minister Chrétien made his Johannesburg commitment to ratify the Kyoto Protocol.

Conclusions

Energy regulation in Canada has been transformed over the last fifteen years by the extended horizontal reach of environmental regulation and by the idea and partial practice of sustainable development. Institutionally, this has been portrayed in this chapter mainly through an understanding of how the relationship between NRCan and Environment Canada has changed. Building on earlier chapters on the OEB and AEUB, we have also referred further, but very briefly, to similar kinds of changed policy and regulatory dynamics at the provincial level in Quebec, New Brunswick, and British Columbia, as the paradigm of sustainable development was stated to be a part of provincial policies

as well. But some provinces, such as Ontario, also reduced the resources and compliance capacities of their environment departments.

The analysis has shown that the initial era of 'end of pipe' traditional regulation, which was characterized by many as command and
control regulation, was conflictual at its core. Though it has been
complemented by other incentive approaches, it has not been fully or
totally replaced by the latter. Indeed, this chapter has shown that it is
essential to understand that energy-environmental regulation involves
a process of regulatory stacking in which command and control regulation and incentive-based regulation are both needed to change
behaviour. But stacking also implies that such systems are not el-
egantly planned, but rather are 'layered in' in complex and at times
even random ways.

The nature of inter-regime energy-environment regulatory relations
began to change in the late 1980s, in part under the common impetus of
the sustainable development paradigm. Because of its implied intellectual and policy focus on preventative action, it partly changed the
relations between NRCan and Environment Canada. Somewhat more
room emerged for cooperative action, especially in the incentive-
regulatory realms and in the use of the larger set of policy tools that
were ultimately needed to broker the key regulatory bargains between
the sectoral energy regime and the horizontal environmental regime.

The chapter has also shown that the climate change process and the
Kyoto Protocol negotiations have brought the horizontal scope within
the federal government of energy and environmental regulatory institutions to their necessary zenith. These processes and issues are global
in scope, and federal-provincial and multi-sectoral in an overall national context. They have involved massive cooperation and learning
between the two core federal departments, but they also involve both
end-of-pipe command and control regulation and sustainable development approaches. Both are still ever present as the new politics of the
carbon economy and society are really confronted for the first time in a
more serious way.

Both aspects of the aggressive U.S. Bush administration's agenda, the
Bush National Energy Plan and the U.S. alternative to Kyoto, have
forced changes in the fundamental Canadian domestic equation. The
Chrétien Liberal government wants to sell oil and gas to the United
States for its obvious economic and employment benefits. It wanted,
initially, to avoid alienating Alberta over energy policy for the second
time in a political generation. It knows that it wants to be a significant

green player in global politics, but, on Kyoto, it can no longer pretend that it is more virtuous than the United States simply by saying so. The command and control crunch of environmental regulation on climate change will soon have to be faced and decisions made, but those actions will need to be complemented as well by incentives and new technology to ensure that energy-environmental sustainable development has some chance of occurring.

Conclusions

Canadian energy regulatory governance has changed markedly in the last twenty years. In the early twenty-first century, the regulatory governance of Canada's energy sector is characterized by a much more complex interaction between two energy regulatory regimes, the traditional sectoral regime and the horizontal regime. The former regulates energy as a distinct industrial sector with its own unique industrial and economic characteristics, and the latter horizontal regulatory regime seeks to establish framework rules and regulations, such as those for the environment and competition, the two aspects of the horizontal regime we have explored in this book. The interaction between these two regimes has altered the nature of energy regulatory governance in Canada, and has had significant implications for both the process and substance of energy regulation.

We reiterate that the book has not been about energy policy in a full sense nor about all aspects of energy regulation. Nonetheless, we have sought to provide a broad and comprehensive examination of energy regulatory governance and an explanation of how and why it has changed. The recent U.S. Bush administration's National Energy Policy and its alternative approach to the Kyoto Protocol, and the Chrétien Liberals' federal energy policy response, have provided the immediate context for our analysis, but these key developments in the early 2000s have also been set against the longer trajectory of Canada's energy politics and policy history in chapter 1, as well as in the context of crucial U.S. influences via the decisions and approaches adopted by the U.S. Federal Energy Regulatory Commission examined in chapter 3. The separate chapters on the changing roles of sectoral regulators such as the NEB, the OEB, and the AEUB show some similar directions of change, but also quite diverse rates and rhythms of change in response to further and more precise institutional settings at the provincial and national levels and in response to the different configurations of business and NGO interests in these jurisdictions.

But, as a set of regulators, they supply a very good sample of the nature of regulatory change and its causes, and of the kinds of challenges inherent in energy regulatory governance as the early twenty-first century evolves. So, too, does the coverage in chapters 7 and 8 of the competition and environmental examples of horizontal energy regulatory governance. The institutional mix here has been complex with regulators and policy entities including, at the federal level, the Competition Bureau, Natural Resources Canada, and Environment Canada, as well as many provincial and international counterpart institutions with views about, and the power to influence, what is meant in practice by key concepts such as competition, fair markets, pollution control, and inter-generational sustainable development.

We have sought overall to characterize and explain the key changing features of energy regulatory governance in the twenty-first century. The factors and framework presented in chapter 2 formed the basis of our analysis and the starting point for examining the 'power switch' that has taken place and continues to take place in Canadian energy regulation. The first part of our approach examined the power switch in relation to a set of key factors, including the following: the Bush administration's NEP and alternatives to Kyoto; the role of ideology and its links with ideas about incentive-based regulation; other economic ideas linked to technical change and the reduced monopoly rationale; the emergence of sustainable development rationales, free trade commitments, and continental energy market integration; and changing configurations of interests in the politics of energy regulation among both NGOs and industrial lobbies. The second part of our overall approach has been our characterization of energy regulatory governance through the two interacting regimes.

Our four main themes, set out in the Introduction and examined throughout the book, reflect in different ways the inter-regime complexities, interactions, and collisions which flow from, and are informed by, our basic overall framework. With the empirical institutional portraits supplied by chapters 3 to 8, we return in our conclusions to comment further on these four key themes and on our related arguments. We also make some final observations on the U.S. Bush administration's energy agenda and the Liberals' challenges and choices in energy regulatory development in the transition from a Chrétien to post-Chrétien era. We also offer some concluding observations on the possible relevance of the inter-regime framework for other realms of regulatory governance.

Key Themes

Less Regulation, More Rules, and Opaque Regimes

First, at the broadest level, we have argued that the regulatory governance of energy in Canada has been transformed from a relatively uncomplicated and clear system of sectoral energy regulators oversee-ing the activities of a relatively small number of large homogeneous industrial players, to a far more complex, dense, and opaque system of multiple sectoral and horizontal regulators regulating the activities of a large number of diverse energy companies. In this sense, contemporary energy regulation constitutes a power switch from a relatively central-ized and jurisdictionally insulated governance arrangement to a far more decentralized governance structure, in which power, in the form of information, financial and other resources, and statutory jurisdiction, is distributed among multiple public, private, and civic players.

This was clearly visible in all of the jurisdictions and regulatory agen-cies we examined. At the federal level, for example, the National Energy Board works closely with Environment Canada's Canadian Environ-mental Assessment Agency, including the use of joint NEB/CEAA pan-els rather than single NEB processes. The development of natural gas pipelines in Canada's North involves difficult and conflictual relations among several energy and environmental regulators in the greatly changed system of northern territorial and Aboriginal governance. As we have shown, these changes include departments such as Fisheries and Oceans Canada and its custody over the Oceans Act. At the provincial level, the energy regulatory system in Ontario, for example, now consists of mul-tiple players beyond the Ontario Energy Board, such as the new Ontario Hydro successor companies, the Independent Market Operator, and the federal Competition Bureau. In Alberta, this same tendency is apparent in the now much broader institutional and organizational membership in the province's energy regulatory milieu, which includes not only the Alberta Energy and Utilities Board, but federal and provincial competi-tion and environmental regulators as well, in addition to a multiplicity of diverse industrial players.

As a result, energy regulatory governance is now characterized by less regulation in some respects and more rules in other respects, owing to the contradictory impulses of sectoral deregulation, on the one hand, and expanded horizontal regulatory rule-making, on the other. This paradoxical feature is perhaps most visible in the opposing tendencies between incentive-based regulation at the sectoral level and expanded rule-making in the horizontal and environmental regulatory regime. At the NEB and the AEUB, we saw how the use of negotiated settlements has supplanted some areas of traditional command and control regulatory approaches with incentive-based regulation. In negotiated settlement processes, the energy regulators do not seek to determine energy deliverables, rates, and terms of service on industry participants, but rather the regulator provides energy industry stakeholders with the guidelines and framework that permit them to come to agreement among themselves.

This tendency towards distributed deregulated decision-making is coupled, however, with an opposing impulse towards expanded rule-making. This is particularly evident in the environmental regulatory regime, where the adoption of the sustainable development paradigm has involved command and control style regulation in setting basic initial standards. So while energy regulators undertake less rule-making in their traditional sectoral responsibilities, on the environmental framework side, they, along with environmental regulators like the CEAA, are expanding their rule-making activities. This is evidenced, for example, in Alberta, by the AEUB's acting as a single window for energy development applications, which must be reviewed by as many as a dozen government departments and agencies, and by the AEUB's initiatives to reduce the volume of solution gas flared in Alberta, prompted largely by recommendations made by Alberta's Clean Air Strategic Alliance.

Managed Competition for a Still Essential Service Industry

The second line of argument we advanced is that while energy regulatory governance has been moving in a pro-competition direction, with the implication that energy is just another set of products and services, the system still needs to be seen as one encompassing managed or workable competition rather than full competition per se. We argue that energy is in many ways not just another product or service. This is especially the case regarding electricity, but it is also the case regarding complex energy grids that are now fully North American or regionally North American in scope. Oil and gas are examples of full integration, although this is mainly Canada-U.S. integration rather than full Mexican integration. Electricity is becoming regionally integrated in areas contiguous to the Canada-U.S. border rather than fully integrated across the full expanse of both countries. We believe that Canadians, as well as sectoral and horizontal regulators, are much wiser to think of energy as an essential service industry. This is especially true regarding electricity, but it is also an important feature of oil and gas. Historically, the energy industry has been considered both politically and economically as an industry with natural monopoly features, and therefore one in which society would be better served by substituting government regulation for market forces. This was to protect consumers from abuse of monopoly power, but also, importantly, to protect consumers as *citizens* with the right to access an essential service industry. In the contemporary energy regulatory environment, where public intervention in the sector is premised on an understanding that certain elements of the energy industry are no longer natural monopolies, we maintain that the view of energy as an essential service industry must be sustained, and integrated into current and future energy regulatory thinking and decision-making.

While citizens are of course consumers desiring reasonably priced and delivered energy products and services, they are still, quite importantly, citizens functioning in diverse socio-economic circumstances. These citizen-consumers may be poor, vulnerable, or sick, and therefore political and social considerations such as equity, access, and need continue to be crucial components of government intervention in the energy sector. Contemporary energy regulatory governance involves a power switch to some extent from the citizen, government, and the energy industry to the consumer, in the form of more choice for consumers through competition and therefore a certain power to consumers through their energy-spending decisions. Consumers in this context crucially include major business users and buyers of energy products. But there are clear limits to such choices. When it comes to energy, consumers are also citizens, who require access to this essential service industry but who also have views about how it is produced and what sources of supply are used. Safeguards must be put in place to ensure that energy products and services, such as electricity or home heating fuel, can be accessed by Canadian citizens at reasonable and affordable prices. The Ontario and Alberta experiences with electricity restructuring also show that governments, even when they create new market processes in price-setting, will often not in fact allow such price-setting if consumers and voters protest too greatly or vocally at higher prices or at prices that change too rapidly. Thus, even if the *direction* is towards more competition, this is not the same as the net resultant *destination*. The destination, in fact, is a world of workable competition, not only because monopoly aspects remain, but also because existing political institutions and political-regulatory authorities seek accommodations with each other and ultimately must manage both a networked industry or grid and an interacting world of imperfect markets and imperfect governments, neither of which has been designed by some single all-knowing all-purposeful actor. It may be tempting to believe everything is moving towards a more perfectly competitive world, but we argue that this is an illusion. Governments and particular regulatory bodies also compete for regulatory space, and hence for the chunk of territory they need to manage markets. The analysis in chapter 7 shows how the Competition Bureau's principles of engagement with sectoral regulators, in general, and energy regulation, in particular, reflect this careful treading of water through the shoals of workable competition. The workable electricity competition experiments and/or debates in Alberta, Ontario, and Nova Scotia, with the California crisis as a cautionary backdrop, are an important change in energy regulation and governance, but one whose outcomes are not wholly predictable nor always desirable. Again, this is because inter-regime accountability and coordination are more complex and opaque. As we have seen, electricity markets were described as being 'restructured' rather than deregulated. Some deregulation did occur, but, as the analysis has shown, there were major new areas of regulation precisely because electricity markets are not fully real markets because of the inherent characteristics of electricity compared to oil and gas.

Energy-Environment Regulatory Stacking

Our third key theme with inter-regime implications and tensions has centred on the concept of regulatory stacking as a major feature of energy-environmental regulation. Our argument here is that the overall pattern is not that of the replacement of command and control regulation with incentive-based regulation. Some lessening of detailed control is certainly evident in the move towards incentive-based regulation. This has been shown to be the case in oil and gas. But the role of key commands by the state is still pivotal. Because of this reality, a key institutional pattern is one of regulatory *stacking*, in which regulatory systems are layered on top of each other, but often not in an orderly fashion. Partly, this is because of the pressure and demands of interests operating through complex sets of environment and energy regulators within Canada (and globally). These produce decisions to adopt, adapt, and delay environmental initiatives concerning everything from lead in gasoline to climate change. But it is also because of the central reality that effective incentive-based environmental regulation demands and crucially depends on some form of 'command' in the setting of reduced pollution levels or levels of sustainability.

Thus we traced in chapter 8 the continuing importance of traditional environmental regulation, or so-called end-of-pipe regulation or emission and pollution control, but also the regulatory institutional change which has accompanied the adoption of the paradigm of sustainable development. Though the latter's inter-generational time frame tends to imply that regulation becomes more incentive-based and flexible rather than founded on 'command and control' approaches, we argued again that 'command' remains crucial. This was shown through a brief account of the regulatory and institutional implications of climate change policy and of Canada's commitments under the Kyoto Protocol to reduce greenhouse gases. Not only does it bring the obvious global regulatory dimensions into play it is also an energy and environment regulatory challenge which engages both the 'clean-up' and hence 'command' aspects with the 'preventative' and incentive aspects of environmental regulation. The analysis also showed the massive co-operation and conflict ultimately between the two core federal departments involved, NRCan and Environment Canada, but propelled by the larger pressures from business and NGO interests which use these two departments (and others federally and provincially) as their respective favoured political arenas of representation and choice for their preferences.

The New Energy Regulatory Accountability Grid: Trust Us?

The fourth question involving inter-regime interaction and conflict zeroed in on the nature of political accountability in the new energy regulatory governance system, in which energy is regulated not just by particular regulators but by complex regimes of regulation. The recent changes in Canada's energy regulatory environment render basic political accountability much more difficult in a number of ways. First, as the sectoral and horizontal regimes interact and meld with one another, there is, at a most basic level, the issue of accountability *by whom*. As we have seen, Canadian energy regulatory governance is a distributed governance system involving multiple public players negotiating, cooperating, and often conflicting with one another over regulatory decisions and processes. This complex interdependence and institutional opaqueness may render the determination of accountability within the system vulnerable to finger-pointing between institutions of the state when dramatic events require a rendering of accounts. It is not difficult to imagine a number of sectoral and horizontal regulators abdicating responsibility for mistakes while pointing their fingers at one another. This has certainly happened in the new restructured electricity markets of Ontario and Alberta. Second is the question of accountability *for what*. Here, as we have shown, the chief alternatives are *performance* criteria, such as the price of electricity, equity among different users, and terms of service, versus *process* criteria, such as the right to have hearings and be consulted in decision-making processes. The desirable accountability criteria would probably represent some combination of these two approaches, but, when combined, they add up to complex and even conflicting criteria. The third element of accountability is accountability *to whom* – to the energy industry? to citizens? to Cabinet and Parliament? Answering this question is potentially quite tricky in that each of these groups – the industry, citizens, Cabinet and Parliament – is likely to have different, even contradictory, ideas about *what* regulators should be accountable for. A fourth aspect of accountability that is rendered more complicated in the contemporary period is accountability *over what time frame*. This is an important consideration because the intended outcomes of some of the changes taking place in Canadian energy regulation are of a long-term nature (e.g., transition to workable competition in the electricity industry, the adequacy of Canada's long-term gas supplies and oil sands reserves). As such, the appropriate time frame may be measured in years rather than in quarters or months. A final dimension of accountability challenged by the new regulatory milieu is accountability *by what means*. The increase in incentive regulation, for example, can have the effect of reducing transparency in decision-making. In the NEB's negotiated settlement process, for instance, once agreements have been reached and approved, the NEB cannot easily track whether the agreement is fully implemented.

The Bush Energy Agenda and the Chrétien Liberals' Response

These key themes arise from forces and changes over the last two decades and thus reflect our concern in the book as a whole to analyse energy regulatory governance in a historical manner from an institutional perspective. But the energy regulatory governance system in the early 2000s is now also dealing with the actual and possible impacts of the U.S. Bush administration's energy agenda and with how the Liberal government in the post-Chrétien era responds to this agenda, in concert with other global and Canadian factors and forces.

We have traced these developments at several points in the book. The Bush energy agenda has a number of key elements with actual or potential impacts on Canada and its energy policy and regulatory governance system. We offer further concluding comments on each of these elements, in the light of our analysis up to the end of 2002.

The first issue is obviously the reality of a heightened and intensified U.S. interest, on security and economic grounds, in Canadian oil and gas supplies, including long-term supply. We have seen that the September 11th terrorist attacks have given a double meaning to the notions of energy security for the United States and for Canada. The recent impetus is to provide extra physical security for pipelines, power grids, and nuclear power facilities in the context of overall critical infrastructure in Canada and the United States, as well as Mexico. This sense of vigilance is added to the older notions of energy security, which have usually meant the avoidance of dependence on Middle-Eastern oil supplies. For Canada, energy security has also meant that Canada would have appropriate access to its own petroleum reserves and that these are adequate for its long-term needs. It is likely that the security of supply agenda within energy policy will resurface in more overtly institutional ways. It does not appear likely that Canada would revisit the NAFTA energy provisions about sharing supply in emergency contexts, but it is likely that more overt political attention will focus on how regulators such as the NEB deal with supply and demand estimations and scenarios. It is likely that market processes will still determine such supply concerns, but it must be remembered that U.S. energy actions in the Bush plan are themselves not all market driven. There are significant elements of state intervention to ensure production, many in the form of explicit forced policies to lessen or quicken regulatory requirements.

A second element, closely tied to the first, is the great economic opportunity that arises for Canada to sell more natural gas and also more oil to the United States. Markets in the United States have always been crucial to the economics of the Canadian oil and gas industry, and, of course, the prosperity of Alberta and other oil and gas producing areas can be enhanced greatly by these expanded sales. There is an extra political impetus for this optimum-sales position, and this is, as we have argued, that the process allows the federal Liberals to attempt to ensure that Alberta sees a more supportive federal policy than was the case in the early 1980s era of the Trudeau National Energy Program. This seemed a distinct possibility in 2001 when a re-elected Prime Minister Jean Chrétien sought to woo Alberta amidst the then obvious collapse of the Canadian Alliance in the brief Stockwell Day era. As we have seen, the prime minister initially promised support for expanded oil and gas sales in the wake of the Bush energy plan. But the 2002 Kyoto Protocol ratification debate, triggered by Chrétien's Johannesburg announcement, quickly saw a fast deterioration in federal-Alberta relations. However, Alberta is not the only player. Economic benefits from the U.S. Bush plan will also accrue to Atlantic Canada's now maturing energy production industry. The post-Chrétien Liberals may still want to turn federal energy policy into something that is conducive to national unity. Their policy on climate change, as we have seen, is also rooted in the concept that no single region or province will be required to absorb an unfair burden of the adjustments required by climate change policy. But this is easier said than done, and the Kyoto Protocol debate of 2002 has tested this principle to the limit.

The third element of U.S. policy centres on the linked issues of the Bush administration's alternative-to-Kyoto approach and its diverse and potentially quite subtle impacts on Canada's position on the Kyoto Protocol. The Bush administration's overall agenda, centred on incentive- and technology-based approaches to climate change in general, has already altered Canada's position on the details of how to cast and implement the Kyoto Protocol. This is because of an economic concern that Canadian industry (energy and non-energy) will face competitive disadvantages in the North American market since U.S. competitors will not face Kyoto-induced higher costs. As we have argued, Canada's position on Kyoto was slippery and not very robust to start with, and too often seemed to be driven more, in terms of basic targets, by making sure that Canada looked good compared with the United States in the overall global politics of climate change. This at least seems to have been the raw calculus at the prime ministerial level. As the time for real decisions emerges in 2002, the Chrétien Liberals seem, in part, to be altering their rhetoric on Kyoto; but, in fact, their policy will probably be closer to the overall federal-provincial agreement on principles reached several years ago, centred on fairness of burden sharing and the notion that the Kyoto Protocol commitments – somehow and through some package of rules and incentives – will not be another federal Liberal NEP imposed unfairly on the producer provinces.

Another element relates to the U.S. use of new technologies and incentives. This approach may complement Canada's own existing technology incentive initiatives. Indeed, increased U.S. incentives may be an advantage to Canada's alternative energy industry players if they can take part in large U.S. and linked Canadian initiatives aimed at innovation. This includes such developments as fuel cells (British Columbia has a Ballard-centred fuel cells industry). Another potential impact of the overall U.S. 'alternative to Kyoto' agenda is that the United States may have an even greater interest in Canadian natural gas because it is a cleaner source of energy than oil or coal in terms of carbon emissions. This is already fostering greater exploration and has led to concrete proposals for new pipelines in the North.

All of these developments mean that there will undoubtedly be a renewed northern focus for Canada's energy policy and regulation. But, as we have seen, this means that pipeline regulation, on economic and environmental grounds, will involve a very complex set of regulators which include not only the NEB but also territorial and Aboriginal governance structures, as well as new statutory governance regimes regarding oceans, governed by concepts such as the precautionary principle, integrated resource management, and sustainable development.

Finally, we reiterate the impacts of the restructured electricity markets. The considerable increase in North American electricity markets, and the need for linked and managed electricity grids, will likely continue to raise concerns about whether they are being designed properly. The complexity of networked industries and inter-regime networked regulators will induce some institutional caution to ensure that the right balance is struck between what governments must do and what markets can do.

All of these developments strengthen the point that the North American energy market is increasingly integrated. Energy market integration (especially of oil and gas) has been enabled, on the one hand, by bilateral and trilateral trade agreements and, on the other, by electricity restructuring reforms in Canada and the United States, industrial convergence in gas as a source of electricity, and developments in information technology that permit instantaneous market exchanges to take place. One of the key questions for Canada, then, is the nature of tri-country continental energy bargaining compared to bilateral Canada-U.S. bargaining. While there has always been a trilateral aspect to North American energy relations, bilateral U.S.-Canadian and U.S.-Mexican relations have tended to supersede trilateral relations, largely because Mexico did not open up its energy markets the way the United States and Canada have. In more recent times, however, this hub-and-spoke configuration appears to be giving way to a more complete tri-country energy-environment relationship, propelled in part by NAFTA, but also by the other drivers of market integration just mentioned, domestic deregulatory reform, industrial convergence, and developments in information technology. Perhaps the most visible manifestation of the move to energy trilateralism is the newly minted North American Energy Working Group, announced following the April 2001 meeting of Presidents Bush and Fox and Prime Minister Jean Chrétien during the Summit of the Americas in Quebec City.

The power switch in energy regulatory governance traced in the book as a whole will undoubtedly be influenced significantly by the events and pressures of the early 2000s. If the longer past trajectories of Canadian energy policy have seen a movement from pro-market to government intervention eras, and then to the longish cycle of market-driven development since the mid-1980s, the early 2000s may need a more qualified summary label. The conjoined world of dual regulatory regimes traced in this book suggests a structure of energy regulatory governance in which markets and the state are entwined in a complex web of joint cooperation and conflict.

While we have applied the inter-regime framework to the energy realm, we believe it has some potential relevance to other realms of regulation, such as telecommunications, banking and finance, biotechnology and human genome regulation, and transportation. Indeed, in the U.S. debacle of 2001–2, which involved the toxic mix of the Enron affair, electricity restructuring in California, and fraud by the accounting and financial sectors, the first three of the above mentioned realms were all involved in ways which compellingly showed that complex regimes of regulation and failures to regulate were at play and that both imperfect governments and imperfect markets do not make a pretty or reassuring sight. Sectoral and horizontal regulatory regimes are interacting and colliding in many different ways. Each industrial sector on which one might focus has, of course, differences and unique characteristics. Biotechnology is not the same as energy, though even here there are links. Financial products differ from oil, gas, and electricity as products, but they are both part of the power switch in regulatory governance. Regulatory governance in the twenty-first century needs to be examined on its own terms, with frameworks or at least analytical reference points that begin with complexity and with a more considered sense of how institutions and regimes of rule-makers interact and fail to act.

References

Abele, Frances. 2002. 'Aboriginal People and Energy Policy in the North.' Paper presented to the Conference on Canadian Energy Policy in the Sustainable Development Era, Carleton Research Unit on Innovation, Science and Environment (CRUISE), Ottawa, 17–18 October.

Alberta. 1994. *Alberta Energy and Utilities Board Act*. R.S.A. 1994, c.A-19.5.

– 1999. Alberta Resource Development. 'Power of Competition: A Guide to Alberta's New Competitive Electric Industry Structure.' May.

– 2000. Provincial Advisory Committee on Public Safety and Sour Gas. *Public Safety and Sour Gas, Findings and Recommendations Final Report*. December.

– 2002. 'Proposed Plan on Climate Change Balances Environmental Action with Economic Prosperity.' www.gov.ab.ca/home/news/dsp_feature.cfm (accessed 14 July).

Alberta Energy and Utilities Board (AEUB). 1996. *Annual Report for 1995/96*.

– 1998a. 'Negotiated Settlement Guidelines: Tolls, Tariffs, and Terms and Conditions of Service.' Informational Letter IL 98-04. 15 May.

– 1998b. 'EUB Emphasizes Responsible Regulatory Compliance.' News Release. 30 June.

– 1998c. 'Appointment of Three New Board Members.' General Bulletin GB 98-25. 30 September.

– 1999a. *Regulatory Highlights for 1998*.

– 1999b. 'EUB Adopts New Enforcement Process – Enforcement Ladders.' News Release. 10 June.

– 1999c. 'EUB Organizational Restructuring.' General Bulletin GB 99-13. 30 June.

– 1999d. 'Upstream Petroleum Industry Flaring Requirements.' Interim Directive ID 99-6. 29 July.

– 1999e. 'New Board Member Appointed.' General Bulletin GB 99-21. 16 December.

- 2000a. *Regulatory Highlights for 1999.*
- 2000b. *Guide 60: Upstream Petroleum Industry Flaring Guide.* January.
- 2000c. 'New Chief Operating Officer Appointed.' General Bulletin GB 2000-01. 6 January.
- 2000d. *Guide 64: Facility Inspection Manual.* April.
- 2000e. 'EUB Announces Successful Stakeholder Consultation on Appropriate Dispute Resolution (ADR) Initiative.' News Release. 20 June.
- 2000f. 'Provincial Advisory Committee on Public Safety and Sour Gas Releases Final Report: Findings and Recommendations.' News Release. 18 December.
- 2001a. 'Appropriate Dispute Resolution (ADR) Program and Guidelines for Energy Industry Disputes.' Informational Letter IL 2001-1. 8 January.
- 2001b. 'EUB Initiates Review of Alberta's Wholesale Electricity Marketplace.' News Release. 18 January.
Alberta Energy Resources Conservation Board. 1989. 'Public Involvement in the Development of Energy Resources.' Informational Letter IL 89-4. 22 June.
- 1991. *Energy Alberta 1990, ERCB, Review of Alberta Energy Resources in 1990.*
- 1992. *Energy Alberta 1991, ERCB, Review of Alberta Energy Resources in 1991.*
- 1993a. *Energy Alberta 1992, a Review of Alberta Energy Resources in 1992.*
- 1993b. *Into the Next Century.*
- 1994. *Energy Alberta 1993.*
Alberta Ministry of Energy. 1996. *Alberta Ministry of Energy 1995/96 Annual Report.*
- 1997. *Alberta Ministry of Energy 1996/97 Annual Report.*
- 1998. *Alberta Ministry of Energy 1997/98 Annual Report.*
- 1999. *Alberta Ministry of Energy 1998/99 Annual Report.*
- 2001. *Environmental Regulation of Natural Gas Development in Alberta.*
Alberta Ministry of Resource Development. 2000. *Alberta Ministry of Energy 1999–2000 Annual Report.*
Anderson, David. 2000. 'The Clean Air Challenge.' Notes for speech at Hart House, University of Toronto, March 21.
Armstrong, Christopher, and H.V. Nelles. 1986. *Monopoly's Moment: The Organization and Regulation of Canadian Utilities 1830–1930.* Philadelphia: Temple University Press.
Aucoin, Peter. 1997. *The New Public Management: Canada in Comparative Perspective.* Kingston and Montreal: McGill-Queen's University Press.
Ayres, Ian, and John Braithwaite. 1992. *Responsive Regulation: Transcending the Deregulation Debate.* Oxford: Oxford University Press.
Bailey, Vicky A. 1999. 'Reassessing the Role of Regulators of Competitive

Energy Markets, or: Walking the Walk of Competition.' *Energy Law Journal* 20(1): 1–22.

Bankes, Nigel, and Mike Wenig. 2002. 'Canadian Energy Pipeline Policy in the North: Then and Now.' Paper presented to the Conference on Canadian Energy Policy in the Sustainable Development Era, Carleton Research Unit on Innovation, Science and Environment (CRUISE), Ottawa, 17–18 October.

Barrett, Scott. 1999. 'Montreal versus Kyoto: International Cooperation and the Global Environment.' In *Global Public Goods*. Ed. Inge Kaul, I. Grunberg, and M. Stern. Oxford: Oxford University Press. 192–219.

Baumol, W.J., J.C. Panzar, and R.D. Willig. 1988. *Contestable Markets and the Theory of Industrial Structure*. New York: Harcourt, Brace, Jovanovitch.

Bellamy, Christine, and John A. Taylor. 1998. *Governing in the Information Age*. Buckingham: Open University Press.

Benidickson, Jamie, G. Bruce Doern, and Nancy Olewiler. 1994. *Getting the Green Light: Environmental Regulation and Investment in Canada*. Toronto: C.D. Howe Institute.

Braithwaite, John, and Peter Drahos. 2000. *Global Business Regulation*. Cambridge: Cambridge University Press.

Breen, David. 1993. *Alberta's Petroleum Industry and the Conservation Board*. Edmonton: University of Alberta Press.

Bregha, François. 1980. *Bob Blair's Pipeline*. Toronto: Lorimer.

British Columbia. 2001. *Strategic Considerations for a New British Columbia Energy Policy*. Interim Report of the Task Force on Energy Policy.

Brown, Paige. 1998. *Climate, Biodiversity, and Forests*. Washington, DC: World Resources Institute.

Brown, Paul M. 1992. 'Organizational Design As a Policy Instrument: Environment Canada in the Canadian Bureaucracy.' In *Canadian Environmental Policy: Ecosystems, Politics, and Process*. Ed. Robert Boardman. Toronto: Oxford University Press. 22–42.

Brown, Peter A., and Carmel Letourneau. 2001. 'Nuclear Fuel Waste Policy in Canada.' In *Canadian Nuclear Energy Policy: Changing Ideas, Institutions, and Interests*. Ed. Bruce Doern, Arslan Dorman, and Robert Morrison. Toronto: University of Toronto Press. 129–46.

Brownsey, Keith. 2002. 'Alberta's Oil and Gas Industry: The Rise and Retreat of the State.' Paper presented to the Conference on Canadian Energy Policy in the Sustainable Development Era, Carleton Research Unit on Innovation, Science and Environment (CRUISE), Ottawa, 17–18 October.

Burke, Terry A., A. Genn-Bash, and B.Haines. 1991. *Competition in Theory and Practice*. London: Routledge.

Burton, John. 1997. 'The Competitive Order or Ordered Regulation? The UK

Model of Utility Regulation in Theory and Practice.' *Public Administration* 75(2): 157–88.

Bush, President George W. 2001. 'Climate Change Policy Options.' White House statement, 11 June.

– 2002. 'Climate Change Initiatives.' White House statement, 14 February.

Butt, Roger. 1986. 'Regulating Deregulation: The National Energy Board and Tory Energy Policy.' Unpublished research essay, School of Public Administration, Carleton University, Ottawa.

Byfield, Mike, and Philip Hope. 1998. 'Why Did the EUB's Boss (Céline Belanger) Depart So Quickly?' *Alberta Report* 25 (37): 17–18.

Calamai, Peter. 2001a. 'Doubters Struggle to Make Voices Heard.' *Toronto Star*, 7 April: 3.

– 2001b. 'Forecast Hazy.' *Toronto Star*, 7 April: 3.

– 2001c. 'Burying the Problem.' *Toronto Star*, 8 April: 5.

Cameron, Maxwell, and Brian Tomlin. 2000. *The Making of NAFTA: How the Deal Was Done*. Ithaca, NY: Cornell University Press.

Cameron, Peter. 2001. *Competition in Energy Markets*. Oxford: Oxford University Press.

Canada. 1988. *Energy and Canadians into the Twenty-First Century*. Ottawa: Minister of Supply and Services.

– 1996. *Environment Canada's Science and Technology: Leading to Solutions*. Ottawa: Minister of Supply and Services.

– 2001a. *Canada's Position on Forests and Agriculture Sinks*. Ottawa: Government of Canada.

– 2001b. 'Removing Carbon Dioxide: Credit for Enhancing Sinks' and 'Why Canada Wants Carbon Sinks.' http://climatechange.gc.ca (accessed July 24).

– 2002. *A Discussion Paper on Canada's Contribution to Addressing Climate Change*. Ottawa: Government of Canada.

Canadian Dispute Resolution Corporation. 2000. *Report for Implementation of an Appropriate Dispute Resolution System for Alberta's Upstream Petroleum Applications*. 1 May.

Canadian Electricity Association. 2000. 'Canadian Electricity Association Brief to Energy Ministers' September.'

– 2001a. 'Canadian Electricity and the Economy.' May.

– 2001b. 'Canadian Electricity and the Economy: Investing in Canada's Energy Future.' Brief to the Council of Energy Ministers. September.

– 2002. 'Electricity and Climate Change: Towards a Sustainable Future.' February.

Carter, Neil. 2001. *The Politics of the Environment*. Cambridge: Cambridge University Press.

Chase, Steven. 2002. 'Ottawa Slams Alberta over Kyoto Estimates.' *Globe and Mail*, 15 March: 1.

Claussen, Eileen, and Lisa McNeilly. 15: 1. 1999. 'Equity and Global Climate Change: The Complex Elements of Global Fairness.' Pew Centre on Global Climate Change.

Commission for Environmental Cooperation. 2001. 'Environmental Challenges and Opportunities of the Evolving North American Electricity Market.' Discussion paper. Montreal, 5 November.

Commissioner on the Environment and Sustainable Development. 1999. *Report to the House of Commons*. Ottawa: Minister of Public Works and Government Services.

Comnes, G.A., E.P. Kahn, and T.N. Belden. 1996. 'The Performance of the U.S. Market for Independent Electricity Generation.' *Energy Journal* 17(3): 23–39.

Competition Bureau. 1996. *Staff Analysis of the Report of the Advisory Committee on Competition in Ontario's Electricity System*. 6 September. Ottawa: Competition Bureau, 6.

– 1997. *Submission of the Director of Investigation and Research, Competition Act to the British Columbia Utilities Commission*. 10 March. Ottawa: Competition Bureau.

– 1998a. *Comments of the Competition Bureau on the First Interim Report of the Ontario Electricity Market Design Committee*. 29 May. Ottawa: Competition Bureau.

– 1998b. *Submission of the Director of Investigation and Research, Competition Act to the Ontario Standing Committee on Resources Development on Bill 35: The Energy Competition Act, 1998*. August. Ottawa: Competition Bureau.

– 2001. *Realizing the Benefits of Competition in the Nova Scotia Electricity System: An Evolutionary Approach*. Submission to the Nova Scotia Energy Strategy Review, Department of Natural Resources, 31 May. Ottawa: Competition Bureau.

Conklin, David, ed. 2001. *Canadian Competition Policy: Preparing for the Future*. London, ON: Richard Ivey School of Business, University of Western Ontario.

Connelly, James, and Graham Smith. 1999. *Politics and the Environment*. London: Routledge.

Cordon, Sandra. 2001. U.S. Wants Canadian Gas, Oil, Electricity More than Ever, Says Ambassador. *National Post*, 19 December: 5.

Corporate Knights. 2002. 'Green Machines.' *Corporate Knights* 1(2): 20–4.

Czamanski, D.Z. 1999. *Privatization and Restructuring of Electricity Provision.* London: Praeger.

David Suzuki Foundation. 2000. *Negotiating Climate Change.* November. Vancouver: David Suzuki Foundation.

Davis, Evan, and S. Flanders. 1995. 'Conflicting Regulator Objectives: The Supply of Gas to UK Industry.' In *The Regulatory Challenge.* Ed. M. Bishop, John Kay, and C. Mayer. Oxford: Oxford University Press. 43–66.

Desveaux, James A. 1995. *Designing Bureaucracies: Institutional Capacity and Large-Scale Problem Solving.* Stanford: Stanford University Press.

Dewar, E. 1980. 'Groping the Dark.' *Canadian Business.* May. 13–16.

Dewees, Donald. 2001. 'The Future of Nuclear Power in a Restructured Electricity Market.' In *Canadian Nuclear Energy Policy: Changing Ideas, Institutions and Interests.* Ed. Bruce Doern, Arslan Dorman, and Robert Morrison. Toronto: University of Toronto Press. 147–73.

– 2002. 'Electricity Restructuring in Canada.' Paper presented to the Conference on Canadian Energy Policy in the Sustainable Development Era, Carleton Research Unit on Innovation, Science and Environment (CRUISE), Ottawa, 17–18 October.

Dimensions Planning, Western Environmental and Social Trends Inc. 1989, *Public Consultation Guidelines for the Canadian Petroleum Industry.*

Doern, G. Bruce. 1977. *The Atomic Energy Control Board.* Ottawa: Law Reform Commission.

– 1980. *Government Intervention in the Canadian Nuclear Industry.* Montreal: Institute for Research on Public Policy.

– 1982. 'Liberal Priorities 1982: The Limits of Scheming Virtuously.' In *How Ottawa Spends 1982: National Policy and Economic Development.* Ed. G. Bruce Doern. Toronto: Lorimer. 1–36.

– 1990. *Getting It Green: Case Studies in Canadian Environmental Regulation.* Toronto: C.D. Howe Institute.

– 1993. *Green Diplomacy.* Toronto: C.D. Howe Institute.

– 1995a. *Fairer Play: Canadian Competition Policy Institutions in a Global Market.* Toronto: C.D. Howe Institute.

– 1995b. 'The Formation of Natural Resources Canada: New Synergies or Old Departmental Fiefdoms?' Paper presented to the Workshop on the 1993 Federal Reorganization, Canadian Centre for Management Development.

– 1998. 'Managing Relations among Sectoral versus Framework Regulators.' In *Changing Regulatory Institutions in Britain and North America.* Ed. Bruce Doern and Stephen Wilks. Toronto: University of Toronto Press. Chapter 11.

– 2002. 'Environment Canada As a Networked Institution.' In *Canadian*

Environmental Policy: Context and Cases. Ed. Debora L. VanNijnatten and Robert Boardman. 2nd ed. Toronto: Oxford University Press. 107–22.

– ed. 1978. *The Regulatory Process in Canada.* Toronto: Macmillan of Canada.

Doern, G. Bruce, and Tom Conway. 1994. *The Greening of Canada.* Toronto: University of Toronto Press.

Doern, G. Bruce, Arslan Dorman, and Robert Morrison, eds. 2001. *Canadian Nuclear Policies: Changing Ideas, Institutions and Interests.* University of Toronto Press.

Doern, G. Bruce, and Monica Gattinger. 2001. 'New Economy–Old Economy? Transforming Natural Resources Canada.' In *How Ottawa Spends 2001–2002.* Ed. Leslie Pal. Toronto: Oxford University Press. 223–46.

Doern, G. Bruce, M.Hill, M. Prince, and R. Schultz, eds. 1999. *Changing the Rules: Canadian Regulatory Regimes and Institutions.* Toronto: University of Toronto Press.

Doern, G. Bruce, and Mark MacDonald. 1999. *Free Trade Federalism: Negotiating the Canadian Agreement on Internal Trade.* Toronto: University of Toronto Press.

Doern, G. Bruce, and Robert Morrison, eds. 1980. *Canadian Nuclear Policies.* Montreal: Institute for Research on Public Policy.

Doern, G. Bruce, and Ted Reed, eds. 2000. *Risky Business: Canada's Changing Science-Based Policy and Regulatory Regime.* Toronto: University of Toronto Press.

Doern, G. Bruce, and Markus Sharaput. 2000. *Canadian Intellectual Property: The Politics of Innovating Institutions and Interests.* Toronto: University of Toronto Press.

Doern, G. Bruce, and Brian W. Tomlin. 1991. *Faith and Fear: The Free Trade Story.* Toronto: Stoddart.

Doern, G. Bruce and Glen Toner. 1985. *The Politics of Energy.* Toronto: Methuen.

Doern, G. Bruce, and Stephen Wilks, eds. 1996. *Comparative Competition Policy: National Institutions in a Global Market.* Toronto: University of Toronto Press.

– 1998. *Changing Regulatory Institutions in Britain and North America.* Toronto: University of Toronto Press.

Dotto, Lydia. 1999. *Storm Warning: Gambling with the Climate of Our Planet.* Toronto: Doubleday Canada.

Doyle-Bedwell, Patricia, and Fay G. Cohen. 2001. 'Aboriginal Peoples in Canada: Their Role in Shaping Environmental Trends in the Twenty-First Century.' In *Governing the Environment.* Ed. Edward A. Parson. Toronto: University of Toronto Press. 169–206.

Duane, Timothy P. 2002. 'Regulation's Rationale: Learning from the California Energy Crisis.' *Yale Journal on Regulation* (19)2: 471–540.

Dukert, Joseph M. 2000. 'The Evolution of the North American Energy Market: Implications of Continentalization for a Strategic Sector of the Canadian Economy.' *American Review of Canadian Studies* (30)3: 349–59.

Dunfield, Allison. 2002. 'Ottawa Need Plan Before Ratifying Kyoto, Producers Say.' *Globe and Mail*, 4 March: 3.

Dunn, Seth. 2001. 'Decarbonizing the Energy Economy.' In *State of the World 2001*. Ed. Lester Brown. New York: Norton. 83–101.

Economic Council of Canada. 1985. *Connections: An Energy Strategy for the Future*. Ottawa: Minister of Supply and Services.

Ellerman, A.D., Paul Joskow, R. Schmalensee, J. Montero, and E. Bailey. 2000. *Markets for Clean Air: The U.S. Acid Rain Program*. Cambridge: Cambridge University Press.

Ernst, John. 1994. *Whose Utility? The Social Impact of Public Utility Privatization and Regulation in Britain*. Buckingham: Open University Press.

Farrell, J.H., and P.F. Forshay. 1994. 'Competition versus Regulation: Reform of Energy Regulation in North America.' *Journal of Energy Resources and Law* 12(4): 385–405.

Federal Energy Regulatory Commission (FERC). 1996a. *Promoting Wholesale Competition through Open Access Non-discriminatory Transmission Services by Public Utilities and Recovery of Stranded Costs by Public Utilities and Transmitting Utilities, Order No. 888*. Washington: Federal Energy Regulatory Commission.

– 1996b. *Open Access Same-Time Information System (Formerly Real-Time Information Networks) and Standards of Conduct, Order No. 889*. Washington: Federal Energy Regulatory Commission.

– 1996c. *Inquiry Concerning the Commission's Merger Policy under the Federal Power Act: Policy Statement, Order No. 592*. Washington: Federal Energy Regulatory Commission.

– 1997. *Order Clarifying Order No. 888 Reciprocity Condition and Requesting Additional Information*. Washington: Federal Energy Regulatory-Commission.

– 1999. *Regional Transmission Organizations, Order No. 2000*. Washington: Federal Energy Regulatory Commission.

– 2000. *Regulation of Short-Term Natural Gas Transportation Services, and Regulation of Interstate Natural Gas Transportation Services, Order No. 637*. Washington: Federal Energy Regulatory Commission.

Ferlie, Ewan, Lynn Ashburner, Louise Fitzgerald, and Andrew Pettigrew. 1997. *The New Public Management in Action*. Oxford: Oxford University Press.

Fife, Robert. 2002. 'Premiers Ambush Chrétien on Kyoto.' *National Post*, 16 February: 1.

Flavin, Christopher. 1998. 'The Next Energy Revolution.' In *The World Watch Reader on Global Environmental Issues: 1998 Edition*. Ed. Lester Brown, and Ed Ayres. London: Norton. 56–76.

Flinders, Matthew. 2001. *The Politics of Accountability in the Modern State*. London: Ashgate.

Ford, Robin, and David Zussman, eds. 1997. *Alternative Service Delivery: Sharing Governance in Canada*. Toronto: Institute of Public Administration of Canada.

Freeman, Neil B. 1995. *The Politics of Power: Ontario Hydro and Its Government, 1906–1995*. Toronto: University of Toronto Press.

'Future of Fuel Cells, The.' 1999. *Scientific American*, July: 72–93.

Gallick, E.C. 1993. *Competition in the Natural Gas Pipeline Industry*. Westport, CT: Praeger.

Gattinger, Monica. 2002. 'Alternative Dispute Resolution in Energy Regulation: Opportunities, Experiences and Prospects.' Paper presented to the Conference on Canadian Energy Policy in the Sustainable Development Era, Carleton Research Unit on Innovation, Science and Environment (CRUISE), Ottawa, 17–18 October.

Geddes, Ashley. 1999. 'Klein Admits Power Struggle Prompted Kowalski's Ouster: Premier to Speak at 20th Anniversary of Barrhead MLA.' *Edmonton Journal*, Final Edition, 26 November 1999: B8.

Gilbert, R.J., and E.P. Kahn. 1996. 'Competition and Institutional Change in U.S. Electric Power Regulation.' In *International Comparisons of Electricity Regulation*. Ed. Richard J. Gilbert and Edward P. Kahn. Cambridge: Cambridge University Press. 179–230.

Gomez-Echeverri, Luis. 2000. 'Most Developing Countries Are Neither Prepared to Address nor Interested in Climate Change.' In *Climate Change and Development*. New Haven: Yale University. 309–19.

Government of the United States. 2001. *Reliable, Affordable and Environmentally Sound Energy for America's Future*. Washington: U.S. Government Printing Office.

Grabosky, Peter N. 1995. 'Using Non-Governmental Resources to Foster Compliance.' *Governance* (8)4: 527–50.

Gray, Jeff. 2001. 'Energy Equals Opportunity, PM Says.' *Globe and Mail*, 7 April: 1.

Grubb, Michael, Christiaan Vrolijk, and Duncan Brack. 1999. *The Kyoto Protocol: A Guide and Assessment*. London: Royal Institute of International Affairs.

Hancher, L. 1997. 'Energy Regulation and Competition in Canada.' *Journal of Energy and Natural Resources Law*. 15(4): 338–65.

Harris, R.A., and S.M. Milkis. 1989. *The Politics of Regulatory Change*. New York: Oxford University Press.

Harrison, Kathryn. 1996. *Passing the Buck: Federalism and Canadian Environmental Policy*. Vancouver: UBC Press.

Harrison, Kathryn, and George Hoberg. 1994. *Risk, Science and Politics*. Kingston and Montreal: McGill-Queen's University Press.

Hart, Michael. 1994. *Decision at Midnight*. Vancouver: UBC Press.

Hartle, Douglas. 1979. *Public Policy Decision Making and Regulation*. Montreal: Institute for Research on Public Policy.

Hawkin, Paul, Amory Lovins, and Hunter Lovins. 1999. *Natural Capitalism: Creating the Next Industrial Revolution*. New York: Little, Brown. 234–59.

Helm, Dieter, and Tim Jenkinson, eds. 1998. *Competition in Regulated Industries*. Oxford: Oxford University Press.

Hoberg, George. 1993. *Pluralism by Design: Environmental Policy and the American Regulatory State*. New York: Praeger.

Hoffman, Peter. 2001. *Tomorrow's Energy*. Cambridge, MA: MIT Press.

Hood, Christopher. 1986. *Administrative Analysis*. London: Harvester Wheatsheaf.

Houghton, John. 1997. *Global Warming: The Complete Briefing*. 2nd ed. Cambridge: Cambridge University Press.

Hunt, Sally, and Graham Shuttleworth. 1996. *Competition and Choice in Electricity*. London: Wiley.

International Energy Agency (IEA). 1996. *Energy Policies of IEA Countries: Canada 1996 Review*. Paris: International Energy Agency.

– 1998a. *Energy Policies of IEA Countries: 1997 Review*. Paris: International Energy Agency.

– 1998b. *Energy Policies of IEA Countries: The United States 1998 Review*. Paris: International Energy Agency.

– 1998c. *Natural Gas Pricing in Competitive Markets*. Paris: International Energy Agency.

– 1999. *Energy Policies of IEA Countries: 1998 Review*. Paris: International Energy Agency.

Jaccard, Mark. 1994. 'Changing Canadian Electricity Markets and the Future Role of Government.' *Energy Studies Review* (6)2: 103–26.

– 1997. *Reforming British Columbia's Electricity Market: A Way Forward*. Victoria: British Columbia Task Force on Electricity Market Reform, Second Interim Report.

– 2002. *California Shorts a Circuit: Should Canadians Trust the Wiring Diagram?* Commentary, No. 159. Toronto: C.D. Howe Institute.

Jaccard, Mark, John Nyboer, and Bryn Sadownik. 2002. *The Cost of Climate Change*. Vancouver: UBC Press.

Jackson, David, and John de la Mothe. 2001. 'Nuclear Regulation in Transition.' In *Canadian Nuclear Energy Policy: Changing Ideas, Institutions and*

Interests. Ed. Bruce Doern, Arslan Dorman, and Robert Morrison. Toronto: University of Toronto Press. 96–112.

Jackson, Tim, K. Begg, and S. Parkinson. 2001a. 'The Language of Flexibility: Operational Forms of Joint Implementation.' In *Flexibility in Climate Policy: Making the Kyoto Mechanisms Work*. Ed. Tim Jackson, K. Begg, and S. Parkinson. London: Earthscan. 17–27.

– eds. 2001b. *Flexibility in Climate Policy: Making the Kyoto Mechanisms Work*. London: Earthscan. 1–15.

Jang, Brent. 2002. 'It's Not Easy Being Green in Alberta.' *Globe and Mail*, 12 June: B10.

Janisch, Hudson. 1999. 'Competition Policy Institutions: What Role in the Face of Continued Sectoral Regulation?' In *Changing the Rules*. Ed. Bruce Doern, Margaret Hill, Michael Prince, and Richard Schultz. University of Toronto Press, 101–21.

Jarvis, Bill. 2002. 'Accounting for the Uncountable.' Paper presented to the Conference on Canadian Energy Policy in the Sustainable Development Era, Carleton Research Unit on Innovation, Science and Environment (CRUISE), Ottawa, 17–18 October.

Jennings, Rick, and Russell Chute. 2001. 'Ontario Policy on Nuclear Energy.' In *Canadian Nuclear Energy Policy: Changing Ideas, Institutions, and Interests*. Ed. G. Bruce Doern, Arslan Dorman, and Robert Morrison. University of Toronto Press. 129–46.

Joskow, Paul. 1996. 'Introducing Competition into Regulated Network Industries: From Hierarchies to Markets in Electricity.' *Industrial and Corporate Change* (5)2: 341–82.

– 2000. 'Deregulation and Regulatory Reform in the U.S. Electric Power Sector.' In *Deregulation of Network Industries: What's Next?* Ed. Sam Pelzman and Clifford Winston. Washington, DC: Brookings Institution. 113–88.

Kahn, A.E. 1997. 'Competition and Stranded Costs Re-revisited.' *Natural Resources Journal* 37(1): 29–42.

Kaul, Inge, I. Grunberg, and M. Stern, eds. 1999. *Global Public Goods*. Oxford: Oxford University Press.

Keeping, Janet. 1993. *A Citizen's Guide to the Regulation of Alberta's Energy Utilities*. Calgary: Canadian Institute of Resources Law.

Kickert, Walter J.M., Erik-Hans Klijn, and Joop F.M. Koppenjan, eds. 1997. *Managing Complex Networks: Strategies for the Public Sector*. London: Sage.

Kinnie Smith Jr., S. 1995. 'Future Structures for the Regulated Energy Industries in the United States.' 13(2): 73–95.

Krajnc, Anita. 2000. 'Wither Ontario's Environment? Neo-Conservatism and the Decline of the Environment Ministry.' *Canadian Public Policy* 26(1): 111–27.

Kuhn, Richard G. 1998. 'Social and Political Issues in Siting a Nuclear-Fuel Waste Disposal Facility in Ontario.' *Canadian Geographer* (42)1: 14–28.

Lafferty, William M., and James Meadowcroft, eds. 2000. *Implementing Sustainable Development*. Oxford: Oxford University Press.

Lafond, Andre. 1999. 'The Roles and Responsibilities of the Industry Regulator versus the Competition Bureau As Regulated Industries Become Competitive.' Address to the Conference Board Regulatory Reform Program Meeting, Ottawa, 19 February.

Laughren, Floyd. 1998a. 'Remarks to Industrial Gas Users Association 1998 Natural Gas Conference.' Sheraton Centre, Toronto, 3 November.

– 1998b. 'Speaking Notes for 10th Annual Canadian Independent Power Conference and Trade Show.' Sheraton Parkway North, Toronto, 17 November.

– 1999. 'Remarks to the Municipal Electrical Association's 1999 Annual Meeting.' Royal York Hotel, Toronto, 1 March.

– 2001. 'Ontario Energy Network: Expectations of Market Opening and Role of the Ontario Energy Board.' Ontario Energy Board, 6 November.

Levi-Faur, David. 1999. 'The Governance of Competition: The Interplay of Technology, Economics, and Politics in European Union Electricity and Telecom Regimes.' *Journal of Public Policy* (19)2: 175–207.

– 2001. 'Herding towards a New Convention: On Herds, Shepherds and Lost Sheep in the Liberalization of the Telecommunications and Electricity Industries.' University of Oxford and University of Haifa.

Lowndes, Vivien. 1996. 'Varieties of New Institutionalism: A Critical Appraisal.' *Public Administration* 74: 181–97.

Lucas, A. 1977. *The National Energy Board*. Ottawa: Law Reform Commission.

– 1978. 'The National Energy Board.' In *The Regulatory Process in Canada*. Ed. G. Bruce Doern. Toronto: Macmillan of Canada. 259–313.

– 2002. 'Energy Policy and Climate Change: The Energy Sector's Voluntary Approach.' Paper presented to the Conference on Canadian Energy Policy in the Sustainable Development Era, Carleton Research Unit on Innovation, Science and Environment (CRUISE), Ottawa, 17–18 October.

Lyon, Thomas P. 1990. 'Natural Gas Policy: The Unresolved Issues.' *Energy Journal* 11(2): 23–49.

Macdonald, Douglas. 1991. *The Politics of Pollution*. Toronto: McClelland and Stewart.

– 2002. 'The Business Response to Environmentalism.' In *Canadian Environmental Policy: Context and Cases*. Ed. Debora VanNijnatten and Robert Boardman. 2nd ed. Toronto: Oxford University Press. 66–86.

Mackie, Richard. 2002. 'Ontario Power Deregulation Blasted.' *Globe and Mail*. 2 November: A8.

Martin, Don. 1999. 'Govier's Name Still Carries Clout: George Govier – No. 49.' *Calgary Herald*, Final Edition, 13 November: A2.

McDougall, John N. 1982. *Fuels and the National Policy*. Toronto: McClelland and Stewart.

McNeil, Patrick D. 1999. 'The Future of the Ontario Nuclear Program.' Paper presented to the CRUISE Conference on the Future of Nuclear Energy in Canada, Ottawa, 1 October.

Mertl, Steve. 2002. 'Canada May Not Ratify Climate-Change Agreement, Dhaliwell Suggests.' *National Post*, 14 March: 2.

Midttun, A., and Svein Kamfyord. 1999. 'Energy and Environmental Governance under Ecological Modernization: A Comparative Analysis of Nordic Countries.' *Public Administration* 77(4): 873–95.

Mittelstaedt, Martin. 2001. 'Power Plant Is Canada's Top Polluter.' *Globe and Mail*, 18 April: B1.

Mol, Arthur P.J. 2001. *Globalization and Environmental Reform*. Cambridge, MA: MIT Press.

Moore, Oliver. 2002a. 'Hydro One Sale Only One Option, Eves Says.' *Globe and Mail*, 1 May: 2.

– 2002b. 'Klein, Hamm Voice Support for Kyoto Alternative.' *Globe and Mail*, 3 May: 1.

Morrison, Robert. 1998. *Nuclear Energy Policy in Canada: 1947–1997*. Ottawa: Carleton University.

– 2002. 'Energy Policy and Sustainable Development.' Paper presented to the Conference on Canadian Energy Policy in the Sustainable Development Era, Carleton Research Unit on Innovation, Science and Environment (CRUISE), Ottawa, 17–18 October.

Morrison, Robert, David Layell, and Ged McLean. 2001. 'Technology and Climate Change.' Paper presented at Climate Change 2: Canadian Technology Development Conference, Toronto, 3–5 October.

Morse, Edward, and James Richard. 2002. 'The Battle for Energy Dominance.' *Foreign Affairs* 81 (March–April): 16–31.

Muller, Markus M., and Ian Bartle. 2000. 'Regulation, Competition and Competitiveness: Convergence or Conflict?' Discussion paper for Project on Causes and Consequences of Regulatory Transformation: A British–German Comparison, University of Exeter.

Nakicenovic, N., A. Grubler, and A. McDonald. 1998. *Global Energy Perspectives*. Cambridge: Cambridge University Press.

National Climate Change Process. 2000. *Canada's National Implementation Strategy on Climate Change*. Ottawa: Government of Canada.

National Energy Board (NEB). 1987. *The Regulation of Electricity Exports*. Ottawa: National Energy Board.

- 1994a. *Annual Report 1993*. Ottawa: National Energy Board.
- 1994b. *Canadian Energy: Supply and Demand 1993–2010*. Ottawa: National Energy Board.
- 1994c. *The Public Hearing Process*. Ottawa: National Energy Board.
- 1994d. *Review of Inter-Utility Trade in Electricity*. Calgary: National Energy Board.
- 1995. *National Energy Board Annual Report 1994*. Ottawa: National Energy Board.
- 1996a. *National Energy Board Annual Report 1995*. Ottawa: National Energy Board.
- 1996b. *Protection of the Environment*. Information Bulletin IX. Ottawa: National Energy Board.
- 1996c. *Ten Years after Deregulation*. Ottawa: National Energy Board.
- 1997a. *Long-Term Canadian Natural Gas Contracts: An Update*. Ottawa: National Energy Board.
- 1997b. *1997 Annual Report*. Ottawa: National Energy Board.
- 1997c. *Welcome to the Transformation*. Ottawa: National Energy Board.
- 2000. *Annual Report*. Ottawa: National Energy Board.
- 2001. *2001–2002 Estimates: Part III – Report on Plans and Priorities*. Ottawa: Public Works and Government Services Canada.

National Round Table on the Environment and the Economy. 1999. *Canada's Options for a Domestic Greenhouse Gas Emissions Trading Program*. Ottawa: National Round Table on the Environment and the Economy.

Natural Resources Canada. 2000. *Energy in Canada 2000*. Ottawa: Natural Resources Canada.

- 2001. *Sustainable Development Strategy*. Ottawa: Natural Resources Canada.

Newbery, D. 1999. *Privatization, Restructuring and the Regulation of Networked Utilities*. Cambridge, MA: MIT Press.

New Brunswick. Department of Natural Resources and Energy. 2001. White Paper on New Brunswick Energy Policy.

Newell, Peter. 2000. *Climate for Change: Non-State Actors and the Global Politics of the Greenhouse*. Cambridge: Cambridge University Press.

Nivola, Pietro S. 1993. 'Gridlocked or Gaining Ground? U.S. Regulatory Reform in the Energy Sector.' *Brookings Review* 11 (Summer): 36–41.

Nordhaus, William D., ed. 1998. *Economics and Policy Issues for Climate Change*. Washington, DC: Resources for the Future.

Norman, D.A. 1999. 'Competition and Electric Power Generation.' In *Advances in the Economics of Energy and Resources: Fuels for the Future*. Vol. 11. Ed. John R. Moroney. London: JAI Press. 187–214.

Nova Scotia. 2001a. *Powering Nova Scotia's Economy*. Halifax: Government of Nova Scotia.

– 2001b. *Seizing the Opportunity: Nova Scotia's Energy Strategy*. Halifax: Government of Nova Scotia.

O'Brien, Paul, and Ann Vourc'h. 2001. *Encouraging Environmentally Sustainable Growth: Experience in OECD Countries*. Paris: OECD.

Olewiler, Nancy. 1994. 'The Impact of Environmental Regulation on Investment Decisions.' In *Getting the Green Light: Environmental Regulation and Investment in Canada*. Ed. Jamie Benedickson, G. Bruce Doern, and Nancy Olewiler. Toronto: C.D. Howe Institute. 53–113.

– 2001. 'North American Integration and the Environment.' Paper presented to Industry Canada Conference on North American Linkages, Calgary, June.

Ontario. 1996. *A Framework for Competition*. Report of the Advisory Committee on Competition in the Ontario Electricity System to the Ontario Ministry of Environment and Energy.

Ontario Energy Board. 1992. *Annual Report 1991–1992*. Toronto: Queen's Printer.

– 1993. *Annual Report 1992–1993*. Toronto: Queen's Printer.

– 1997. *Annual Report 1996–97*. Toronto: Ontario Energy Board.

– 2001. *Annual Report 2000–2001*. Toronto: Ontario Energy Board.

Ontario Legislature. 1998a. *Hansard*. 9 June. Toronto: Queen's Printer.

– 1998b. *Hansard*. 17 June. Toronto: Queen's Printer.

– 1998c. *Hansard*. 22 June. Toronto: Queen's Printer.

Ontario Ministry of Energy, Science and Technology. 1997. *White Paper: Direction for Change*. Toronto: Ontario Ministry of Energy, Science and Technology.

– 2001. 'Ontario's New Electricity Market: Safeguarding Ontario's Electricity Future.'

Parson, Edward A., ed. 2001. *Governing the Environment*. Toronto: University of Toronto Press.

Pelzman, Sam, and Clifford Winston, eds. 2000. *Deregulation of Network Industries: What's Next?* Washington, DC: Brookings Institution.

Peters, Guy. 1999. *Neo-Institutional Theory*. London: Pinter.

Plourde, Andre. 2002. 'The Changing Nature of National and Continental Energy Markets.' Paper presented to the Conference on Canadian Energy Policy in the Sustainable Development Era, Carleton Research Unit on Innovation, Science and Environment (CRUISE), Ottawa, 17–18 October.

Poelzer, Greg. 2002. 'Aboriginal Peoples and Environmental Policy in Canada: No Longer at the Margins.' In *Canadian Environmental Policy: Context and Cases.* Ed. Debora L. VanNijnatten and Robert Boardman. 2nd ed. Toronto: Oxford University Press. 87–106.

Portney, Paul. 1999. 'Environmental Policy in the Next Century.' In *Setting National Priorities: The 2000 Election and Beyond.* Ed. Henry J. Aaron, and Robert D. Reischauer. Washington, DC: Brookings Institution. 359–92.

Prakash, Aseem. 2000. *Greening the Firm: The Politics of Corporate Environmentalism.* Cambridge: Cambridge University Press.

Pratt, Larry, and John Richards. 1979. *Prairie Capitalism: Power and Influence in the New West.* Toronto: McClelland and Stewart.

– 1980. *Prairie Capitalism.* Toronto: McClelland and Stewart.

Princen, Thomas, Michael Maniates, and Ken Comca. 2002. *Confronting Consumption.* Cambridge, MA: MIT Press.

Prosser, Tony. 1999. 'Theorizing Utility Regulation.' *Modern Law Review* 62(2): 197–217.

Quebec. 1996. *Energy at the Service of Quebec.* Quebec City: Government of Quebec.

Ratushny, Ed. 1987. 'What Are Administrative Tribunals? The Pursuit of Uniformity in Diversity.' *Canadian Public Administration* 30(1): 1–13.

Reich, Simon. 2000. 'The Four Faces of Institutionalism: Public Policy and a Pluralistic Perspective.' *Governance* 13(4): 501–22.

Reiter, Doris F., and Michael J. Economides. 1998. 'Structure and Economics of the Natural Gas Industry Following Deregulation.' In *Advances in the Economics of Energy and Resources: Fuels for the Future.* Ed. John R. Moroney. Vol. 11. London: JAI Press. 161–85.

Riley, Allan. 2000. 'A Unique Antitrust Regulatory Problem: Coordinating Concurrent Competition Powers.' *Utilities Law Review* 11(2): 48–62.

Ringling, Arthur. 2002. 'An Instrument Is Not a Tool.' Paper presented to the Conference on Instrument Choice in Global Democracies, Policy Research Initiative, Montreal, 26–8 September.

Rochefort, Terry. 1997. 'Reforming the Regulation of Canadian Pipelines.' Paper presented to the Regulatory Reform Program of the Conference Board of Canada, Calgary, 7 May.

Rowlands, Ian H. 1995. *The Politics of Global Atmospheric Change.* Manchester: Manchester University Press.

– 1997. 'International Fairness and Justice in Addressing Global Climate Change.' *Environmental Politics* 6(3): 1–30.

– 2000. 'Beauty and the Beast? BP's and Exxon's Position on Global Climate Change.' *Government and Policy* 18: 339–54.

Ruff, Larry E. 2001. 'Competition in Electricity for Nova Scotia: Report on the Nova Scotia Energy Strategy Review.' Prepared for the Competition Bureau. 31 May.

Sagar, A.D., and Tariq Banuri. 1999. 'In Fairness to Current Generations: Lost Voices in the Climate Change Debate.' Paper, Program in Science, Technology and Public Policy, Harvard University.

Salamon. Lester M. 2002. *The Tools of Government: A Guide to the New Governance*. Oxford: Oxford University Press.

Sato, Ken. 1997. 'Integration of Environmental Assessment with the Regulatory Process.' National Energy Board, Calgary. Presentation to CAMPUT 97, Whistler, BC.

Schelling Thomas C. 2002. 'What Makes Greenhouse Sense?' *Foreign Affairs* 81(3): 1–9.

Schott, Stephan. 2002. 'Energy Source Combinations and Market Structure for Efficient and Sustainable Electricity Production: Will Ontario Satisfy the Criteria?' Paper presented to the Conference on Canadian Energy Policy in the Sustainable Development Era, Carleton Research Unit on Innovation, Science and Environment (CRUISE), Ottawa, 17–18 October.

Schrecker, Ted. 1984. *The Political Economy of Environment Hazards*. Ottawa: Law Reform Commission of Canada.

Schultz, Richard, and Alan Alexandroff. 1985. *Economic Regulation and the Federal System*. Toronto: University of Toronto Press.

Schultz, Richard, and G. Bruce Doern. 1998. 'Canadian Sectoral Regulatory Institutions: No Longer Governments in Miniature.' In *Changing Regulatory Institutions in Britain and North America*. Ed. G. Bruce Doern and Stephen Wilks. Toronto: University of Toronto Press. 108–32.

Schwanen, Daniel. 2000. *A Cooler Approach: Tackling Canada's Commitments on Greenhouse Gas Emissions*. Toronto: C.D. Howe Institute.

Seaver, Brenda M. 1997. 'Stratospheric Ozone Protection: IR Theory and the Montreal Protocol' *Environmental Politics* 6(3): 31–67.

Shukla, P.R. 1999. 'Justice, Equity, and Efficiency in Climate Change: A Developing Country Perspective.' In *Fair Weather Concerns in Climate Change*. Ed. Ference L. Toth. London: Earthscan. 145–59.

Sidak, J.G., and Daniel F. Spulber. 1998. 'Deregulation and Managed Competition in Network Industries.' *Yale Journal on Regulation* 15(1): 117–48.

Sioshansi, F. 2001. 'California's Dysfunctional Electricity Market: Policy Lessons on Market Restructuring.' *Energy Policy* 29: 735–74.

Sparrow, Malcolm K. 1994. *Imposing Duties: Governments Changing Approach to Compliance*. London: Praeger.

Stanbury, W.T. 2000. *Environmental Groups and the International Conflict over the*

Forests of British Columbia. Vancouver: SFU–UBC Centre for the Study of Government and Business.

Stephanick Lorna, and Kathleen Wells. 1998. 'Staying the Course or Saving Face? Federal Environmental Policy Post-Rio.' In *How Ottawa Spends 1998–99: Balancing Act: The Post-Deficit Mandate*. Ed. Leslie A. Pal. Toronto: Oxford University Press. 243–70.

Stiglitz, Joseph. 2002. 'The Roaring Nineties.' *Atlantic Monthly*, October: 77–89.

Stueck, Wendy. 2001. 'Study Alleges Californians Were Gouged.' *Globe and Mail*, 12 April: B2.

– 2002. 'Canadian Companies Ensnared in Enron Debacle.' *Globe and Mail*. 9 May: B1.

TerraChoice Environmental Services Inc. 1999. 'The Relationship between Products, Services and Climate Change.'

Toner, Glen. 1986. 'Stardust: The Tory Energy Program.' In *How Ottawa Spends 1986–87*. Ed. Michael Prince. Toronto: Methuen, 1986. 119–48.

– 1994. 'The Green Plan: From Great Expectations to Eco-Backtracking ... to Revitalization?.' In *How Ottawa Spends: 1994–95: Making Change*. Ed. Susan Phillips. Ottawa: Carleton University Press. 229–60.

– 2000. 'Canada: From Early Frontrunner to Plodding Anchorman.' In *Implementing Sustainable Development: Strategies and Initiatives in High Consumption Societies*. Ed. William M. Lafferty and James R. Meadowcroft. Oxford: Oxford University Press. Chapter 3.

– in press. *Sustainable Production in Canada: Building Capacity*. Vancouver: UBC Press.

Toulin, Alan. 2002. 'Oil Patch Will Be Hammered by Kyoto Protocol, Study Says.' *Financial Post*, 4 December: FP5.

Trebilcock, Michael. 1991. 'Requiem for Regulators: The Passing of a Counter-Culture?' *Yale Journal of Regulation* 8(2): 497–510.

Trebilcock, Michael, and Ronald Daniels. 1995. 'The Future of Ontario Hydro.' *Utilities Law Review*, Winter: 152–61.

Trebilcock, Michael, and Robert Howse. 1999. *The Regulation of International Trade*. 2nd ed. London: Routledge.

Tupper, Allan. 2002. 'Toward a New Beginning? The Chrétien Liberals and Western Canada.' In *How Ottawa Spends 2002–2003: The Security Aftermath and National Priorities*. Ed. G. Bruce Doern. Toronto: Oxford University Press. 88–101.

VanNijnatten, Debora. 2002. 'The Bumpy Journey Ahead: Provincial Environmental Policies and National Environmental Standards.' In *Canadian Environmental Policy: Context and Cases*. Ed. Debora VanNijnatten and Robert Boardman. 2nd ed. Toronto: Oxford University Press. 145–70.

VanNijnatten, Debora, and Robert Boardman, eds. 2002. *Canadian Environmental Policy: Context and Cases.* 2nd ed. Toronto: Oxford University Press.

Vass, Peter. 1998. 'UK Regulatory Reform and Relations among Regulatory Authorities.' In *Changing Regulatory Institutions in Britain and North America.* Ed. G. Bruce Doern and Stephen Wilks. Toronto: University of Toronto Press. 236–62.

Vieira, Paul. 2001. 'Ontario Selling Hydro for $5.5 B.' *National Post*, 13 December: 1.

Vollans, Garry E. 1995. 'The Decline of Natural Monopolies in the Energy Sector.' *Energy Studies Review* 7(3): 247–61.

Ward, Hugh, Frank Grundig, and Ethan R. Zorick. 2001. 'Marching at the Pace of the Slowest: A Model of International Climate-Change Negotiations.' *Political Studies* 29: 438–61.

Watkins, G. Campbell. 1991. 'Deregulation and the Canadian Petroleum Industry: Adolescence or Maturity.' In *Breaking the Shackles: Deregulating Canadian Industry.* Ed. Walter Block and George Lermer. Vancouver: Fraser Institute. 215–52.

Watson, Robert. 2000. 'Presentation of the Intergovernmental Panel on Climate Change to the Sixth Conference of the Parties.' www.unfcc.de/

Webb, Kernaghan, eds. 2002. *Voluntary Codes: Private Governance, the Public Interest and Innovation.* Ottawa: Carleton Research Unit on Innovation, Science and Environment.

Wells, Jennifer. 1999. 'Power Play.' *Report on Business Magazine*, June: 36–46.

Wilson, Carter A. 2000. 'Policy Regimes and Policy Change.' *Journal of Public Policy* 20(3): 247–73.

Wilson, Robert. 1998. *Efficiency Considerations in Designing Competitive Electricity Markets.* A Report Prepared for the Competition Bureau. Ottawa, Competition Bureau.

Zorn, Michael. 1999. 'The Rise of International Environmental Politics: A Review of Current Research.' *World Politics* 50: 617–49.

Index